D0363920

I CHOSE TO CLIMB

I CHOSE TO CLIMB

by

CHRISTIAN BONINGTON

with a Foreword by
ERIC SHIPTON

LONDON
VICTOR GOLLANCZ LTD
1973

© Christian Bonington 1966

First published September 1966
Second impression November 1966
Third impression April 1969
Fourth impression January 1973

ISBN 0 575 00347 2

Printed in Great Britain by
The Camelot Press Ltd., London and Southampton

To
my Mother
and Wendy

CONTENTS

	Foreword	13
I	The Choice	15
II	Winter in Scotland	29
III	Between Air Force and Army	41
IV	First Alpine Climb—on the Eiger	51
V	Fiascos on the Aiguilles	62
VI	South-west Pillar of the Dru	69
VII	Direttissima	87
VIII	Outward Bound	96
IX	Annapurna II—The Build-up	106
X	Annapurna II—The Summit	118
XI	Nuptse	128
XII	Eigerwatching	145
XIII	The Central Pillar of Frêney	155
XIV	Eigerwandering	170
XV	Rescue on the Eiger	178
XVI	The Walker Spur	187
XVII	Success on the Eiger	195
	Epilogue	208

MAPS AND DIAGRAMS

The Annapurna Range   110

Camps on Annapurna   119

Camps on Nuptse   134

The South Side of Mont Blanc   163

LIST OF ILLUSTRATIONS

The author in Patagonia (*photo Don Whillans*)   *Frontispiece*

Facing Page

The author at Harrison's Rocks, a sandstone outcrop near London.   30

The author at the age of sixteen, just after he had started to climb.   30

Buachaille Etive Mor from the north.   31

Hamish MacInnes on our bivouac ledge on the lower slopes of the North Wall of the Eiger.   64

The Leschaux Hut.   64

Approaching the Walker Spur up the Leschaux Glacier.   65

Chamonix Aiguilles from the south showing route of attempt on the Aiguille du Lépiney.   76

Crossing the top of the couloir leading to the start of the first rock pitch on the South-west Pillar of the Dru.   77

Don Whillans in the lead on the South-west Pillar.   77

The Petit Dru from Montenvers.   84

End of the second day on the South-west Pillar.   85

Climbing a Dolomite overhang.   85

Half-way up the Direct on the Cima Grande on our first day.   96

Gunn Clark coming up through the overhangs on the Cima Grande.   97

Annapurna II from the north.   108

Sherpas ferrying loads above the Dome on Annapurna II.   109

Sherpas resting on the Shoulder of Annapurna II.   116

Chris Bonington, using oxygen, on the ridge leading to the Summit Pyramid of Annapurna II.   117

Tachei.   128

Village at the end of our walk across Tilicho Pass.   129

Back to the "Main Road" after our walk across the
Tilicho Pass: goat carrying loads down valley.   129

Nuptse: ferrying loads on the arête leading into the upper
part of the face.   140

Les Brown on a gendarme on the arête between Camps
III and IV on Nuptse.   141

Tachei reaching the summit of Nuptse.   148

Everest from the summit of Nuptse.   149

The Central Pillar of Frêney from the Col de Peuterey.   160
The Central Pillar of Frêney in profile. In the foreground
is the Peuterey Ridge.   161

Clough and Djuglosz on the first bivouac ledge on the
Central Pillar.   164

Don Whillans on the Central Pillar.   165

Don Whillans and Chris Bonington on the top of Mont
Blanc after climbing the Central Pillar.   168

Looking south from the southern flanks of Mont Blanc.   169

Don and Chris setting out from Hampstead for the Eiger
in the summer of 1962.   184

Brian Nally at the top of the Second Ice-field.   185

The Grandes Jorasses and Rochefort Ridge from the
north-west.   188

Ian eating some spaghetti we found in the Jorasses bivouac
hut, on the col between the Jorasses and the Rochefort.   189

Ian Clough at the bivouac below the Difficult Crack.   196

Chris at the bivouac below the Difficult Crack.   197

Chris, wearing duvet and pied d'éléphant, settled down
for the night in the bivouac below the Difficult Crack.   198

The North Wall of the Eiger.   199

Chris on the Hinterstoisser Traverse.   202
Looking back on to the Second Ice-field from the top of
the Flat Iron.   203

On the Third Ice-field.   204

Cutting steps into the White Spider from the end of
the Traverse of the Gods.   205

AUTHOR'S NOTE

I am most grateful to those of my friends who have kindly allowed me the use of their photographs in this book. Acknowledgment is made individually beneath each reproduction. All other photographs are my own with the exception of the unacknowledged photograph facing page 30 which is in my possession.

I am also grateful to Messrs. Van den Berghs Ltd. and Unilever Ltd. for giving permission to reproduce the letter on page 15, and to my wife for drawing the diagrams.

C. B.

FOREWORD

by Eric Shipton

THERE IS TODAY a wide gulf between the "classical" mountaineer and the expert in modern climbing techniques; and there are many famous climbers still in their prime who would be quite incapable of tackling the more difficult routes in the Alps, or even of using modern methods and equipment effectively. This curious anomaly is due to the fact that until comparatively recently the development of these techniques was virtually confined to the Alps, while those who made their reputations in other ranges, where competition was far less keen and where the new methods were often still not applicable, had no need to employ them to break new ground.

The revolutionary development of modern mountaineering began in the twenties and was a direct result of the greatly increased popularity of the sport. Hitherto, mountain climbing had been largely confined to the comparatively affluent; but with the practice of guideless climbing, which became general after the First World War, it was found to be one of the least expensive of pastimes, available to a vast number of young people who lived within easy reach of the Alps. Increased popularity led inevitably to keener competition for the dwindling supply of possible new routes, and this to the evolution of bold new techniques, novel equipment and, it must be said, to the acceptance of narrower margins of safety. The inter-war years saw in the Alps a spectacular advance in standards of achievement, which at that time was matched nowhere else in the world.

The British, who can be said with some justice to have started the sport of mountaineering and who had the field almost to themselves during the Golden Age of the mid-nineteenth century, played almost no part in the developments of this great era in the Alps. Certainly they were not inactive in the more distant ranges, and our rock climbers achieved great forward strides in the perfection of their art. But the latter were largely content to remain in their home environment, and British crag climbing seemed to have become a separate sport, almost divorced from the field of greater mountaineering.

In the last two decades, however, there has been an astonishing reversal of this trend. Shortly after the War, Tom Bourdillon (who was fired by an almost missionary zeal to put British Alpine achievement back on the map), Arthur Dolphin and others began to climb some of the great new routes of the thirties, on which British climbers had never ventured before, and even to pioneer new lines of their own. Their lead was followed by scores of young men trained on British rock, who quickly adapted themselves to the Alpine environment, the ice and snow and rotten rock (the old bugbears of the pure cragsman), the enormously greater scale of the climbs; they soon mastered the techniques of "artificial" climbing and learnt the art of survival in bivouacs in the most rigorous and terrifying situations, which are unavoidable on the great modern routes. They have made a truly remarkable breakthrough into this world of achievement; and their performance has often astonished their continental colleagues as, for example, when Joe Brown and Don Whillans made the fourth ascent (in record time) of the West Face of the Dru, a climb which a short time before had been hailed as opening a new chapter in the history of mountaineering.

Since the War the advance in Alpine standards has been fully maintained; but a more significant development has been the increasing application of modern Alpine techniques in the Himalaya, the Karakoram, the Andes and elsewhere. Thus in these great ranges, too, the limits of possibility are being thrust further and further back to open a boundless horizon of fresh endeavour.

By his ability and his dedication, Chris Bonington has won a prominent place among climbers of the younger generation. Written with frankness and perception, his book illustrates well the relentless spirit which inspires some of his contemporaries and is a fine record of his own achievements.

E. S.

CHAPTER ONE

THE CHOICE

"WE have considered your letter and regret that we cannot accede to your suggestion that we should release you to join this mountaineering expedition. . . . That you should be very anxious to go on this expedition is understandable enough but you should see the problem exactly for what it is. If you were to regard mountaineering as a holiday pastime, that would be one thing; but if you still want to pursue it to the point of long-term expeditions in distant parts of the world, then you must see mountaineering not as something which can be combined with your business career but as something which is incompatible with it. Put as plainly as possible, the time has come for you to make up your mind whether you leave mountaineering or Van den Berghs.

"It was very much in our minds when you joined us after returning from an expedition to the Himalayas that it was your intention to settle down uninterruptedly to a business career, particularly as you were a few years older than most people who join us as Management Trainees. I also think that from a business point of view an interruption of some six months in your training would not be advantageous to yourself or the Company."

I read the letter a second time. It went straight to the root of my problem, the question I had been struggling to solve for the previous few weeks—this conflict between my love of climbing and the need to find a worth-while career.

And then I looked up and glanced round our furnished room, at the big double bed in one corner, at the half-opened door that led into the cupboard-like kitchenette, at the washing in front of the gas fire. My wife, Wendy, was crouched over the table, at work illustrating a children's book, her paints and papers overflowing on to the floor. We were cramped, overwhelmed by the narrow limits of our room whose every drawer and cupboard seemed to bulge with our possessions. Our landlady, an elderly and fragile Russian, who none the less possessed an iron will, passed our french window (we were on the ground floor), and glanced into the room with a disapproving glare. A few seconds later, as she stormed up the stairs outside the room, we could hear her mutter, "They do not care. They make my room untidy. They live like animals." She was used to young bachelors and unmarried girls who were out at work all day, had the bare minimum of possessions and kept their rooms at a barrack-room standard of tidiness.

I picked up the other letter that lay on my desk. It was an invitation to climb the Towers of Paine in South Patagonia. The leader was taking his wife with him, so, presumably, I could do so as well. There were some photographs showing three spectacular, almost improbable rock spires that looked more like huge, windowless skyscrapers than natural mountains. They seemed to jut straight up from the rolling Pampas and there was an impression of boundless space, of exciting, unknown land. But it was not just a question of whether to go on another expedition or not—the letter from Van den Berghs made that quite clear. I now had to choose between a career with an assured future, or a life based on mountaineering. Up till then, I had effected an uneasy compromise between my work and climbing. Now I should have to make a choice one way or the other.

My background and early years gave little hint of my erratic future as a mountaineer. I was born in London in 1934. Neither of my parents had the slightest interest in the mountains though my father had had the wanderlust. After my parents' marriage broke up, he passed the years before the war drifting about the Far East and Australia. He had plenty of physical courage and joined the Special Air Service during the war, but was captured on his first operational mission and spent the rest of the war as a prisoner. As a result I saw him only a few times in my first fifteen years and he had no influence on my upbringing. In my early years I was brought up by my grandmother, while my mother went out to earn a living.

Looking back, it is only too easy to see signs of future behaviour in childhood escapades, but I did seem to have inherited my father's wandering nature. I had a passion for running away that dated from the age of three, when I took flight with a girl-friend on to Hampstead Heath. We were caught only three hours later by a policeman and taken to the police-station. They were heartily glad to return us to our parents, for by that time we had emptied the Inspector's bottle of milk over his desk and torn up the contents of his filing cabinet.

During the war I was evacuated to a boarding-school in Westmorland. I was still an enthusiastic escaper and twice ran away from school, not to go home, but just for the sake of it.

I saw mountains for the first time during this period, but I was too young for them to make a real impression. Nevertheless, I scrambled around the hills near Grasmere in the Lake District with immense enthusiasm, my patient and very devoted grandmother plodding behind me.

Towards the end of the war, when I was eight, I was brought back to the South of England, first to a boarding-school near Letchworth where I was desperately unhappy and then, after only half a term, home to London, where my mother now looked after me. After a year at a small private school I was sent to the junior branch of University College School—a public day school. Both there, and at the Senior School, I was neither wildly happy nor unhappy—I made a few friends but was never particularly popular. I was shy and very unsure of myself. Games, at first, were sheer purgatory. I detested cricket, was frightened of the hard ball and was thoroughly bored by the game, surreptitiously reading a book when on the field. I was slightly better at playing rugger and even came to enjoy it, eventually reaching the giddy heights of the Third Fifteen, where I made up for a complete lack of ball sense with a great deal of enthusiasm and a certain amount of brute force. In school work I was average to bright, though tended to be lazy, working only at the things that interested me. I had a passion for military history, read a great deal about it and fought imaginary battles in my head.

I was sixteen when I went to stay with my grandfather who lived near Dublin. The line to Holyhead skirts the Welsh coast, and the hills thrust it on to the very shore. I gazed out of the carriage window, enthralled. There was something strangely exciting about the way the deep-cut, utterly desolate valleys wound their ways into the mountains. There were no crags, just big rounded hills that gave a feeling of emptiness, of the unknown.

When I reached Dublin, I found that my grandfather's house was on the very doorstep of the Wicklow Hills. These had not got quite the atmosphere of the mountains I had seen from the train but they were still exciting. I wanted to explore them, to find out more about them, but at the same time I was frightened by their size and my own lack of experience. I stayed with my grandfather for two weeks. He was nearly eighty, very short, shrivelled by years in the tropics, though you could still see how tough he had been in his prime: his shoulders were still very broad, his chest deep, and you could feel the power of his personality. He had led a fascinating life. He was born in Denmark in the late 1860's; his family had a shipyard, building sailing ships, but he was unhappy at home, and ran away to sea in his early teens. He spent the next few years before the mast on a variety of sailing ships and had any number of adventures. He rounded the Horn, jumped ship in Nova Scotia and served for a time in the U.S. Marines; deserted and joined another sailing ship, which finally was wrecked off Cape Hatteras in a storm, but he managed to swim ashore.

Eventually he ended up in Bombay and secured a commission in the Royal Indian Marine. He was serving on the troopship *Warren Hastings* when it was wrecked off Mauritius, and distinguished himself by going down below as the ship, sank to secure the water-tight doors; in doing this he had very little chance of survival. For his courage he was awarded a permanent billet in the dockyard at Bombay.

He was then offered a position in the Andaman penal settlement, in the Indian Ocean, to establish a shipyard; he spent the rest of his working life there, for he loved the islands and became particularly interested in the pygmy inhabitants. He transferred to the Forestry Service and became officer-in-charge of aborigines. He did a great deal to help these fierce and very primitive people and probably saved them from being wiped out altogether by various punitive expeditions. He also made a complete survey of both the Andaman Islands and the Nicobars, which must have been a monumental task for the archipelago comprises literally hundreds of densely forested islands.

His home was filled with relics of his work in the Andamans and presentations from the many people he had helped. Even in his eighties he managed a large greenhouse and was known and respected by all his neighbours.

On my way back from Ireland at the tail-end of the summer holiday I stayed with an aunt in the flat surburbia of Wallasey in the Wirral Peninsula. One night we called on some of her friends. While they talked, I idly picked up a book of photographs of Scotland and suddenly my imagination was jolted in a way I had never previously experienced. The book was full of photographs of mountains: the Cairngorms, huge and rounded; the Cuillins of Skye, all jagged rock and sinuous ridges; but what impressed me most of all was a picture taken from the summit of Bidean nam Bian in Glencoe, with the serried folds of the hills and valleys merging into a blur on the horizon. To me it was wild, virgin country, and yet it was just within my reach: I could imagine exploring these hills for myself. A book of Alpine or Himalayan peaks could never have had the same effect, for they would have been unattainable. I spent the rest of the holiday examining every picture; I no longer planned battles but worked out expeditions through the mountains instead.

Once back at school, I started to put my dreams into practice; the first thing was to find someone to share my enthusiasm. Shortly before Christmas I persuaded one of my form-mates to join me in an expedition to Wales. We set out just after Christmas and hitch-hiked up to Snowdonia. Anton had only his shoes to walk in, while I had bought a pair of ex-army boots that had a few studs in the soles. We had no windproofs, but relied on our school burberries.

We had chosen one of the hardest winters of recent years for our introduction to the hills. There was barely any traffic on the road and we spent the entire day getting from Llangollen, near the Welsh border, to Capel Curig in the heart of Snowdonia, but this did not matter, it was all so new and exciting; even the walks between lifts were enjoyable, as the country got progressively more bleak and wild and the hills got higher. Just as it grew dark we reached Capel Curig. There are few views to beat that of Snowdon from Capel, especially when the mountains are covered with snow. The three peaks of the Snowdon Horse Shoe stood isolated a good seven miles away, but in the crisp, clear air it seemed even farther. They had all the grandeur of Himalayan giants yet were within our grasp.

That night, in the Youth Hostel, Anton and I made our plans. We had not the faintest idea of what mountaineering would entail, and looking round the common-room at all the confident, experienced climbers, I felt very green. We sat huddled in a corner, very conscious of our complete ignorance and the fact that we did not look the part, that we had none of the right clothes. I longed for a pair of proper climbing

boots with plenty of nails in the soles, or real climbing breeches
and a well darned sweater.

The conversation for the most part was in a climbing jargon
that was difficult to understand, every one talking at the top of
his voice about the day's exploits, and, as far as one could see,
no one really listening. A big, bearded man with a hole in the
seat of his camouflaged ex-army windproofs was sitting immediately behind us and was describing, with a wealth of gestures, a
narrow escape that day.

"The ice was at least eighty degrees with an inch of powder
snow on top. I'd run out sixty feet without a runner and Roy
only had an axe belay. Near the top it got even steeper and
turned to black ice. There was only an inch of it and you hit
rock. It was all I could do to get up it."

I couldn't really understand what he was talking about
though it sounded most impressive. I was much too shy to talk
to anyone, but just sat in a corner and listened. I looked ridiculously young for my age anyway; though I was nearly six foot
tall and of average build, I had a fresh complexion and smooth
skin that made me look little more than fourteen. I was always
intensely aware of this, and this as much as anything made me
shy and tongue-tied at first in the company of strangers.

We had a map, and there was a path marked all the way up
Snowdon from Pen y Pass, so we decided to follow it the next
day. We did not like consulting anyone about our plans, but if
we had done, I am sure we should have been warned off Snowdon, for in severe winter conditions even the easiest way up can
be dangerous and has claimed many lives. The next morning,
happily ignorant, we hitch-hiked to Pen y Pass, just below
Crib Goch. The path, marked on our maps, ran along the side
of the ridge above the deeply glaciated cwm of Glas Llyn, but
standing by the roadside it did not seem to be much help. The
weather had changed overnight; the cloud was down and it was
beginning to snow. From the road, the white of the snow, broken
only by black gashes of exposed rocks, merged imperceptibly with
the cloud. There were a few tracks in the snow but whether
these were the paths marked on the map, who could tell?

We were about to turn back when a group of three climbers,
who looked very professional with their ice-axes and windproofs, strode past and plunged into the snow. We followed
them; soon we had not the faintest idea where we were as the
snow swirled around us, and we floundered up to our waists in

it. My feet quickly lost all sense of feeling, it was so cold. Anton was in an even worse state without proper boots, and continually slipping. The figures in front were vague blurs in the rushing snow; above us loomed black cliffs, below, the steeply dropping white slope merged into the cloud and only occasionally could we see the dull black surface of Glas Llyn through a momentary break. We ended up in a minor avalanche when we must have been quite high on the slopes of Crib Goch. Suddenly, everything around us was moving and we rolled and slid in a steadily moving chute of snow down the slope. We had no real comprehension of danger, and arrived at the bottom laughing. If there had been a cliff on the way down we could have been seriously injured. The people we had followed had not had any more sense than us and had floundered about in the soft snow just as incompetently. I returned to the Hostel that night soaked to the skin, exhausted but completely happy —it was the most exciting and enjoyable day I had ever had. Anton did not share my enthusiasm; he returned to London the next day and never came back to the hills. I stayed on by myself for a few more days. For the most part I kept to the roads and walked from one Youth Hostel to the next, but I could never pluck up courage to talk to anyone in the evenings until my last night. The Youth Hostel at Capel Curig was full, and so I found a little bed-and-breakfast place to spend the night in. Two climbers arrived just as it got dark and we spent the evening together. It was easy to talk to them, to find out something about real rock climbing, and what they told me confirmed my ambition to be a climber.

Back at school I dreamt of the mountains and of rock climbing. I read every book I could lay my hands on. But the real problem was to find someone to climb with. In Wales I had seen the danger of solitary wandering, and anyway wanted to climb properly with a rope. Today, even in the last twelve years, climbing has expanded out of all recognition: in London there are many local clubs all of which encourage beginners and welcome new members; there are organisations such as the Mountaineering Association and the Central Council of Physical Recreation, that organise training courses, so that it is not too difficult to learn how to climb. In 1951, however, there were few local clubs anywhere and none in London. No one at school was interested in the mountains and there seemed no way of finding anyone to teach me to climb.

Finally, I ran down a friend of the family who had done some climbing. He agreed to take me/down to Harrison's Rocks, an outcrop in Kent only forty miles south of London. It seemed incredible that there could be crags so close to the city in Southern England. I had always associated climbing with the bleak hills of Scotland and Wales, certainly not with the hop fields of Kent. I met Cliff one Sunday morning at the end of March on Victoria Station. I had an irrational feeling of superiority over all the thousands of other travellers who were merely going down to the coast for a day by the sea and was intensely conscious of the length of old hemp rope in my rucksack; I longed to take it out and sling it round my shoulder but felt too self-conscious to do so. We were not the only mountaineers travelling down to Tunbridge Wells—you could tell them from the patches in their trousers and the battered anoraks. We all piled out of the train at Groombridge and walked up an ordinary country road. There was still no sign of any rocks, even when we went through a wood of young trees; and then, suddenly, we came to the top of a sandstone cliff. It was only thirty feet high; the trees growing at its base towered above its crest; a railway ran along the bed of the valley through fields of hops and past an oast house. I could not help being disappointed: it was all so peaceful and rustic. We scrambled to the foot of the cliff and walked along a path, looking up at the rocks as we went. There was nearly a mile of them—all very steep, seamed with cracks, weathered by wind and rain, sometimes completely hidden by the trees or covered with an uninviting black slime, but where the trees had receded there were stretches of clean grey-brown rock. As we walked along the foot, Cliff sounded like a guide in a stately home showing off the prized possessions to his visitors.

"That's Dick's Diversion up there," pointing to a seemingly holdless, vertical wall. "It's one of the hardest routes here; I've never done it." I wondered how anyone could, except perhaps a human spider—and then a bit farther on, he said, "There's Slim Finger Crack—you can see why it's called that." I could. The wall was overhanging at the bottom, and the crack that split it seemed barely wide enough to take one's fingers. It was difficult to believe that practically every square foot of rock had been climbed and had then been mapped and recorded, given a name and a standard of difficulty.

People were beginning to climb; for the most part they

looped their climbing rope round a tree at the top of the rocks, tied on to one end, while a friend pulled it in at the bottom, so that they could not possibly hurt themselves if they slipped. This precaution was particularly advisable since the sandstone holds were often frail and could easily break off. We stopped to watch one of the climbers perform; there was already a good audience gathered at the foot of the cliff. The climb, called Long Layback, ran up a steep crack of about thirty-five feet. He started off in fine form, his feet pressing against the rock at the side of the crack, his body almost parallel to the ground, leaning back on his arms. But then as he got higher he began to tire; his body sagged back on to the rope, and then the audience came to life, several climbers shouting different directions all at the tops of their voices.

"Cock your right foot up on to the scrape by your shoulder and layback on the little pock."

While another yelled, "That's no good, Jack, jam your left foot in the crack to your left and reach up for the jug* . . . come on, reach, man reach . . . you're nearly there."

Jack, panting hard—"Tight rope . . . tighter, for God's sake"—gasps and grunts, and forces his unwilling body an inch higher, and the man holding the rope heaves and pulls at the bottom. But it's no good, he slumps back on the rope. Yells and ironic cheers from the audience.

"Let me down," groans Jack.

"Come on, Jack. Have another go. You were nearly there," shout the supporters' club.

"I can't. I've no bloody strength left in my arms and the rope's cutting me in two. Come on, let me down for Christ's sake."

But his tormentors are now enjoying themselves.

"Go on, Jack. Fight it. You'll never make a mountaineer if you give in that easily."

At this stage Jack is hanging unashamedly on the rope, having lost all contact with the rock, and is lowered to the ground. The next man quickly takes his place and starts up the crack, but because he has done the route many times before, climbs it quickly and easily. At Harrison's Rocks climbing becomes almost a spectator sport. People living in the area go there for their Sunday afternoon walk with the dog, and some of the climbers themselves rarely leave the ground but prefer to drift from audience to audience, to watch their friends and to talk about climbing.

* Jug-handle, a large hand-hold.

Cliff soon had me on the end of a rope and I had my first taste of climbing. When he had gone up the narrow little chimney he had chosen for my first climb, it had looked easy, almost effortless—he had seemed to coax his way up the rock, stepping and pulling with a controlled precision; but when I followed I started to fight it and soon exhausted myself to no real effect, for I could make no further upward progress and all my struggles seemed to jam me even more firmly in the crack.

"Try to relax, Chris, you can't hurt yourself, you'll only come on to the rope," Cliff said quietly.

I began to think, to look around me, to try and find somewhere to put my feet, something to pull on, and suddenly it was no longer a struggle, but an absorbing exercise.

I reached the top of that first climb and we went on to more, sometimes using the rope and on the shorter routes doing without it. There were plenty of climbs I could not get up, plenty of times when I began to fight, only to end by hanging on the end of the rope, to be lowered to the ground. By the end of the day my fingers were like strips of limp rubber and opened out the moment I pulled up on them; every limb ached with weariness. But what a day! I felt a sympathy with the rock; I found that my body somehow slipped into balance naturally, without any conscious thought on my part. There was not much height to worry about, for the crag was only thirty feet, but what there was did not worry me; if anything, I found it stimulating. I knew that I had found a pursuit that I loved, that my body and my temperament seemed designed for it, and that I was happy.

Up to that time I had found no complete release in physical expression. Although I enjoyed rugger, I was always aware of my limitations, my instinctive fear of the ball, the slowness of my reactions. Even in the gymnasium, I was limited. I lacked the speed of reaction to control my limbs with quick precision and, perhaps as a result, I always experienced a quick jab of fear as I launched myself into a vault or handspring. This acted as a kind of brake, and I therefore often landed badly or ended the exercise in an uncontrolled tangle of arms and legs. But even on that first visit to the rocks, I experienced none of these limitations; I was conscious only of feelings of confidence and intense enjoyment that I had never experienced before.

On the way back to London, I asked Cliff once again, "Wouldn't you like to go climbing in Wales this Easter, just for a few days?"

He replied, "I wish I could, but I've got too much work to catch up on. I shall have a word with Tom Blackburn, though—I've done most of my climbing with him—he might take you."

Cliff took me round to see Tom Blackburn that same week— I felt like an applicant for an important job, I was so anxious to make a good impression—and be invited to go climbing. Tom was a schoolmaster so he had a good holiday at Easter, but he was married and had three children. Nevertheless, he promised to spend a few days in Wales with me immediately after Easter, and at least to give me a grounding in climbing. I was delighted —it seemed almost too good to be true—that he, a complete stranger, should be prepared to saddle himself with a schoolboy and complete novice to climbing, especially after a term of teaching boys like myself.

I did very little work at school for the rest of that term, but spent my entire time dreaming of the hills. I had a few pounds saved up and went into Black's, a climbing shop in London, to buy my first pair of boots—a magnificent pair bristling with clinker nails and a good two sizes too big. Cliff had given me an old hemp rope that was so worn that it looked as if it had been used by the Victorian pioneers, and my final item of equipment was an old school waterproof that I had cut down to look like an anorak.

At last it was time to set out on my first real climbing holiday. I was to meet Tom Blackburn at a climber's hut in the Llanberis Valley of North Wales. I hitched up to Chester, and then along the coast to Caernarvon, ending with a long walk from Llanberis up the valley. As I walked up, I gazed around me excitedly and wondered which of the myriad of crags that bristled on either side of the road I should climb in the next three days, or whether they were climbable at all. The tops were all covered with snow, and this seemed to increase the scale of everything. I had asked the way to Ynys Etws, the climbing hut, in Nant Peris, and had been told that it was the last house up the valley. It was a long, low building of local stone, with just a few small windows. As I walked along the track towards it I felt shy, rather like a boy going to a new school. I wondered how many people I should find there, and what they would be like; I felt terribly conscious of my complete inexperience and hoped with all my heart that Tom Blackburn would already be there. But there was no sign of him—only a telegram with the brief message—"Children mumps hope arrive Thursday."

The only other occupant of the hut was a man in his mid-twenties. He was sitting in the big kitchen-living-room in front of a roaring fire. He was obviously a full-blooded climber, having a look of quiet ownership in the hut as if he were permanently installed, and in his talk showed that he had an intimate knowledge of the area, which indeed he did, for Tony Moulam was one of the leading rock climbers of that period. I don't imagine he was particularly pleased to find himself suddenly landed with a young lad, who had never been climbing before, but he was very patient with me, especially in answering all my questions, most of which were very naïve.

I spent the next few days wandering the hills on my own. The weather was consistently bad and Moulam, in spite of my broad hints, preferred to sit in front of the fire rather than take a young novice out on to the crags. When Tom Blackburn finally arrived he did his duty manfully, taking me out every day. My first climb was Flake Crack on Dinas Bach, an undistinguished climb on a scruffy little crag, but to me it was the ultimate in excitement and difficulty.

When the weather began to improve Tony Moulam showed signs of emerging from his long hibernation; he offered to take us climbing. We started on Crackstone Rib, a route of *very difficult** standard, that was more steep and airy than anything I had been on up to that time. Having acquitted ourselves well on this, Tony decided to take us up a climb in the next standard, a *severe*. This route had a nondescript name—The Crevice—that gave little indication of what it had in store for us. The first pitch led easily to the foot of a deep-cut vertical corner, roofed by a big overhang, with a narrow chimney up its back. Tony went up first; he climbed with a slow precision, very much in keeping with his personality, resting for long periods, then trying a move, coming back down for another rest and then up again. I was most impressed by the way he safeguarded himself with cunningly contrived running belays,† so that if he fell he could only have fallen a few feet. In the overhang his progress was still slower as he jammed his body into the crack and by sinuous wriggles eased his way up, but his progress was always positive and he seemed part of the rock.

Then it was Tom's turn to go up and the comparison between

* The three lowest standards in rock-climbing are *moderately difficult, difficult,* and *very difficult.*

† Loops of rope placed over minute flakes, or threaded behind stones jammed in the back of a crack with the climbing rope clipped into them by a karabiner —a steel snap-link.

a really good climber on peak form and a lesser one immediately became apparent, for Tom had done little climbing in the last few years. Where Tony had seemed to slide up Tom fought and grunted, but with the help of a pull from the rope, he finally got up; and then came the moment of truth—it was my turn. I felt so alone on the end of the rope; the chimney loomed up above me, threatening and inhospitable. The rope at my waist came taut, pulled from above; a cry to come up sounded very far away, thinned and distorted by the wind, as I started worming my way up the chimney. At first it was not too difficult but soon the rock arched out over my head and I could find no holds to pull on. In my fear I jammed my body firmly in the inmost recesses of the chimney, but then, though I could certainly not slip down, I could make no upward progress. I started to fight the hard, unyielding rock, exhausted myself to no avail, edged my panting body up the chimney and out over the overhang, my feet kicking helplessly in space below me; the rope pulled at my waist, threatening to pull me in two. At last I was up, lying on a small ledge, completely exhausted, sobbing for breath. It was the only time I have ever been pulled up a climb and it was agonizingly uncomfortable, but it was also useful, for I had become over-confident even in my first few days of climbing, and this showed me all too clearly how much I had to learn.

That same afternoon, Tom Blackburn had to return to London, to cope with his mump-ridden family, so that evening I was left once more with Tony Moulam in the hut. I planned the next day to walk over to the Ogwen Valley, where there are many more easy climbs than in that of Llanberis and where I could hope to find other people of similar ability to myself.

That night, in front of the fire, I summoned up all my courage to ask Tony if there was any chance of joining the Climbers' Club—it owned Ynys Etws and was one of the senior clubs in the country, having a long and distinguished history dating back to the last century. I wanted to stay in this warm and comfortable hut, and, much more important, to belong and feel part of the body of climbers. Tony must have been thoroughly embarrassed by my request—he talked about my youth, that I was too young anyway to be allowed into the club, and the fact that I had only just started to climb.

"You know, Chris, there are a lot of lads, just like yourself, who start to climb with just as much enthusiasm. They're keen

on it for two or three years and then they give it up and go on
to something else. Whatever you think now, you might do the
same. If you are still climbing in five years, that's when you
should start thinking of joining the Climbers' Club."

I sat and listened in a state of dumb misery. It sounded like a
sentence of eternal banishment.

A few years later Tony told me that at the time he thought
I would either kill myself in the next few months or go on to
do great things. I had plenty of narrow escapes during that
period, but in many ways it was the best I ever had. Everything was strange and new, a constant process of discovery. My
first *V. diff.* lead, my first *severe*, the first trip to Scotland, the
first iced gully on Tryfan, were all tremendous adventures that
had a freshness one only seems to experience in one's teens.

A year after my first visit to the Llanberis valley, I returned
with a friend of my own age, also still at school. We slept under
a boulder below Dinas Mot and climbed with all the fanaticism
of youth, doing at least three climbs each day; I always felt
cheated if I got off the crags before dark and never dreamt of
going drinking in the pub at nights. Apart from anything else
we couldn't afford it. We slowly worked our way through the
V.S.'s* in the Llanberis guide book and made our first timorous
visit to the dark flanks of Cloggy†—to us it was as frightening
as the North Wall of the Eiger.

Climbing now completely filled my interest, not only when
on the crags but back at home as well, where I read everything
I could lay hands on. At the same time, I realised that I had to
find a career, and was now entering my final school term with
A Levels at the end of it. It had always been assumed that I
should go to University, and I even had a place at University
College, London. After that I was not at all sure what I should
do, but took it for granted that I should have to find some kind
of conventional occupation.

But I failed one of my A Levels—one that I had been convinced I could pass. I felt disillusioned, wanted to get away
from home, and after another term at school decided to do my
National Service. At least it meant I could spend a couple of
weeks in Scotland climbing under winter conditions while I
waited for my call-up papers.

* Climbs of *very severe* grade.
† Clogwyn dur Arddu on Snowdon, on which are found some of the most serious
climbs in North Wales.

CHAPTER TWO

WINTER IN SCOTLAND

THE lorry panted slowly up the hill leading to the Moor of Rannoch. My excitement had steadily increased ever since leaving the drab streets of Glasgow and Dumbarton, and making my way into the hills along the winding road beside Loch Lomond. I had been this way twice before but it had been summer; the road packed with cars; tourists everywhere, and though, at the time, the hills had excited me to a degree I thought could not be exceeded, now, with a covering of snow, they seemed so vast, so utterly remote that I knew I had never seen anything more beautiful.

Each bend in the road brought a new view, higher and wilder mountains, an ever increasing feeling of the unknown. As we reached the crest of the hills, Rannoch Moor stretched before us, the whiteness of the snow patterned with black waters and beyond it, rounded hills, untouched, pure and desolate. The road winds round the edge of the moor and one has the feeling that nobody ever ventures into its midst—it is so featureless—and this adds to its fascination, to make it, in a way, more exciting than the mountains, for one's eyes are drawn inevitably to their tops and one knows that many people have stood there, while on the moor there is nothing on which to focus the eye, no place to reach, just rolling, snow-covered peat hags and water.

We swept round a bend, and Buachaille Etive Mor came into sight, its shapely mass and steep flanks dominating the other hills. The road ran past its foot in a long, straight stretch, before dropping into Glencoe. This was my objective, for I had arranged to meet a friend at Lagangarbh, a climbing hut owned by the Scottish Mountaineering Club, that stands at the foot of the Buachaille. John Hammond arrived the following morning and we spent the next few days floundering in the deep powder snow that completely covered the hills. We saw no one else—it was mid-week—but one evening on our return to the hut we saw a light in the window. Three rough-looking climbers were sitting round the fire, drinking tea, our tea I noticed, for there was no sign of any of their belongings. They ignored us; continued talking quietly amongst themselves.

John tried to break the ice.

"It's been a superb day, hasn't it?"

"Aye."

"Have you done anything today?"

"No. Only came up this afternoon."

"You're stopping here?"

"No. We're in the bothy by the road. It's free."

"Haven't I seen you before?" John asked the largest of the three, a wild-looking individual with straw-coloured hair, hollow cheeks and eyes that for ever peered into the distance. "Wasn't it in Chamonix last summer? You had your leg in plaster and your head was bandaged."

"Aye, that'ld be me. I had a bit of trouble on the Charmoz. I was doing the traverse solo and abseiled* from some old slings on the way down; the buggers broke on me and I fell about fifty feet. I was lucky to get away with it—landed on a ledge. But I only cracked my skull on that. We got pissed the same night and I tried to climb the Church Tower. The drain pipe came away when I was half-way up. That's where I broke my leg. What did you do last summer?"

The conversation now became more friendly. I was still much in awe of established mountaineers and was quite content to listen. I guessed this must be none other than Hamish MacInnes, already a legendary figure in Scottish circles, though he was only in his early twenties. He had started climbing as a lad, hitch-hiked to the Alps just after the war with only £5 in his pocket and had spent his National Service in Austria. There he had earned the nickname "MacPiton", having acquired a taste for pegging,† from the Austrians, on the steep limestone walls of the Kaisergebirge. In the early fifties the use of any artificial aids was still frowned on, but Hamish hammered his pegs into Scottish crags with gay abandon, much to the disgust of the staider members of the Scottish Mountaineering Club. This never worried him, however, for he had a complete disregard for public opinion and was in every respect an individualist.

His two companions were members of the Creagh Dhu

---

* A quick method of descent on steep rock, using the friction of the rope round the body.

† Pegs (pitons): metal spikes hammered into cracks in rock.

Left: The Author at Harrison's Rocks, a sandstone outcrop near London.

Below: The author at the age of sixteen, just after he had started to climb (*photo Geoffrey Gilbert*).

Buachaille Etive Mor from the north (*photo Hamish MacInnes*).

Mountaineering Club, a body even more legendary than
Hamish himself. It had been started on Clydeside before the
war at the height of the Depression. Its members had a fine
tradition of deer poaching behind them, had fought the
Zermatt guides in pitched battle when they had set up their
own guiding agency, and prided themselves on their toughness.
There was even a story doing the rounds that, on a rescue,
several members of the Creagh Dhu had fought over the dead
man's boots; though no doubt many of the tales about them
had been exaggerated in the telling.

At the end of the evening John asked:

"Where are you going tomorrow?"

"Up the Rannoch Wall. We're going to try to do the first
winter ascent," replied Hamish.

"Do you think we could follow you up?" asked John.

A calculating look came into Hamish's eye.

"You can, if you take the gnomie with you. I'll go in front
with Kerr."

The gnomie was the youngest of the three. He had only just
started to climb and was not yet a full member of the Creagh
Dhu; he had to complete his apprenticeship, and so was at the
beck and call of all the members, doing the cooking and making
endless brews of tea. Climbing as a party of three is never much
fun, it is so much slower than a party of two, but we should
never have been able to undertake a first winter ascent by
ourselves, since we had neither the experience nor sufficient
knowledge of the area, so we agreed with alacrity. If we had
known just how slow the gnomie was, we might have had
second thoughts.

Hamish and his party came for us the next day—we had got
up early because we thought it important to make maximum
use of the short hours of daylight, but Hamish evidently had no
such worries for they arrived at the hut in the middle of the
morning. On the previous day the weather had been perfect,
with a clear sky, brilliant sun and a hard, invigorating frost,
but during the night a scum of high, grey cloud had hidden the
sky and there was a cold wind that carried a few stray snow-
flakes. The Buachaille looked grim and menacing in the dull,
flat light, much bigger, more dangerous than on previous days.
It was warm and comfortable in the hut; I had no desire to go
out into the wind and the cold, was suddenly afraid of the
mountain, full of forebodings and yet excited at the same time.

"Do you think it'll go, Hamish?" asked John, voicing my own fears. "The weather seems to be brewing up. There's some snow in the air."

"It'll be all the more interesting," replied Hamish cheerfully. "There's a stack of powder snow on the crag already; a bit more won't do any harm. Anyway, we'd better be getting off— it's dark at six."

We set out, plodding slowly through the deep snow in single file. It's a long way to the Rannoch Wall, nearly to the top of the mountain. We worked our way round the bottom slopes of the Buachaille and Hamish paused only to point out a long slide of water ice, which we had to cross.

"A nig-nog tried it solo last week and came unstuck at the top. He landed down there. We had to shovel his brains back into his head; it was quite messy." I found myself clinging to the hand-holds a little harder and thinking regretfully of the fire we had just left. We were now climbing the Curved Ridge, one of the easy routes up the Buachaille, and I should have loved the security of the rope but was too proud to ask; anyway, everyone else seemed perfectly at ease.

At last the Rannoch Wall came into sight; it looked impossibly steep, jutted into the cloud base just above, with a fluted structure of ribs and grooves, bristling with little overhangs, and from below there seemed to be no ledges at all. Hamish confidently kicked steps across a snow gully to the foot of the wall, and before I caught up with the rest of the party, had already started up the first pitch—he was planning to follow Agag's Groove, a comparatively easy but fine line that started at the lowest point of the Wall and led to the crest of the Crowberry Ridge, near the top of the Buachaille. It had been done hundreds of times in summer and was not particularly hard— but now all the holds were covered with snow and ice; the gully we had crossed to reach its foot, dropped away steeply below us in a snow-chute between steep rock walls, giving us a sensation of isolation.

By the time we had untangled our ropes and tied on, Hamish had disappeared round a corner, somewhere above us. There was a long pause and we soon grew cold huddled together in the snow. We could hear Hamish singing an Irish rebel song high above. The rope to him crept out through Kerr MacPhail's hands with maddening slowness. At last there was a thin cry; another pause and the rope began to move quickly until it was taut, pulling at Kerr's waist. He started to climb and soon vanished into the flurries of snow that were now pouring down the crag.

We soon discovered why Hamish had been so happy that we should follow him up with the gnomie; he was the ultimate of slow climbers. Leading each pitch was all right; I was much too gripped to notice the cold, even enjoyed clearing the holds, balancing up the ice-glazed rock, but the waits in between were sheer agony. Then I had ample time to notice how cold I was, how slow the other two were in coming up. Each pitch* was the same. We were following a series of shallow grooves and seemed to be getting somewhere near the top. The other pair had vanished entirely; we could not even hear their shouts and I felt weak and inadequate against the size of the wall, the strength of the wind and the driving snow. Our windproofs were frozen into suits of armour, and our clothes underneath, warmed by body heat, were by now wet and clammy from melted snow. The groove dwindled into nothing and the face steepened; a feeling of near panic grew inside me as I searched for the route, clearing away snow, only to find sloping ledges.

There was a lull in the wind and much to my relief I heard a shout from below—it was Hamish; they had finished the climb and were on their way down.

"Are you planning to spend the night out?" he yelled. "It'll be dark in another hour. You'll have good bivouac practice for the big North Walls."

I was not amused. "Where the hell does it go from here?" I shouted.

"Traverse left," he replied, "and you'll find a peg. There's a bit of ice on the wall that makes it a wee bit hard."

Across to the left it looked frighteningly steep but there was no time to waste if we were to get off before dark. I started to edge my way across, grateful for the hand-holds that Hamish had cleared from the ice. I could just see the piton about twenty feet away. My fingers had long ago lost all feeling and I was shivering so hard I felt I was going to shake myself off the holds. I was very glad to reach the peg. After that I felt more confident and a few more feet led to the top. It was now nearly dark but I felt reassured for Hamish had settled down on the Ridge below to wait for us. John quickly came up to me, and

* The stretch of the climb between each stance where the climber can belay (tie) himself safely to the rock.

then the Gnomie slowly followed. We were impatient to finish, to move swiftly and freely, to get some warmth back into our limbs. When Gordon reached the peg, we discovered why Hamish had waited for us.

A yell wafted up from the depths.

"Mind you get the peg out, Gordon."

We heard the sound of hammering from below.

"I can't get it out, Hamish. It's bent in the crack and my hands are frozen solid," he cried.

"You're not going up till the peg's out," came the implacable reply. "A night out will do you no harm. Don't let him up, Chris, till he has got it out."

Bugger the peg, I thought. I want to get down. But Hamish has a strong personality and the "gnomies" in the Creagh Dhu are used to an iron discipline, so we sat and cursed and shivered while the unfortunate Gordon hammered at the peg.

At last, a weak gasp of triumph.

"I've got it out, Hamish."

"Well, you can go on up now. Next time you should take a heavier hammer," replied the hard man.

By the time Gordon reached us it was dark. We hurriedly coiled the hawser-like frozen ropes and stumbled across easy-angled but snow-plastered rocks to the top of the Curved Ridge, which was to be our way down. We were greatly relieved that Hamish had waited for us, for, by ourselves, we should never have found the way. The three Scots went back to Glasgow that night saying that there was too much fresh snow to do any climbing, but Hamish said that he might return at the end of the week and told us where to find him.

John and I did some more climbs that week but they were of no particular merit for there was too much fresh powder snow blanketing the rocks and filling the gullies. Wading through it, thigh deep, was an exhausting business. At the end of the week John left for London and on the Friday night, Hamish arrived at Lagangarbh.

"It's no good going for the gullies," he said. "There's too much powder snow. We need a good thaw followed by a hard frost before we can go for the big stuff—but I know a nice little problem that's just waiting to be done on the Crowberry Ridge. We'll do the Direct tomorrow—it's never been done in winter."

I was happy to follow him anywhere for I had complete confidence in him and still could hardly believe my luck that I should be climbing with one of Scotland's best mountaineers. We set out next morning and scrambled to the start of the difficulties, which was fairly high up on the Crowberry Ridge— this was the famous Abraham's Traverse. Hamish quickly un- coiled the rope and tossed me an end. I started to search for a good bollard on which to belay but could not find one.

"Don't worry about that," said Hamish. "You'll be fine sitting down there; it's a grand stance."

I was much too in awe of the master climber to demur, so I sat where he pointed, feeling decidedly unsafe. Hamish stepped round the corner out of sight—the rock above was smooth and sheer, and the route lay round to the left. I was sitting on a small rock-pedestal, my feet braced against a block. Looking down, the ridge that had felt pleasantly easy-angled as we had scrambled up, dropped away steeply below my feet.

There was no movement from the rope in my hands, just the sound of Hamish's nails scraping on the rock round the corner. I began to wish that I had a proper belay, to imagine what would happen if Hamish fell off—the sudden violent pull of the rope that would surely tear me from my stance. I then began to pick out the line we should take as we hurtled downwards: we should hit that snow-covered ledge but inevitably bounce, and so on to the boulder-strewn slopes over a thousand feet below. Ten minutes went by, no movement, just the sound of scraping, of metal on rock. The rope acted as a telegraph wire, transmitting Hamish's struggles out in front even though he was out of sight. There was nothing I could do but sit and wait; I was more worried about being pulled off the ledge than about his safety. Another twenty minutes went by and the rope crept out a few inches. I restrained my longing to ask what was going on, whether it was difficult.

At last, a shout from above: "It's a wee bit hard. I'm coming down for a rest. Take in the rope." A clatter of nails and Hamish appeared.

"There's ice over all the holds. They are all sloping and I can't find anywhere to get a peg in."

"Well, how about finding me a belay," I protested.

"You should be all right as you are, but we'll give you some- thing," and he made a big loop in my rope and dropped it over the pedestal on which I was sitting; it was better than nothing, but if he fell off I should be pulled off my stance before it held me. I resumed my nerve-racking wait—another half-hour and he was back again. I was now on the point of open rebellion but Hamish's enthusiasm disarmed me.

"I've nearly got it," he asserted, full of optimism, "but I'll have to take my boots off—the nails skid straight off the holds, but I might just stay on in socks." He set out once again in his stockinged feet; at least there was no more scraping of iron on rock, though perhaps this was even worse for the silence allowed my imagination even more play. The rope ran out slowly; there was a sound of hammering, the rope continued to move, and then a shout: "I'm up." I had been sitting in the same position for an hour-and-a-half, and when I stood up to follow, it was all I could do to move my limbs, they were so frozen. I soon discovered why he had found it so hard: the rock was covered by a thin but tenacious skin of ice that did not shatter under the blows of our axes. The place that Hamish had found so difficult was a gently sloping slab. He had managed to hammer a piton half an inch into a hairline crack, while his feet had been steadily slipping down the slab, and then, hand-ling the peg with loving care, had stretched for the top where the holds improved. His position had been even more precari-ous than I had imagined. In comparison, the rest of the climb was easy and we quickly reached the top of the Buachaille.

That night Hamish was in high spirits.

"Conditions are much better than I had expected. Tomorrow we'll go on to the big-time stuff," he told me.

"What's that?" I asked, full of apprehension.

"We'll have a go at Raven's Gully. It will be the best winter route in the Glen, if we can get up it. I've tried it a couple of times already."

I had heard of Raven's Gully; there was a note in the Hut log-book describing Hamish's last attempt when he had been rescued from it. It was the steepest of the gullies on the Bua-chaille and the only one that had not had a winter ascent, though it had been climbed in summer. Huge boulders blocked the gully bed, forming fierce overhangs and the climb, even in summer, was rated as *very severe*.

"We tried it last year," Hamish told me. "I went up with a big group of Creagh Dhu lads. We got over the first overhang and I was just trying the second one, with the lads waiting on the snow below. Big Bill was fooling around unroped, and must have stepped backwards. One moment he was there and the next he was whistling down the gully. He must have gone a thousand feet before he stopped—we thought he was a goner. He just got up and shouted: 'Come on down—it's great down here.' There were a lot of boulders sticking out of the snow on the way down, so he was lucky to get away with it. We didn't follow him."

"You had a narrow escape yourself last month, didn't you? Weren't you pulled out of the gully?"

"I wasn't pulled out. They dropped me a rope and I climbed out. I was only ten feet from the top anyway. I went up with Charley Vigano and John Cullen, two Creagh Dhu lads. The gully was heavily iced but we had got over the crux* and just had a couple of hundred of feet up an icy groove to get out. I ran out a hundred feet, using a few pegs; it was bloody thin climbing and pitch dark by that time; then the rope jammed. The lads wouldn't leave their ledge, said they couldn't get up without the help of the rope. They were all right where they were, for they had heavy motor-cycle suits and were sitting on a big ledge, but I only had my jeans and a thin shirt under my anorak. I had to get up or freeze to death, so I took off the rope and went up solo. I got to within ten feet of the top; I was jammed across a little chimney. There were no real holds and it was all covered in verglas.† I couldn't get up or down so I just stayed there. I thought I'd had it, it was so bloody cold and I was there for eight hours. Fortunately someone in the valley saw the torch signals the lads were making and a rescue party came up and gave me a top rope and then pulled the lads up."

I was impressed by his story at the time but when I saw the spot where he had remained precariously jammed for over eight hours in a temperature that was well below freezing I understood just how tough Hamish was. The slightest loss of consciousness, or even relaxation of his muscles, would have caused him to fall, his position was so insecure. It was characteristic of him that he was so lightly clad, for he never seemed to feel the cold.

We settled down for the night, Hamish on the floor, though there were fifteen unoccupied beds in the hut, for he believed that a hard bed was essential to health. He was also very keen on health foods and advocated a diet of brown, stone-ground bread and honey; he was so persuasive that he even got some of the Creagh Dhu on to this diet.

* The hardest part of a climb.
† A thin, hard layer of water-ice coating rock.

The next morning it was a fine, warm day; perfect, Hamish claimed, for attempting the Gully. We set out early to make the maximum use of daylight, and weighed down by a rucksack full of pitons, crampons* and spare clothes, plodded up the lower slopes of the Buachaille. The Gully is in an intimidating setting; it is a deep-cut, dark gash, flanking one of the most impressive walls in Glencoe, so steep that there was no snow to vein the rock, just black streaks of water ice. On the other side of the Gully was a steep but slender buttress; it was obvious from below that there was no easy escape out of it.

At first we cramponned up a slope of easy-angled ice but it quickly narrowed and steepened into a chute, enclosed by sheer walls, that was finally barred by a big overhang formed by a boulder jammed in the gully. This was the first obstacle. I was ensconced in the cave formed by the boulder; it was like being in a refrigerator. Hamish set to work on the ice-coated walls below the overhang, chipped away the ice and hammered in several pitons. The time dragged slowly; it took him an hour-and-a-half to climb this pitch; but worse horrors were in store. Above the overhang there was a stretch of simple snow climbing, but then the gully steepened and narrowed; there were several boulders jammed in the chimney, and the route seemed to go inside these, but everything was covered with a thick coat of ice. I had thought my stance at the back of the cave unpleasant, but this was infinitely worse for a stream of water was pouring down the back of the gully and the only possible stance was in its bed. We were both soaked to the skin. Hamish unroped and threw the end over the boulder just above our heads and tied on again. With this protection, he began cutting hand and footholds in the thick ice and slowly worked his way up the chimney. The water poured over him, running down his legs in streams. A grunt of relief, and he was able to pull out on to the wall, clear of the torrent—but a steep groove barred his way.

"I'll have to take my boots off, Chris," he shouted. "Bring them up with you. I'll leave them on the ledge." I paid out the rope slowly, winced away from the stream of water and gazed out through the slit formed by the walls of the gully at the sunlit hills on the other side of the valley, longing to be there. My enthusiasm for first winter ascents had been washed away by the shower-bath of icy water that hammered on my head,

* Framework of steel spikes strapped to the boots.

and my one ambition was to escape the dank confines of these steep walls—I even began to regret ever having met Hamish.

The rope was now tugging at my waist. I could not hear Hamish shouting for the sound of falling water, so assumed he was belayed and nerved myself to plunge into the full force of the torrent. I was glad to feel the rope pulling at my waist: I could hardly co-ordinate the movement of my limbs, they were so cold, and the ice-covered gully wall was vertical. After a few feet I escaped the waterfall, and reached the ledge on which Hamish had left his boots. The groove above was steep and holdless, with the occasional knob of rock protruding from the black ice. Hamish had balanced up these in his stockinged feet; I followed in crampons, the points scratching ineffectively on rock and ice alike, very glad of a tight rope. I found Hamish standing on a snow ledge in his stockinged feet, showing no sign of cold though my teeth were chattering like a machine-gun.

"Aren't your feet cold, Hamish?"

"No, I can't feel them. I won't bother to put my boots on; I think I'll be needing socks again for the next pitch. It's a grand climb, isn't it?"

I agreed, without enthusiasm. At least we were now out of the waterfall, the rock above was less steep though very smooth, and the gully had opened out a bit, giving us a feeling of greater freedom. Hamish had started to edge his way across the smooth left-hand wall of the gully; he hammered in a couple of pitons on the way, as there was a thin glaze of ice over it—a shout of triumph and he reached the top of the pitch.

"Let's have my boots," he called.

He had led two iced pitches and had stood on the stance in between for over an hour in his stockinged feet. It seemed a miracle that he was not frostbitten. I was quite sure I would have been, in his place; my feet were like blocks of ice, though I was wearing boots and two pairs of socks.

It was now my turn to follow him; my boots skidded on the iced rock and the rope gave me little help since it was running up from me at an angle. I reached the last peg; had I come off, once I had unclipped from it, I would have swung some thirty feet into the rocky bed of the gully.

"Make sure you get the peg out," cried Hamish.

"I can't. I need it to hold on to."

"Use the holds, man—they're there if you look for them. A swing won't do you any harm. That peg cost two bob."

"I'll pay you for the bloody peg. I'm coming across."

I teetered somehow across the wall, more off than on, but just managed to maintain contact with the rock.

The gully now deepened into a dark chasm.

"This is where the lads waited when we got stuck last time," Hamish told me. "I had to solo up those grooves to the right. That's where we go now. They don't look too bad today. Would you like to go in the lead?"

I jumped at the chance, for the rock was almost entirely clear of snow; there even seemed to be a few proper holds.

"It was completely covered last time," Hamish went on. "That's where I ended up—in that wee chimney up there."

I could see why he had been stuck; the walls were as smooth as a bottomless coffin, about three feet apart and seemingly holdless. It was difficult to conceive how he had survived eight hours jammed across it.

"You should be able to get out to the left," Hamish shouted from below. "I took the chimney because the ordinary way up was covered in ice."

I was only too glad to avoid it and started to traverse across broken rocks towards a welcoming band of sunlit snow. A few minutes later we were both standing near the top of the Buachaille, our wet clothes steaming in the sun.

CHAPTER THREE

BETWEEN AIR FORCE AND ARMY

My call-up papers arrived shortly after my return from Scotland, and in early March, 1953, I joined the Royal Air Force to do my National Service. Much to my surprise I found that I enjoyed Service life. Perhaps after leading a rather solitary, fatherless childhood, when I had always felt oddly different, in some ways inferior, to other boys at school, I was now an integral part of a large organisation, in effect a family, in which I could submerge myself.

Because I had the right academic qualifications I was automatically put up for a National Service commission, and passed the selection board; questioned, I was asked if I wanted to apply for a permanent commission and decided to have a try, choosing the R.A.F. Regiment, which sounded more exciting than one of the administrative branches. One of the selecting officers on the Regular Commissions Board talked me into trying for a flying commission.

"Why don't you want to be a pilot?" he asked.

I didn't like to say that the idea had little appeal for me, as I thought this would doom my chances from the start: flying tends to be a holy word in the Air Force.

"I don't think I've got fast enough reactions, sir," I told him.

"We've got experts who are paid to find that out. Shall I put you down for Air Crew?"

"Yes, please do, sir. I've always dreamt of flying."

It did not really matter what I said, as I was sure I should never get through the aptitude tests.

I passed the board, and to my amazement, got through the aptitude tests. It was quite a job conditioning myself to the thought that I was going to be a pilot. I went to Cranwell, the Royal Air Force College, in the autumn, but for the first two terms we got no nearer to an aircraft than the planes constantly buzzing over our heads. We were submitted to an intensive and very unpleasant basic training. The only thing that kept us going was dreaming of the pleasures ahead, when we would become full flight cadets, each have a room of our own, and learn to fly.

Once we did start flying, however, my own doubts about my aptitude proved more accurate than the tests of the experts. I was ham-handed in the cockpit of the aircraft and was completely incapable of judging height and distance in relation to the manipulation of the controls. My instructor couldn't even trust me on the ground after I nearly ran the plane, a Chipmunk, into a petrol tanker!

One by one, the other members of my term were judged to be sufficiently competent to go solo, and soon I was the only one to be flying with an instructor. I never really enjoyed flying; it was too foreign to me. I was like a person with a strong aversion to heights, trying to climb. Nevertheless, I hated the thought of being beaten, and wanted to make a success of this.

At last I was told I was going to have a flight with the Chief Flying Instructor; this was usually the last step before getting the "chop".

At first it went quite well; I even had hopes of being able to put up a creditable performance. I got the plane off the ground without too much trouble and was ready to take it on the old familiar circuit round the airfield. I knew it off pat— that I had to turn over the cricket pavilion, cut my engine above the clock tower, and lower the flaps above the parade ground. I should then have been at just the right height to bring the plane down at the end of the airfield.

But the Chief Instructor was full of guile.

"We'll go for a bit of a run," crackled over my earphones. "I'll take over for a bit."

He took me to another airfield.

"You can put her down there," he told me.

I knew none of the landmarks, but thought I could manage it. The landing strip looked absurdly small from a thousand feet as I made my circuit, came into the final leg, and realised with a blank horror that I had not lost sufficient height; I was still five hundred feet up, when I came opposite the caravan at the end of the runway, when I should have been just above the deck. I did another circuit, firmly kept cool, but it was no good, I was still a hundred feet up.

I was getting desperate; I had forgotten all about passing or failing; I just wanted to get the bloody plane on to the ground. I did an extra long circuit, was limping along at stalling speed only fifty feet from the ground when we were still some miles from the field; my passenger displayed immense powers of self-control in remaining silent. At last we reached the end of the field; one wing was lower than the other, we were askew to the runway, but the only thing I could think of was to get her down at all costs. I slammed back the stick, we lost airspeed and dropped to the ground, bounced crazily from one wheel to the other, much too fast, nearly out of control.

A tired voice came from the back.

"I think I'd better take over."

We roared away from the airfield and back to Cranwell. I could not stop the tears coming to my eyes for I knew that this was the end of my flying, that I had failed.

I was given the chance of becoming a navigator or transferring to the ground side of the Air Force, but realised that I could never enjoy being entirely dependent on machinery, or cope with the wealth of technical knowledge one needed as a navigator, and the ground jobs were even less attractive, being entirely desk-bound. I had been happy at Cranwell, however, and had enjoyed the Service life; I therefore decided to transfer into the army and try to get into Sandhurst.

It was now midsummer and the Sandhurst term did not start until September; for two months I was in a happy limbo between Army and Air Force. I received the princely sum of £3 a week and was technically on duty at home—this meant that I could not leave the country. I spent the entire summer in North Wales, in the road-menders' hut by the Cromlech Boulders in the Llanberis Valley. During the week there were never more than a couple of other inhabitants, but at weekends there were sometimes up to fifteen, squeezed sardine-like on its floor. We were happy enough to put up with the discomfort, however, for the weekenders usually left a good stock of provisions to fill our own scanty larder; after nightly visits to the Pen y Gwryd Hotel, there was little money left for food.

The other permanent inhabitant of the hut was Ginger Cain. He was in his early twenties and had just left university prematurely. In a way we were both in the same boat, for we were both awaiting "Boards", mine the Regular Commissions Board and his the Conscientious Objectors' Board. He was a born rebel, with a shock of undisciplined ginger hair, a big nose and a quick, wolf-like grin. Our routine in the hut could not have been further removed from Service life, and Ginger could never understand why I wanted to give it all up and return to bondage; looking back, neither can I, but at the time, although I loved the feckless, irresponsible way of life in Wales, I felt I had to have a steady career, and, in fact, actively looked forward to life in the army.

I was summoned before the Regular Commissions Board at the end of July. We spent three days crossing "crocodile-infested rivers" on the lawns of a large country house, competed in discussion groups and worked on intelligence tests. I now felt quite an old hand, having survived two similar boards. My final interview was with a colonel who was a caricature of the traditional Colonel Blimp. He had a swollen, red nose, a bristling moustache, and a black labrador who barked at regular intervals. When I was in full flight, describing why I wanted to make the army my career, he would roar—"Shut up, you bastard! No, not you—the dog."

After the Board I returned to Wales, and a few days later learnt that I had passed. Ginger also was successful, being registered as a conscientious objector, so we both got drunk in celebration of our mutual success. We quickly settled down into a pleasant, easy rhythm of existence; there was little incentive to climb, for that summer was an unusually wet one, even for Wales. The crags were rarely dry, and Clogwyn dur Arddu was swathed in slime for the entire summer. We snatched our climbs between showers or on the odd fine day, but since we had no transport and little enthusiasm for walking, were restricted to those within easy reach of the hut. Each night we made a pilgrimage to the Gwryd, not so much for the beer, as for the favours of the girls working there.

The history of climbing in the Llanberis Valley is fairly recent: the crags are steep and vegetated, merging into the hillside, and until the 1930's were avoided by climbers; but then Menlove Edwards, a man of immense strength and pioneering zeal, who was fond of steep and mossy rock, put up a number of routes on them. In many ways he was the real father of modern climbing in this country. There was a pause during the war, but in 1947, Peter Harding and Tony Moulam filled in some of the obvious gaps left by Menlove Edwards. They were able to push the standard a little higher, making full use of their technical competence gained in practising on gritstone outcrops and of the improvement in equipment—the use of nylon ropes and running belays. Peter Harding produced a guide-book to the valley in 1950 and in recognition of the increased difficulty of his new routes, introduced two new standards—*extremely severe* and *exceptionally severe*.

In the previous three years, I had slowly worked my way through the new guide book, ticking off routes with a youthful enthusiasm, and that summer I ventured on to the extremes. I had now nearly finished the book and so nerved myself to take a step into the unknown, to attempt some of the routes put up by Joe Brown.

In 1954 a fog of myth surrounded his name; he had made a large number of first ascents in the Llanberis Pass and on Clogwyn dur Arddu, on stretches of rock that seemed so steep and intimidating that they had been dismissed as impossible by other climbers. The Cenotaph Corner on Dinas Cromlech, a right-angled gash between sheer walls, that from below looked completely holdless, was typical of his climbs. He had made many of these routes as early as 1951 and yet no one outside his own close circle had plucked up courage to repeat them. I had never seen him, for the Rock and Ice, the club he belonged to, tended to keep to themselves, and anyway I was only on the fringe of the climbing world, never having climbed on gritstone from where this new wave of climbers originated. There were any number of stories told about him, that he was small and light, that his arms hung down to his knees, that he had superhuman strength; one imagined an ape-like creature. It was said that no one of normal build could possibly repeat his climbs; a depressing thought, for I was nearly six foot tall and of very average strength. Nevertheless, I resolved to try one of his routes and chose Sickle, on Clogwyn y Grochan, because it was rated as only *very severe* and not *XS*. This did not do much to reassure us, however, for we took it for granted that a "Brown *VS*" would be much harder than anything that had ever been done before.

In the course of the summer we did a few more of his climbs, but familiarity made them no easier or less intimidating. They still held an aura of mystery and terror that is difficult to comprehend today, in 1966. Although few other climbers were trying them, their ascent did not require the build of a superman; it was more a question of a refined, very precise technique. Brown's routes tended to take lines that at first glance looked impossible and had been dismissed as such by earlier climbers, but once on them we found that there were just sufficient holds.

Our best effort was Surplomb, another route on Clogwyn y

Grochan, up a series of particularly savage grooves. It started up a blank wall, which was crossed by standing in a sling,* balanced on a spike the size of a thumbnail; then came a fiercely overhanging crack, followed by a V groove that slowly opened out, until at the top I was barely braced across it by my toes and the small of my back, and felt that it was about to spew me out. There was no protection† and it was now necessary to pivot round on one's toes to grasp the smooth, square-cut edge of the bulge that thrust one out of the seeming security of the groove. It was the hardest climb I had ever done, and I was a good hour braced at the top of that groove. Our bubbling egos were slightly deflated when we learnt that Brown had made the first ascent in nailed boots during a snow storm. Even so, the climb still has the reputation of being one of the hardest in the Llanberis Pass.

Towards the end of August, the weather went from bad to worse; it was almost a relief to leave Wales for the next stage in my career. Before going to Sandhurst I had to be absorbed into the Regular Army as a recruit. I had chosen my own county regiment, the Royal Fusiliers, whose depot was in the Tower of London. I spent three days there as a private, employing every dodge I had learnt in the Air Force to avoid doing any fatigues. It was certainly an interesting time—the barracks, of Victorian vintage, are on one side of the Inner Bailey of the fortress, immediately opposite the White Tower. We recruits felt like prisoners in the Tower, for we were not allowed in any parts of it which were used or even in view of the public—this put everywhere out of bounds except a narrow lane between the walls and the back of the barracks; its entire length was in full view of the regimental policemen, whose mission in life was to terrorise newly joined recruits. The barracks, in 1954, were full of the atmosphere of the past. Tiny windows, one lavatory for about thirty recruits and no hot water. We ate in a vault that would have done good service as a dungeon. The other recruits, who came from the East End of London, were not quite sure what to make of me, but treated me with good-humoured indulgence and gave me any amount of advice.

After three days, dressed in ill-fitting khaki, I went on to the Royal Military Academy, Sandhurst. We spent most of the first two months on the drill square, being bellowed at by Guards sergeant-majors.

* A rope-loop   † Nowhere to place a running belay.

We each had our own small room, a great luxury, and six of us shared a servant. Most of these were nearing retiring age and had been at the Academy for years; Jack, my servant, was the second oldest, with over thirty years service to his credit. A confirmed snob, he delighted in telling me of the young gentlemen who had been through his hands in the past.

"They were a much better class than we get today, such nice young gentlemen, all from the best public schools. The Academy just isn't the same today," he'd murmur, looking at me reproachfully. I am afraid I did not measure up to his standards. My next door neighbour came closer to his ideal, for he had been to Winchester, rushed off to London in mid-week to attend deb parties and was going into the Scots Guards.

There were many others like John, and they naturally formed a well-knit group within the Academy. They had the same backgrounds, went to the same parties, all knew each other or had mutual friends, and were going into the same kind of regiments—the Brigade of Guards, Cavalry and so on. They were full of self-confidence, at times were arrogant and had a firm though unspoken code of what was, or was not, good form. They undoubtedly had a strong influence on the rest of the Academy. For a start, one could not help being a little envious. I also should have liked to flit off to London to deb parties, to attend hunt balls, to have the same self-confidence. As a result, many of us with very ordinary, middle-class backgrounds aped some of their ways, conforming with the atmosphere that pervaded Sandhurst. I hid in the back of my wardrobe the unfashionable, double-breasted blue suit which I had bought whilst at Cranwell, and acquired the Sandhurst leisure uniform: tight cavalry twill trousers, plain coloured waistcoat and tweed jacket. I even equipped myself with a bowler hat—bought second-hand, and an umbrella, for my forays in London which rarely got farther than my home in Hampstead. My only girl-friend at the time, a straight-thinking, Northern lass, who was at a domestic science college in Leicester, was, I think, slightly appalled by my affectation. I became acutely conscious of my own social limitations and quite unconsciously began to add an exaggerated public school veneer to my ordinary south-country accent. I, and many others, were simply conforming to the Sandhurst mould, not consciously but because we were adaptable and wanted to be part of this society.

I thoroughly enjoyed my stay at Sandhurst, and flung myself

into everything with immense enthusiasm; the study of war had always interested me, and playing at soldiers in the woods behind Camberley was great fun, just like cowboys and Indians, except that we had real rifles and thunderflashes. I was even made an under-officer in my final term—this meant that one carried a sword around on parade—and passed out quite high in the Order of Merit.

I had chosen to join the Royal Tank Regiment, and, after a short introductory course was sent out to Germany to join the 2nd Tanks. It was a real awakening, for suddenly I realised that the two years spent learning to be an officer had taught me nothing of how to handle a small group of men and supervise the care and maintenance of three fifty-ton Centurion tanks. I was full of ideas learnt at Sandhurst, was very keen, impatient and headstrong; shy and unsure of myself, yet determined to impose my will, to have complete command. My predecessor, a National Serviceman, had been happy-go-lucky and fairly idle, yet had had a sound mechanical knowledge of his tanks and a likeable, friendly personality. I knew the tanks were badly maintained, were not sufficiently clean, that the crews were lazy, but I did not know how to put things right. I plunged into the fray, often with insufficient thought, too proud to ask my sergeant's advice. As a result, I often demanded the impossible and then had to back down. I was too conscious of the pips on my shoulders and my own dignity—I hesitated to work in with the lads, thinking that my job was to supervise.

It took me a good year to repair the damage done in those first weeks. A troop of tanks is a small, close-knit unit, and the crew of each tank a still smaller one—just four people with different jobs, one to drive, one to fire the gun, one to load it and operate the wireless, one to command and help the other three members whenever necessary. At Sandhurst we had been warned of the dangers of 'familiarity breeding contempt', but in the close confines of this mobile, steel box, one had no choice. One's crew were soon familiar with one's personal habits, weaknesses and character. It was no good erecting a stockade of discipline, of stiff upper lip; one had to earn their friendship and, at the same time, maintain their respect—discipline and obedience followed quite naturally from that.

Being an armoured regiment, there was never much likelihood of our going into real action—tanks were not used for internal security of the Malayan and Cyprus variety. We therefore trained in Germany for a full-scale war. If one paused to think, it all had a touch of make-believe; our equipment and organisation could not possibly stand up to a full-scale nuclear fight. But in exercises, atom bombs were flung around with gay abandon and we reluctantly dug our six-foot-deep trenches with eighteen inches overhead cover, or cowered for hours on end, inside our tanks, all hatches closed to gain protection from enemy fall-out. It was then that one's powers of persuasion were most needed to convince the soldiers that it was all worth while.

But for the most part, tank training was a really magnificent game, the best I have ever played. The big exercises were the best. They often lasted several days and we got little or no sleep, reaching a state of complete exhaustion. I always felt sorry for the unfortunate infantry plodding along through the fields with very little idea of where they were going or what was going on beyond their own narrow field of vision. They were the pawns in the fight, but we raced across the country—Juggernauts encased in steel, smashing through walls, scything through young trees, the wireless crackling in our headphones with messages to other tanks or troops, giving us a picture of the course of the battle.

Although I enjoyed my work as a troop commander, I began to wonder after a time, if I fitted into the Regular Army, or anyway, into this particular regiment. I soon found that I had little in common with the other regular officers, with the exception of a couple who had the same doubts as myself. But, most of all, I missed the company of climbers, even more than the actual climbing. We were stationed in the centre of the North German plain, there were no hills for miles around and I had been unable to find anyone even remotely interested in climbing. There could not be a greater contrast than between the free-and-easy relationships of mountaineers and the rank-consciousness of a foreign garrison. In England, while at Sandhurst, I had been able to escape at weekends, but in the Regiment, I was part of a tightly knit community. We worked together during the day, saw each other every mealtime and went to the same cocktail parties. We might just as well have been stationed on an oasis in the middle of the desert, we had so little social contact with officers from other Regiments—and none at all with our German neighbours. In a country with a large surplus of women, some of us fought a highly competitive struggle for the favours of a handful of English Nursing Sisters and the rest bottled up their sexual instincts until they returned home on leave—very few had German girl-friends.

Unless one was completely immersed in the Regiment, its work, social life and intrigues, one could not help finding it all a bit empty; but there were no other outlets, no escape. I was unable to plunge myself into its life, much as I wanted to; my companions spoke a different language, had different values. At times, in my first year, I felt very lonely.

CHAPTER FOUR

FIRST ALPINE SEASON—ON THE EIGER

THERE was a distant clatter of falling stones; the gurgle of running water. My ears still tingled with the maniacal buzz of flies from the Alpine pasture we had just left. The sun was hot on my neck, my clothes wet with sweat. My foot slipped on a patch of steeply banked scree and I cursed under my breath; cursed the heat, the smooth, rounded, grey rock, the piles of debris and, above all, Hamish who was scrambling so quickly, with such confidence, just ahead. Beyond him and all around, stretched the rock, grey, yellow, black, more of it than I had ever before seen. The scale was so vast. Even on that hot, still afternoon the Face held a lurking threat. I asked myself yet again what I was doing on the North Wall of the Eiger.

Back in Münster, a few weeks before, I had received Hamish's letter suggesting that we should attempt it. I suppose I should have laughed outright at his suggestion and refused, for I had not yet been to the Alps and had little experience of ice climbing, but back in 1957 the Eiger was not nearly so much in the news as it is today, and I had read very little about it. I knew it had claimed several lives before the war when fanatical young Germans had hurled themselves at its defences, and that was all. I had great confidence in Hamish's ability, however, so shrugged my shoulders and thought, "Well, it'll be a good start to my Alpine career". In fact, at that time, it had been climbed twelve times and had claimed fourteen lives. Perhaps, had I known this, I should not have been so blasé.

I travelled down from Germany in early July, to meet Hamish at Grindelwald, the village below the Eiger. I craned out of the open window of the crowded little train that rattled its way up the deep, pine-clad valleys of the foothills, past precipitous limestone walls larger than any crag in Britain— yet here no one had even thought of climbing them. At the head of the valley I caught exciting glimpses of snow peaks; but it was only just outside Grindelwald, when the train crept round a spur, that I saw the North Wall of the Eiger. It was in deep shadow, tier upon tier of dull grey ice and dark rock, on a

scale greater than I had ever imagined. Perhaps I had been
ridiculously naïve, over-confident in my ability as a rock
climber, to think of pitting my strength against such a face, but
one glance at it was enough: I felt afraid and began heartily to
regret ever having agreed to go on to it.

There was no sign of Hamish at the station. Only a couple of
days before I had received a cryptic telegram: "Meet me
Grindelwald 7 July Manx Norton." Who or what was Manx
Norton? Could it be the name of a chalet or restaurant in
Grindelwald? It did not seem likely but I could think of no
better explanation. I had imagined Grindelwald as a tiny
Alpine village, packed with climbers. In fact it was a rambling
little town crowded with tourists and had all the amenities of a
resort. Prices were high and there were very few climbers in
the streets. I searched for Hamish all day and began to wonder
if I should ever find him. I even asked at the tourist bureau if
there was a place, or person, called "Manx Norton".

That evening, quite by chance, I met him coming down the
path from the Kleine Scheidegg—the hotel immediately below
the Eiger. He was full of enthusiasm, greeting me as if we had
parted only a couple of days before, rather than three years.

"Ah, hello, Chris. I'm glad you got here all right. I've been
up to the Face today; it's in perfect condition. We'll go on it
tomorrow." His enthusiasm was overwhelming. He had discovered a flat in a chalet at only three francs a day, had found
the only cheap food-shop in the town, and had picked up any
amount of gossip about the Face. I have never known anyone
get himself settled into a place so well as Hamish does. I even
discovered the identity of 'Manx Norton'.

"Oh, that's my bike. I thought it might help you to find me.
There can't be any like it in Europe. It's stripped down for
racing. Did a hundred on it all the way down the Autobahn.
The only trouble with it is there's no silencer, so you have to be
careful in the towns, and I've taken off the lights, so you can't
ride it at night," he told me.

That night we sorted out our gear. I was blissfully ignorant
of the equipment needed for a major Alpine climb.

"Have you got a duvet?" he asked.

"What's that?" I replied.

"A down-filled jacket. You can take a sleeping-bag, it will
be just as warm if not warmer. How about a bivvy sack?" I
looked blank. "You'll need something in case the weather

breaks. I've got a plastic bag that I made specially." He got it out. It was big enough to cover him in a long, waterproof cocoon. "But there is no room for you in it," he went on. "Let's see—you'll be all right in this."

He produced a length of plastic material in the shape of a tube, about four feet long. In the event of bad weather I could use it to protect either my head and shoulders, the lower part of my body or my legs. Such was the force of his enthusiasm that I accepted it without a murmur. We had no ice-pitons,* but bought a couple the next morning; we should have had at least six. My anorak was made of light nylon and was more suitable for ski-ing than tackling a hard climb. Hamish borrowed my commando frame-rucksack since his was falling to pieces.

Our only clue to the route was a postcard he had bought that day. I was happily ignorant of how badly equipped we were, while Hamish was quite accustomed to climbing with the bare minimum. In the three years since I had seen him, he had emigrated to New Zealand, made many first ascents in the New Zealand Alps and had taken part in a two-man Himalayan Expedition, operating on a shoe string.

"We had hoped to try Everest," he told me. "The Swiss, who were on it in 1952, left big dumps of food all the way up to the South Col and we were going to use these. It's a pity that John Hunt and his boys got there first. All the same we went to Khumjung and tried Pumori—carried 190 pounds each on the approach march. We could only afford one Sherpa and he wasn't much good, he didn't carry much at all but was a good sort. When we paid him off at Namche he offered to give us his knife, fork and mug. We paid him for them as eating with pitons and tent-pegs wasn't very hygenic. We reached over 22,000 feet on Pumori but the weather was bloody awful and our equipment was none too good: my sleeping-bag was a thirty-shilling, boy scout model and even colder than I had expected."

Hamish was a hard man but I was not sure if I was. That night I got very little sleep as I thought round and round every possible disaster and began to wish that I had chosen a slightly less formidable companion. If only we could have some bad weather before we were established on the Face!

* An extra-long piton for hammering into ice; nowadays supplanted by screw-pitons.

Unfortunately, it was a perfect morning with not a cloud in the sky, so we completed our preparations and early that afternoon caught the train to Kleine Scheidegg. The Face drops straight into Alpine pastures; there are no introductory ice slopes or glaciers. One moment you are walking through lush grass, the air heavy with the smell of moist hay, and the next you are embarked on the lowest rocks.

The first thousand feet or so give relatively easy climbing and we were planning to scramble as high as possible that afternoon, ready for a quick start the next morning on the first difficult step. Or, at least, Hamish was hoping, for I was still praying for a miracle; anything to give us an excuse for retreat. As I struggled up behind him I took careful note of the way back and on seeing a good ledge protected by an overhang and still fairly low on the Face—well below the top of the First Shattered Pillar—I persuaded Hamish to stop for the night. We had only climbed about eight hundred feet but I was already tired, for our rucksacks weighed forty pounds each and I had never before climbed with a sack on my back.

As Hamish prepared our evening meal, I gazed down at the comforting safety of Grindelwald sprawled far below us, and across the rolling foothills towards the setting sun. Just before dark my prayers were answered: a thin scum of cloud spread over the western horizon and slowly crept towards us. The clouds were not particularly threatening in appearance, and since that time I have often started a long Alpine climb in very much more threatening weather, but that night they were the heaven-sent excuse for me to remark: "Hamish, I reckon the weather is breaking. Look at those clouds."

"They're nothing to worry about. They will probably have cleared by morning," he replied.

"Well, I don't want to be caught out in bad weather. We could easily be trapped here if it breaks during the night. I'm going down now." And I started to pack my rucksack. Hamish followed suit, no doubt thinking dark thoughts about cowardly Sassenachs.

We stumbled down in pitch dark, our head torches throwing small pools of light around us. A drop of three feet vanished into deep shadow just the same as a drop of three hundred. The scree skidded under our feet and the little walls and slabs that had seemed so easy when we had scrambled up them, now felt treacherously holdless. It was past midnight when we reached the final drop above the bergschrund* at the foot of the Face. I only began to feel safe again as I took the last jump on the rope over the gap between snow and rock. We were off the Eiger. The Face loomed above us: huge, black, menacing.

We spent the night in the meadow immediately below the Face. Next morning, to my relief, heavy clouds hid the tops of the peaks and there could be no question of returning immediately to the Wall. I, certainly, had no desire ever again to set foot on it. Given good conditions I think we might well have climbed it, for Hamish had sufficient experience and ability to contend with all the complex mountaineering problems the Face set and I was capable of following him up it and of taking a share in the lead on the rock pitches, but if the weather had turned while we were on the Face, something that happens all too often, we had nothing in reserve. Our equipment, as I have said, was appallingly inadequate and the lack of balance in the party would then have told to our cost. When struggling for one's life in a maelstrom of rushing snow and wind, every member of the party needs to be equally capable, for one slip can bring disaster to all.

However, at the time, my ignorance was so complete that I did not fully realise just how great a risk we had taken. My fears were more a matter of instinct: I had become used to taking the lead on climbs, to making the decisions. But on the Eiger, or for that matter on any Alpine climb, it was inevitable that I should be out of my depth. The scale of everything was so great; there was snow and ice to contend with as well as rock. I wanted to go on easy climbs where I could gain experience as a leader and then progress to harder routes, in the same way as I had done on British hills. But Hamish was still full of ambition. Having escaped one great North Face, he wanted to take me on to another: the Walker Spur of the Grandes Jorasses.

"But it's rock all the way, Chris. You'll have no difficulty at all. Nothing on it is harder than *very severe*. It's just like one of your Welsh rock-climbs but a bit longer."

In fact, 4,000 feet longer but we had to find a compromise somewhere, so, with some misgivings, I agreed to our new venture. We set off for Chamonix that afternoon, Hamish on his Manx Norton and I on foot, intending to hitch-hike, being short of funds.

---

* Bergschrund (or rimaye): a large crevasse between a glacier or snow-field, and steeper snow or rock above.

The atmosphere of Chamonix was completely different from that of Grindelwald. The former hugged the bottom of a sombre valley dominated by the jagged teeth of the Aiguilles and the massive snow hump of Mont Blanc, whose glaciers seemed ready to engulf the town. Grindelwald, on the other hand, was set in spacious meadows, a pretty toy village looking across to the mountain. Once in the streets of Chamonix the contrast was even greater. There was nothing beautiful about the town and it was crowded with trippers who had come in coaches for the day. It had the atmosphere of a third-rate sea-side resort, but for all that it was a real climbing centre. The camp site in the woods at the back of the town was filled with the tents of climbers—it was easy to recognise the British for they were by far the most untidy. In the streets, too, there were climbers of every nationality, reading the weather forecast in the C.A.F. bureau, drinking at the bars, lounging in the pavement cafés.

Hamish was anxious to reach the foot of the Jorasses that same evening for the weather was once again perfect and the local experts told us that the rock was free from snow. There was no time to be lost, therefore, for the Walker Spur rarely comes into good condition, since it only gets the sun in the early morning and late evening and the Face is one of the highest in the Alps. As a result, snow takes a long time to clear from its smooth, granite slabs, which are impassable when covered with a veneer of ice. In some seasons, it never comes into condition.

But before setting out we had to buy food and get some better equipment. Hamish also found any number of acquaintances with whom to discuss the weather and other mutual friends. As morning crept into afternoon, I began to wonder if we should ever get away.

"We'd better hurry, Hamish, or we shall never reach the Leschaux Hut before dark," I ventured.

"It's all right, Chris, I know the Aiguilles like the back of my hand. I'll find the hut all right. We'll just go and see my old friend Contamine. He might have some useful information about the Walker," and we went to see Contamine, one of Chamonix's outstanding guides.

It was five o'clock before we were finally ready to leave, catching the train up to Montenvers, about 3,000 feet above the town. From there we had to walk. The Grandes Jorasses stand at the head of the Leschaux Glacier—a tributary of the huge Mer de Glace that forms the main high road into the centre of the Mont Blanc massif. We shouldered our way through the crowd of tourists who were thronging round the picture-postcard stalls and trooping down the path to see "the wonders of nature" in a man-made ice grotto.

The top of the North Face of the Grandes Jorasses, its rock a rich brown in the evening sun, jutted above some lower, intervening mountains. It looked remote, untouchable, but it did not have the air of menace that I experienced when I looked up at the Eiger. I felt a little apprehensive, but beyond that was excited at the thought of feeling the rough granite; of finding a way up the huge Face. Even the walk to its foot was exciting for I had never stood on a glacier before. As we scrambled down the steep bank, I could feel a breath of cool air, from the expanse of bare ice, brush my cheek. The surface under foot was rough, and crunched crisply. Everywhere was the gurgle of running water: from the bowels of the glacier, from little runnels down its surface. There were others beside ourselves, all walking purposefully towards their different objectives, yet united in the same aim, the same feeling of expectation and hope.

Distances were deceptive. From Montenvers our turning had seemed close at hand but as we plodded up the glacier it never seemed to get any closer. Meanwhile, the light was rapidly fading. By the time we reached the Leschaux Glacier and had negotiated the piles of boulders swept together by the junction of the two rivers of ice, it was totally dark, but Hamish was still full of confidence; he was now on his home ground.

The novelty of walking over crisp ice was beginning to pall, my rucksack to feel heavier, its straps to bite into my armpits; and the angle of the ice began to steepen. Deep shadows of open crevasses appeared on either side and a dusting of fresh snow thickened into a heavy covering.

"We're nearly there now, Chris. It's on the left-hand side of the glacier. There it is"—pointing to a dark mass some distance away. We increased our pace but as we drew closer, we saw that it was only a boulder.

"It can't be far, Chris. It's just a matter of keeping going until we hit on it."

At that point he vanished from sight. He had fallen into a covered crevasse. Fortunately it was a narrow one and he was able to jam his shoulders on its lip. I helped him up and we continued our plod with greater care. I felt as if I was in the middle of a mine-field where one false step could spell disaster. Even Hamish's invincible optimism seemed slightly shaken and he admitted that we might have gone past the hut.

"We had better doss out for the night, Chris. We can sleep under this boulder. I've slept in a lot worse places," he said, when we stumbled on a rock, jammed across a half-filled crevasse. Having made the decision, Hamish dived under the boulder, formed a platform in the snow and in a matter of minutes was completely encased in a plastic cocoon. I did as best I could with my short tube. We had sleeping-bags, so were sufficiently warm. Hamish immediately dropped into a deep sleep; he never seemed to notice either discomfort or cold. I took longer, for our position was cramped and I was unable to keep the snow from touching, and therefore wetting, the sleeping-bag. Also, there is something claustrophobic about sleeping in a crevasse: I can never help fearing that the walls are going to close in during the night, making an icy trap. To add to our discomfort, it began to rain and by dawn the entire sky had clouded over. We could see the foot of the Walker Spur only a few hundred feet above us, and far below we could just discern the Leschaux Hut, a tiny blob, clinging to the hillside beside the glacier. I consoled myself with the thought that I had experienced my first Alpine bivouac, though the circumstances could not have been much more ignominious.

The weather was much too threatening to think of going on to the Spur and anyway, everything we had was wet, so we walked back down to the hut. It was little more than a shell, for an avalanche had swept it some years before. The roof was left standing, supported by a skeleton of wooden struts, but the walls had vanished save for a small, box-like enclosure in one corner that gave shelter from the wind and rain. It was derelict in a pleasing way: there was just room for two in the tiny compartment, and it was warm and cosy inside. We stayed there for three days and in that time I felt very close to the mountains.

Most alpine huts are packed with people, throb with activity and, strongly built against the forces of weather, are bastions of man; but the Leschaux hut had fallen to the power of the mountain, had been abandoned by its guardian and, as a result, this crazy pile of wood and corrugated iron seemed part of the hillside. Lying in my sleeping bag, the rain hammering on the roof, I was soon asleep.

It quickly became obvious that we should be unable to attempt the Walker Spur, for this high face takes a long time to clear of freshly fallen snow, but opposite the hut, on the other side of the glacier, was a smaller peak—the Aiguille de Tacul. Its upper part offered a fine rock buttress which, after carefully examining the guide-book, we found had never been climbed. Hamish has always loved new routes so he decided to wait out the weather and tackle it on the first fine day we had.

I now had my first lesson in patience: much time in the high mountains is spent waiting for the right weather; and the higher the mountain, the longer the wait. In this case we had little food and no books to read, but Hamish was a fine teacher and a good companion. He could spend hours, just lying in his sleeping-bag in a state of semi-coma. I, on the other hand, have always tended to be restless, impatient for action. The hours passed slowly, broken only by meal-times when we had all too little to prepare—a quarter packet of spaghetti or soup with a slice of stale bread. We had brought with us enough food for three days on a climb, and were now trying to make it last four days while we waited. On a climb there is no time to notice hunger, but lying in a small hut all day, there is not much else to think about.

For three days, it rained. We were down to our last hunk of bread and half-packet of soup when, on the third evening, the clouds began to break up and the Grandes Jorasses, all plastered in snow, were dyed an unbelievable crimson by the rays of the setting sun.

"It'll be fine tomorrow," said Hamish. "We'll have a crack at that buttress over the way. It should be quite a good climb and we'll be on new ground." I was only too happy to agree, for the proposed climb seemed very much more suited to my limited experience than our other ventures. It was a fine rock buttress of about fifteen hundred feet, perched on top of a steep little glacier.

We set out early the following morning on my first proper Alpine climb. The fact that we were attempting a new route made it all the more exciting. I felt at home on the rock. The scale, though much bigger than anything in Britain, was nothing like so vast as that of the Eiger. In fact, the summit of

our little peak was barely higher than the base of the North
Wall of the Jorasses. We climbed all day under the hot sun,
slowly working our way up grooves and slabs. It was by no
means a great climb, or even particularly difficult. We were not
painstakingly following a description in a guide-book, but were
picking out our own route, so there were no man-made limitations between us and the mountain, and our freedom was
therefore the more complete. The course we took, and our
success, depended entirely on our own judgement. To me this
has always been the principal attraction of making a first
ascent.

We reached the top just before dark. The pleasure of standing on the summit of my first real mountain was short-lived,
for we now had to get back down. To any climber trained on
British hills, this can be a terrifying experience. I was used to
reaching the top of the crag and walking down round the side,
but now we were perched on a real summit. Hamish had no
doubts. "Come on, Chris, we'll be benighted if we don't hurry
up. We might as well take off the rope. We'll go quicker without it." Yes, I thought, right to the bloody bottom at 'thirty-
two feet per second per second', but I took it off and started
to follow him down.

On steep rock I had been more agile than Hamish but now,
as he scrambled down piled boulders and steep little walls, he
showed his ability as a mountaineer, moving with a confident, easy rhythm. I was thoroughly frightened, tired by a
long day and unaccustomed to climbing down. Hamish
was always drawing away, disappearing into the gathering
gloom.

"Come on, Chris," he yelled, "if you don't want a bivouac,"
and I forced myself on, but the glacier far below never seemed
to get any closer. When we at last reached level ground it was
totally dark. A slow tramp across the glacier, a last, back-
breaking little climb to the hut and we were able to collapse
into our sleeping bags, to lie back and listen to the purr of the
primus as we brewed some tea. There was nothing left to eat
but that did not matter.

I had to return to my regiment the next day. My sole climb
had been an unconventional introduction to the Alps and in
many ways a dangerous one. Hamish had perhaps been over-
optimistic in planning to take a complete Alpine novice on
such long and serious routes. On the other hand he was an

excellent and extremely cautious mountaineer once he had embarked on a climb and I learnt a great deal from him.

On the train, as it raced across Germany, I began to dream of the next summer. Now I wanted to climb some of the easier routes, to gain confidence so that I could feel self-sufficient and at home on the granite walls and ice falls of the Mont Blanc massif.

CHAPTER FIVE

FIASCOS ON THE AIGUILLES

THE following summer Hamish was even leaner and harder. He had spent the winter in the Himalaya, chasing non-existent Yeti through the valleys of Kulu. His face was frighteningly gaunt and he had grown a thin goatee that emphasised the hollowness of his cheeks. He even admitted to feeling run-down but was as full of ambitious plans as ever.

We arrived in Chamonix at the start of July and set up house in a tiny shepherd's hut a few minutes walk from Montenvers, 3,000 feet above the town.

"There will be less temptation to spend any money," said Hamish, "and it's nearer the crags."

It was much too early in the season and even the lowest peaks of the Aiguilles were plastered with snow, but at least this gave Hamish a chance to recoup, for there was nothing we could do but wait patiently. He seldom stirred from his sleeping bag, ate vast meals of army compo that I had plundered from my regiment, and spent hours examining every diagram in the guide-book for spaces unsullied by dotted lines.

"There's a grand route here, Chris. It'll be a real plum," he announced one afternoon.

"What have you found this time?" I asked, full of suspicion.

After my experience of the previous year I was determined to avoid being involved in any more wild-cat ventures. I wanted to tackle some good, established routes, to find my feet in the Alps gradually.

"This really would be good," he replied. "Right up your street, rock all the way, fairly low and no objective dangers. Have a look. It's up the south-east éperon of the Pointe de Lépiney. Nothing's been climbed anywhere near it." I was not going to give in that easily.

"I'll go on it, but only after we have done a practice climb. How about the West Face of the Pointe Albert?" I said.

"Right, that's a bargain. You can lead me up it and I'll get all the pegs out. It'll be like a pin cushion. We might as well get something for our trouble and we could do with some more pegs once we get on to the new stuff."

The Pointe Albert is a small peak, near the end of the Chamonix Aiguilles, whose west face is about seven hundred feet high and very steep. As a result, it is a popular training climb, particularly amongst British climbers, for it is not much higher than one of our own crags and yet gives good practice in the use of artificial techniques.

We intended to rake in the harvest, as pegs are expensive items to buy. I salved my conscience with the thought that the West Face was used as a training climb and that we were therefore doing a good service. It would be much better practice for the parties that followed us if they had to hammer in their own pitons. Hamish worked manfully and removed every peg on the climb. At the end of the day we were thirty the richer. But it was now up to me to meet my side of the bargain, to attempt Hamish's new route.

We walked up to the Aiguilles de l'Envers Hut one afternoon a few days later; the path runs steeply from the Mer de Glace up the south side of the Charmoz. The hut is like a small château, perched on a rocky promontory at the foot of the Tour Verte. Its castellan and only occupant was a young maid of Chamonix (in best story-book fashion). During the evening she displayed a hearty dislike for the English but thought the Scots were very gentle people.

We left the hut just before dawn and set out across the glacier. It was a fine, starlit night; the walls of the Aiguilles, black and jagged, towered to our right; below us swept the Mer de Glace, a great frozen river, gleaming faintly in the light of the quarter moon—its crevasses, like huge ripples, scored the surface.

Getting up in the middle of the night is a painful business; there is a moment when you ask yourself why on earth you do it and wish yourself in a warm bed. But once out in the cold, clear night, your senses are more than normally alert. Excitement at the thought of the climb ahead surges through your body as you stride across the glacier, crampons crunching into crisp snow, and plod, panting hard, up the final snow slope. Eyes search for the faint shadow of a hidden crevasse, pick out the best line through the chaotic shadows of an ice fall.

We had an hour's walk across the glacier and, just as the sun hit the top rocks of the Aiguilles far above us, we came round a buttress and saw our objective. One glance was enough to realise why it had never before been climbed: after a couple of hundred feet of steep slabs, the spur thrust out and upwards in a monstrous overhang.

"We'll never get up that," I exclaimed.

"It always looks a lot worse from below," Hamish replied cheerfully. "Anyway, we can always find a way round it. Let's get our teeth into it and see what it's really like."

We roped up and started up the bottom rocks but after a few pitches were forced off to the left. Soon we were in the gully that bordered our peak. I was almost relieved: we could follow it to the top and perhaps get back to the safety and comfort of the shepherd's hut that night, for it seemed quite easy all the way up, but Hamish was made of sterner stuff.

"We should be able to get back on to the spur from here, Chris. We must be above those big overhangs by now. Those slabs should give some interesting climbing," said the master.

"But what's the point? We've been forced off the route and can easily get up the Col. We might just as well admit defeat and follow the natural line. It's bloody pointless looking for difficulty on a big face like this. Besides, the weather looks as if it is brewing up," I replied.

"But we're going back to the natural line. You don't want to miss a grand new route, do you, when you're nearly up? Don't worry about the weather, that's just afternoon cloud."

I surrendered and we left our nice, easy gully for the smooth, inhospitable slabs on the right. Progress now became desperately slow for there were few holds on the slab and we had to hammer in pitons. As Hamish struggled above, I gazed with longing at the gully we had just left. We were obviously not going to reach the top before dark, for the higher we got the steeper everything became, until our way was barred by a belt of overhangs. Below the overhangs was a fair-sized platform.

"We might as well spend the night here; it looks as if the weather is brewing up after all," announced Hamish. The entire sky was covered by a scum of grey cloud and there were a few flakes of snow in the air. Everything around us was grey and black. Hamish dived into a hollow below a perched boulder and began mining his way into the ice that packed it. Soon only his feet were showing. Feeling rather disconsolate, I searched for my own shelter for the night and ended up in a coffin-like recess at the back of the ledge. With a shroud

Approaching the Walker Spur up the Leschaux Glacier. We spent the night in one of the crevasses immediately below the Spur.

Above: Hamish
MacInnes preparing
the evening meal on
our bivouac ledge on
the lower slopes of
the North Wall of
the Eiger.

Right:
The Leschaux Hut.

formed by my plastic bag, I felt anything but cheerful and spent the night brooding over gloomy thoughts. I was much too cold to sleep.

The dawn was dull grey, and a light dusting of snow covered our ledge, but the storm had not yet broken. After eating a slice of stale bread and some dried fruit, washed down by tea which we had boiled over a spirit stove, I attacked the overhang above our resting place. It thrust my body out over the void, but there was a good, wide crack in the back of a groove and I edged my way up this, hammering in wooden wedges, dangling in my étriers,* I quickly forgot the cold of the night and began to enjoy myself. Hammer another wedge in above, clip in the étrier, swing on to it—and suddenly I'm falling, head first, my legs caught in the rope somewhere above me. There's a violent jerk and I'm gazing into Hamish's upturned eyes and beyond him to the glacier a thousand feet below. My foot is still caught somewhere behind me.

"Your wedge came out," stated Hamish. "Are you all right?" and he lowered me down to the ledge. One of the lower wedges through which the rope ran had remained in place. I was trembling with shock; my heart pumped furiously; and then I was angry, with myself for making a mistake, with the rock for spurning me. My foot was numb and I wondered if I had broken anything. I cautiously took off my boot and worked my toes.

"There's nothing wrong with that," said Hamish. "A bit of a sprain; it might give some trouble if it stiffens up."

"I'll have another go at the bastard," I said, "otherwise I might lose my nerve." I went up again, hammered in another wedge until it was firm in the crack, but this time I used the rock rather than trust my entire weight to the étrier and the wedge. I jammed a hand in the crack, cocked my foot far to one side and, panting with exertion, heaved myself over the overhang on to a tiny ledge. The rock still bulged above my head: if anything it looked more difficult than the stretch I had just struggled up, but at least I had beaten the part I had failed on.

"Come on up, Hamish. It's your turn now."

"What does it look like beyond you, Chris?" he called.

"Bloody awful. It's all overhanging."

"It's going to take a lot of time then," said Hamish, "and

* Three-rung rope ladders.

C

I don't like the look of the weather. Even when we get up, there's going to be too much fresh snow on the other side of the ridge. I think we had better get back the way we came." I did not need any persuading for there was very little fight left in me, but I hated the thought of trying to get back the way we had come. "We should be able to escape on that easy-looking rock over to the left," he added.

That was enough for me, and I abseiled down to him. At first our retreat went smoothly, over the easy-angled, broken rocks on the lower slopes of the Pointe Chevalier, but then we reached a deep-cut gully that plunged down out of sight towards the glacier. Hamish abseiled into it and I followed. Once in its bed we were trapped. The walls on either side were smooth and sheer, a waterfall tumbled down its bed. We started down it. The doubled rope dropped out of sight. Hamish went first; there was a long pause after he had vanished from view and I could hear nothing for the sound of rushing water. At last the rope went slack in my hands and I guessed he was down on the next ledge. It was my turn to follow. At first, I was able to keep out of the stream of ice-cold water, bridging with my feet on either side, but then I came to a bulge, a huge boulder wedged across the bed of the gully. Hamish was about fifty feet below, hanging from a piton hammered into a crack in the smooth wall. The rope hung completely free down to him, and I was soon spinning gently in mid-air with the water thundering about my ears. Hamish was also in the direct line of the waterfall and I had no other choice but to share his peg and single foothold. I couldn't help wondering just how secure it was.

"Get a move on, Chris. If we don't get out of this bloody shower-bath soon, we'll freeze to death. Give me the end of the rope and I'll pull it down." I handed it to him and he heaved on it. "Give me a hand. It's a bit stiff," he cried. We both heaved on the end of the rope, put all our weight on it, but it was no good, it just stretched a little but did not budge an inch.

"I'll try to climb out to one side and pull from over there," said Hamish, "that might free it." He moved with desperate slowness and then came to a stop on the steep slab just beyond us. The water hammered on to my head, spread a freezing numbness over my body. We seemed so helpless and insignificant against the strength of the mountain: I began to think of death. I hated Hamish for being so slow, for landing us in this predicament.

"Let's have a try, Hamish. If I stay here any longer, I won't be able to move at all," I shouted, longing to move, to escape from the pounding of the water. He came back and I took his place. Desperate with cold, I leapt at the slab and managed to get up it. From my new stance I was still unable to shift the rope, but free from the waterfall I could at least think, and I realised I should have to prusik up the doubled ropes. This is a technique in which a form of slip-knot* is tied round the doubled ropes; it grips them when a body's weight is on the knot, but can be slipped up the ropes once it is free of weight. With two knots, used alternately, ropes can be climbed in perfect safety. Using this technique, I hoisted myself laboriously up the gully and cleared the ropes where they had jammed. We were not free of trouble, however, for we were still at least one rope-length above the glacier. The rock bulged out just below us, so we could not see the foot of the crag.

It was now my turn to go down first. As I started out, down the rope, I imagined the worst. Would I reach the end to find myself dangling in space, with no cracks in which to hammer a piton? Soon I stood poised on the bulge: the end of the rope dropped straight into the cavernous jaws of a huge rimaye. It was at least twelve feet wide and I could not guess how deep: it just vanished into impenetrable gloom. Fortunately, just above the gap was a narrow ledge and I slid down to this.

I have always been afraid of jumping, and here was something that seemed beyond my capabilities. Hamish was somewhere far above, and the end of the rope dangled in mid-air. Safety was just twelve feet away but what if I missed the jump, if the edge of the rimaye broke under my feet? Even if I maintained my hold on the rope, I should be dangling, helpless, in the depths of the crevasse. I knew I couldn't do it.

"Hamish, there's a bloody great rimaye. Come on down." At least he'd be company. It was heartening to see him sweep down towards me. He was not daunted by the rimaye but took a bold leap, swinging out on the rope and letting it run through his hands. Even so he landed on the very brink. I followed, very glad to have him on the other side, ready to field me.

The weather had now cleared and it was a brilliant, sunny

* A prusik knot.

afternoon. We presented a sorry sight as we plodded back to the hut, soaked to the skin. People who passed, looked at us strangely. What on earth could we have been up to on such a perfect day! It was nearly dark, but we could not face the prospect of seeing the young guardienne at the Aiguilles de l'Envers Hut; we had cut much too fine a figure the previous night, so we went straight down to the Mer de Glace.

Our trials were not over. The Mer de Glace is a main road, a mountain motorway; hundreds plod up it every day, but at night it looked different. Great shadows turned the glacier into a maze. A mere crease on the surface of the ice looked the same as a crevasse hundreds of feet deep. We were soon hopelessly lost. We could see the point where we should leave the glacier, but turn where we would, there was always a gulf between us and our goal. We were so tired we could have lain down and slept on the ice, but our clothes were sodden and there was a hard frost. Eventually we found the way: what normally takes half an hour, had taken us three.

Another fiasco—I swore to myself not to go on any more new routes until I had some solid experience behind me. At the time I felt depressed but in fact it is this kind of experience that gives some of the richest memories. You quickly forget the agony of icy water hammering on your head and remember only the humorous side of it all.

CHAPTER SIX

SOUTH-WEST PILLAR OF THE DRU

THE war of attrition continued. Hamish had not been daunted by our experience on the Pointe de Lépiney and the following morning was planning the next step in the campaign. I was buried in my sleeping-bag in the darkest corner of the hut for I had a bad cold: my head bulged with catarrh, a never-ending stream of phlegm flowed from my nose and I felt miserable.

"You should be fit by now, Chris," he said. "Here's just the route for us—The Shroud, up to the left of the Walker Spur. There must be a couple of thousand feet of ice on it and we could finish up the summit rocks of the Walker. There might be some stuff coming down it during the day, but we could climb the ice in the dark."

"Look, Hamish, you can keep your new route and stuff it. I couldn't care less if it's the last great unclimbed problem in the Alps. I just want to be sure of getting to the top of one or two good, standard climbs. I can't do anything, anyway, until I've got rid of this cold."

And so the argument went on for the next few days, while I snuffled away in my sleeping-bag and the rain hammered on the roof outside. At least our controversy provided a never-failing topic of conversation. For however heated we became, we continued, somehow, to enjoy each other's company and even the argument itself. At last we came to a compromise.

"I'll go on any route you name, provided that it has been done before," I told him.

Hamish thought it over. "Well, how about the South-west Pillar of the Dru? It's rock all the way and should clear quickly."

In fact, it also had the reputation of being the hardest rock climb in the Mont Blanc massif.

From Montenvers, the Petit Dru is like the steeple of a Gothic cathedral, towering at the end of the mass of the building formed by the ridge of the Flammes de Pierre. Its West Face completely dominates the mountain scene with an upthrust of 3,000 feet of sheer, seemingly featureless, granite. Its ascent in 1952 by a French party marked a major step forward in Alpine techniques. On the right or west, the face is bounded by a spur, the South-west Pillar; this was climbed in 1955 by Walter Bonatti, an Italian and one of the greatest climbers of this century. It was even more difficult than the face and yet he went on it by himself. It would have been a considerable feat for a strong party but as a "solo" effort, it was incredible. Most of the way he could use artificial techniques* for there were plenty of cracks into which he could hammer his pitons. He could get some degree of protection by threading a length of rope through several pegs and then attaching both ends to his body so that it formed a big loop; if a peg came out or he slipped, the rope would still be attached to some of the other pegs and would therefore hold him. But there must have been times when he could not give himself this kind of protection, when a single slip would have meant a fall of some thousand feet.

In effect he had to climb the Pillar twice, for, having made a few feet of upward progress, hammering in pitons as he went, he had to climb back down to take them all out, a labour normally shared between two. In addition, he had to carry nearly as much equipment as a party of two. There is a telling photograph he took when half-way up the Spur, of a rucksack dangling on the end of a rope—rock around it, rock below— entitled: "My only companion—a rucksack".

Solo climbing of this kind is a supreme test of mountaineering skill and self-reliance. Bonatti had five nights by himself, perched on tiny ledges: plenty of time to review the dangers that faced him. Had he lost his nerve he would have had little chance of survival. To add to the strain, he was on new ground, so that he did not even have the benefit of other people's experience on the same route. He had to find his own way, never certain if he could surmount the next obstacle or if he would have to retreat and try another line.

By 1958 four other parties had repeated his route and several more had retreated from it. The fastest party had spent three days on the climb. In the light of these subsequent ascents, Bonatti's achievement seemed all the more unbelievable.

I was both frightened and excited by our plans to attempt

---

* The use of pitons for direct assistance in climbing, and not merely for protection.

the Pillar. It seemed a vast undertaking but at least it was
reputedly firm rock all the way and someone had been there
before us. My confidence was further increased when our
party was reinforced. Two young Austrians came to live in
the room just below ours. They also were interested in attempting the Pillar and were obviously good mountaineers. We got on
well together and soon established a firm friendship. Walter
Phillip, the eldest, was studying at university in Vienna.
Already he had quite a reputation, with several outstanding
new routes in the Eastern Alps to his credit. In the previous
year he had climbed the West Face of the Dru in a particularly
fast time. Richard Blach, his companion, was only nineteen
and slightly built, but we were soon to find that he was a
brilliant climber.

We walked to the foot of the Dru on the first fine afternoon,
across the Mer de Glace and up a long moraine* ridge to a
pile of boulders immediately below the face, where we planned
to spend the night. The Pillar, grotesquely foreshortened,
stretched above us, dyed a rich brown in the light of the setting
sun. On the other side of the glacier we could just see the
tourists, like black ants, milling round the station at Montenvers. The whistle of the last train, clear and sharp in the
evening air; the gurgle of running water; the purr of the
primus; all strengthened the feeling of peace around our
bivouac.

Just before dark I noticed two small figures toiling up the
moraine ridge that led to our boulders.

"I wonder if they're going for the Pillar as well?" I commented.

"That'll be Whillans," said Hamish, "or I'm very much
mistaken. I heard in Snell's that he was asking about the
Pillar. We are going to have quite a party."

I wasn't sorry to see them—I was glad of any addition to the
party. I had heard a great deal about Don Whillans; about his
prowess as a climber and his reputation for toughness. Three
years before, with Joe Brown, he had made the fourth ascent
of the West Face of the Dru.

We watched the two figures slowly come closer. The fore-
most, cloth-cap on his head, was short and powerfully muscled
—it was Don Whillans all right. He was carrying a huge rucksack bedecked with French loaves. His companion, also short

* The debris left by a receding glacier.

but less strongly built, was Paul Ross, a well-known Lakeland climber.

They paused, talked a little: no doubt Don weighed us up, and then the pair carried on to the top of the Rognon.

"See you tomorrow," Don called back from the gathering dark.

We set the alarum to two o'clock and settled down for the night. We had carried up our sleeping-bags, and so were warm and comfortable, but I did not sleep. I listened to the quiet breathing of the others and envied them their peace of mind. My own mind leapt from one thought to another: perhaps the weather would break when we were half-way up; was I capable of climbing nearly 3,000 feet of difficult rock? I was wildly excited by the prospect of our venture, but was too conscious of this conflict between fear and anticipation.

At last the alarum jangled.

"There is much cloud," muttered Walter.

"Aye, and it's too warm. I don't like the look of the weather," added Hamish. "It could do anything."

"I think we should wait till dawn to see if it clears," said Walter.

I was secretly relieved. It felt like a last-minute reprieve and I promptly dropped into a deep sleep, only to be roughly awakened after what seemed a few minutes.

"Wake up, Chris!" shouted Hamish. "The clouds have cleared. It's going to be a good day."

I peered out of my sleeping-bag: there were still some high clouds to the west.

"What about those?" I asked. "It looks pretty changeable to me."

"If we waited for a completely cloudless morning, we'd never get anything done. Those will clear during the day. We'd better get a move on. It's five already," he replied.

We hurriedly cooked some breakfast, packed our sacks and started up the snow slope leading to the couloir which marked the start of the climb. To reach the Pillar we had to follow the gully for nearly a thousand feet.

"Don had a late start as well," said Hamish, as we plodded up the crisp snow. "Look, he is just starting the couloir."

I could discern two small figures in the shadow of the gully.

"We climb solo at first," announced Walter. "It is not difficult and will be quicker."

He stepped on to the edge of the rimaye, to stride across the gap which was only a couple of feet wide, but the edge promptly collapsed and Walter only saved himself by throwing himself backwards. It was an inauspicious start, but undeterred, he hurled himself once again at the rock on the other side and literally leapt up it. The other two followed and I brought up the rear. The angle was not very steep but the rock was worn smooth by ice and falling stones. The holds were all sloping and dusted with gravel that slipped under our feet like ball bearings. I noticed that Don and Paul were roped-up and heartily wished that we were. I was soon left far behind and then I heard a shout from above. Walter had just raced past Don, slipped and landed on top of him. He was lucky not to go down all the way. I felt even more unhappy and was greatly relieved when I caught them up at the start of some steep ice, for at last they had got out the ropes. Hamish now came into his own and took the lead, cutting steps all the way with a steady, easy rhythm. Don and Paul were out to the left, but were able to move faster than we, for they both had crampons whilst we had only one pair in the entire party.

Pitch followed pitch. It was an oppressive place—everywhere there were signs of stone-fall: rocks embedded in ice, the snow grey with debris—and above us towered the Flammes de Pierre ready to engulf us. It was dark and bitterly cold in the gully, but high to our left we could see the plunging skyline of the Pillar, a golden brown in the morning sun. I longed to move swiftly to escape from our icy prison but had to wait for the others. Everything had to be so slow, so methodical, as we worked our way, one at a time, up the ice slope. It was eleven-thirty before we reached the top of the gully and could traverse out on to a small ledge on the crest of the Pillar. We were in the sun: I caressed the warm, rough granite, felt the hot rays of the sun probe through my shirt. I should have liked to have basked in the sun for the rest of the day but the real work was only just beginning. We had over 2,000 feet of sheer rock in front of us.

"You go in front, if you like, Walter. Paul and I can follow and take a turn in the lead if you get tired," suggested Don.

"Aye, we'll bring up the rear," said Hamish. "Chris can do the leading and I'll take the pegs out with the 'message'."

The 'message' was Hamish's extra heavy, chrome-plated, piton hammer. In fact he had volunteered to undertake one of the hardest, yet least exciting, jobs of all. It is very much more awkward taking pegs out than putting them in.

Walter and Riccardo climbed very quickly and soon disappeared from sight. Then Don and Paul vanished up a steep crack that marked the start of the real climbing. Suddenly I felt very lonely, even though I could hear the sound of a peg hammer far above. What did Bonatti feel with the entire face to himself?

I put away my fears and started to climb, eager to catch the others up. Crack followed crack; steep and sustained. My arms began to ache after the first two hundred feet. Could I keep it up for two thousand? This was rock climbing the like of which I had never before known. The granite was cleaved into smooth cracks and grooves: it swept endlessly up, and around us, and below it dropped sheer into the gaping mouth of the gully we had just left.

I heard shouts above, poked my head over the brink of a ledge and found Don and Paul resting in the sun. Above them leaned a big roof overhang. Richard was swinging below it, across a steep slab, in étriers; then he disappeared round a corner. He was still carrying his rucksack.

"That looks too much like hard work," said Don. "I'll leave my sack here and pull them all up when I get to the top."

He started the pitch with a magnificent display of climbing, for he did not use étriers but just pulled up on the pegs and wedges in the crack, and then seemed to walk across the slab on which Richard had dangled. He did not hurry: each move was smooth, calculated and seemingly effortless, and yet, when I came to follow, the rock thrust me backwards. At the end of the overhang Don had swung across a steep slab on the rope clipped into a peg above him, and had vanished. I followed, and found myself in a bottomless groove. Looking down, the first thing I saw was the glacier 2,000 feet below. Far above, quite unattainable, a pair of legs were swinging in the air. A crack, smooth, sheer, unadorned with pitons or wedges, stretched upwards; it was barred by two small overhangs.

"Did you go up here?" I shouted to the legs.

"Yes," came a voice.

"Is it hard?" I asked.

"It's a bit strenuous," came the reply, in a flat Lancashire accent, and the legs kicked idly against the rock.

I thrust myself into the groove. It was vertical but the crack was the right size for a hand-jam, and the toes of my boots just fitted it. Always retaining three points of contact, I clung limpet-like to the rock. At the first bulge the crack was a little wider, I could not jam my hands so firmly. Legs trembling, panting hard, I thrust an arm deep into the crack, leaned out and stepped over the bulge; but there was no rest, nothing to stand on, only another overhang just above. The legs dangling over the ledge looked closer now, but still unattainable. The rope which ran back to Hamish dropped away cleanly for over fifty feet to my last piton. If I came off, I would fall a long way. Should I ask for a top rope? It wouldn't take a minute to drop one. But I was proud, determined to climb on my own. I reached the second overhang. A stone was jammed in the crack just below it and I struggled, frantic, to thread a sling behind it, hanging on one arm. But I could not coax the loop behind the stone. I muttered to myself—I always do when I'm in difficulty —"Can't get it on. Must push on before I plop off. It's only six feet."

I pulled up over the overhang. Another few feet and the dangling legs merged into a body seated comfortably. Once over the edge I collapsed, panting, next to Paul Ross.

"Did you like Don's little variation?" he asked. "The bugger went off route. Look, he should have gone up there," and he pointed down another groove, next to the one I had just climbed. It was bristling with pitons and wooden wedges and would have been comparatively safe and easy to climb.

That was one of the hardest pitches I had ever climbed, and I wondered, with a sinking feeling, if there were going to be many more like it. If so, my strength could not possibly last the course. But that afternoon, as pitch followed pitch, my confidence was restored and I began to enjoy myself again. There were many difficult pitches, shallow chimneys, giddy traverses over bottomless slabs, but none had the unrelenting smoothness, the complete lack of protection, of the Whillan's variation.

Late that afternoon we heard a shout from above. "There's a ledge like a ballroom up here." When I poked my head over the top of the last chimney, I saw that Don had hardly been exaggerating. On the very prow of the Pillar was a platform the size of a night-club dance floor. Don had already unpacked his rucksack and was melting a dixie-full of snow over a gas stove. The ledge was scattered with ropes, climbing equipment and food.

"We might as well stop here for the night," said Don. "There's only another couple of hours of daylight and we shan't find a ledge as good as this higher up." I was only too happy to agree, for I suddenly realised how tired I was. It was the height of luxury just to sit down and relax in the evening sun. The two Austrians were still working, a hundred feet above us.

"We'll peg another pitch and spend the night up here," shouted Walter. Meanwhile, we prepared the evening meal. We pooled our resources. Hamish and I had some nutritious, though totally unappetising, survival rations, while the other two had more conventional food: bread, bacon, sausages.

It was nearly dark and we were just savouring our last brew of tea when the quiet of the night was shattered by a thunderous roar. We craned over the edge of the platform and, through a cloud of dust, watched several tons of rock pour down the bed of the gully we had climbed that morning. Sparks flickered in the dim light and then, as the sound died away into an expectant silence, there was a heavy smell of sulphur in the air. None of us said anything for a few minutes and then Don voiced all our thoughts.

"Just as well that little lot didn't roll this morning. There wouldn't have been much left of us."

The silence of the night was even greater than before, and then, suddenly, it was broken by a thin, high-pitched whine from directly above. I knew instinctively that it was aimed at us. We all ducked. There was a dull thud, and we looked up. Hamish was crouching by a boulder in the middle of the platform, his hands on his head. Blood was gushing through the gaps in his fingers. Fortunately I had a bandage in my rucksack: the only piece of first-aid equipment in the entire party. We strapped it in place but a black stain appeared within seconds, though the bleeding stopped after a few more minutes. Hamish was feeling weak and dazed. We were all stunned by the mammoth rock-fall followed by that single deadly stone. It was the only one that fell anywhere near us during the entire climb.

The platform, which had seemed so safe and comfortable, now felt hideously exposed. We huddled against the rock wall at its back, and without further talk prepared for the night. There was no question of being comfortable. Three of us wedged ourselves into a niche at the very edge of the platform. Paul Ross was standing in the back of it and Hamish sat between his legs, while I jammed myself below Hamish with my legs

The Chamonix Aiguilles from the south showing route of attempted ascent of the Aiguille du Lépiney; ---- line of ascent, ... line of retreat (*photo John Cleare of Gamma*).

Crossing the top of the couloir leading to the start of the first rock pitch on the South-west Pillar of the Dru (*photo Hamish MacInnes*).

Don Whillans in the lead on the South-west Pillar.

straddled across the front of it. I was wearing a down jacket but the cold slowly ate into my feet and spread up my legs. From time to time Hamish slumped on top of me, threatening to force me out of the groove. The night dragged endlessly and I gazed, full of envy, at the chain of lights in the valley far below. People were eating in the restaurants, sleeping in soft beds. I shifted my buttocks from one lump of rock to another. My teeth chattered uncontrollably and I consoled myself with the thought that this was a natural bodily function to help raise one's temperature.

Would day never come? All too slowly the sky outlining the plunging silhouette of the Pillar and the ridge of the Flammes de Pierre, changed from a deep black to a thin, watery blue. Suddenly a white flame of light struck the dome of Mont Blanc; slowly the line between dazzling light and grey shadows crept down the mountain and finally touched the spire of the Aiguille du Midi, colouring it a rich brown. We longed to move, to warm our limbs with exercise, but were so numb with cold that it was difficult to make a start. Facing the west, we could not hope to be in the sun for some hours to come.

We hobbled round the platform like old men, sorted out the litter of equipment carelessly scattered the previous night and made a brew of tea. After that I felt better but Hamish was in a bad way; he was very pale and a streak of dried blood ran down one side of his face.

"How are you feeling?" I asked him.

"Bloody awful," he replied. "I keep feeling dizzy but I think I'll be all right. Once I get going it'll be better."

"Do you think you can make it to the top?" asked Don. "I don't fancy going back down that gully after last night."

"I might need a tight rope some of the way, but I can keep going," he said.

I knew that I should never be able to give Hamish all the help he would need. It was all I could do to lead each pitch of the climb: I had nothing left in reserve so I suggested to Don— "Do you think it would be a good idea if you took Hamish? I am sure you will be able to help him better than I. Paul and I can stay at the back and take all the pegs out."

"Fair enough," agreed Don. "We'd better get going."

The two Austrians had already started and were now far above us, hammering their way up an impossibly smooth-looking groove. On the previous day we had worked our way up a system of cracks, weaving from side to side in search of the easiest way, but now there was only one possible line, up a series of long grooves that stretched up the smooth prow of the Pillar. The rock was just off the vertical, rough to the touch but it offered no incut holds. Walter had hammered pitons into the crack in the bed of the groove at full arms' reach and we pulled from one to the next as if we were climbing a giant ladder. Every now and then you could climb free,* jamming fingers into the crack, legs bridged across the walls of the groove. It was wonderful, exhilarating climbing that made all the discomfort of the night seem worth while.

Hamish from time to time had fits of faintness, but with a tight rope from Don, was able to climb quite quickly. We were all full of optimism. Sometimes Paul and I caught the others up on a stance, sometimes we were left behind so that we felt we had the entire face to ourselves. At midday we reached a fair-sized ledge. Don and Hamish were lounging in the sun which was now beating down with a cruel strength. Richard was paying out the rope, and, glancing up, I could see Walter dangling in the middle of a great bulging wall. The only sound was the sharp clatter of his piton hammer.

"I've run out of pegs," he shouted. "Can you send some more up."

We tied a bundle of ironmongery on to his spare rope and he hauled it up. More hammering from above and he slowly crept up the rock. We lay on the ledge, deadened by the heat of the sun, tired from our sleepless night. There was no snow or water and we were desperately thirsty.

"Can you send any more pegs?" yelled Walter.

We sent up our remaining stock, but he seemed little more than half-way up the wall. It was now late afternoon; the day was slipping by with a frightening speed and we were still a long way from the top.

"I'm sure the route doesn't go up there," said Don. "Hold my rope, Hamish. I'll have a look round the corner."

He shot out of sight, there was a long pause and then a yell of triumph: "I've found it. There's a bloody great overhang round here with pegs all the way up it. Come on round."

We called Walter down. He had to abseil from his top peg and remove all the pitons on the way down, for he had used up our entire stock.

* Climbing on the rock, and using pitons for nothing more than protection.

It was a great relief to move once more, to feel we were getting somewhere, particularly since it was no longer warm: we were now engulfed in cloud.

Don might have found the right way but it was not reassuring. I had never seen such a huge overhang; it thrust out above our heads into the swirling cloud, dark and forbidding. Don was already half-way up it, swinging from peg to peg like an agile monkey, and quickly disappeared from sight.

"What's it like beyond the roof?" I shouted.

"Steep," he replied, "but it will go. I'll need some pegs. There aren't any in place up here. Get some from Walter and send them up."

"It's nearly seven o'clock," I replied. "It'll be dark soon. Are there any ledges there?"

"No," came the reply.

I hated the thought of splitting the party—of some being left below the overhang. I think everyone else felt the same but it would be dark before we could possibly get the whole party and all the rucksacks over the roof.

"I'll come down," shouted Don. "We can stop the night on the ledges."

He pulled the ropes up through the pitons and dropped them down: their ends were swinging in mid-air some feet out from us, the overhang was so big. At the bottom he had to swing back and forth, a human pendulum, to reach us.

We then all climbed back down to the ledges where we had spent most of the afternoon. We had made discouragingly poor progress; the big overhang, like the jaws of a trap, still loomed above us and we were only a few hundred feet above our last bivouac. Hamish, who never complained, and always had a wry joke to crack about his predicament, was obviously feeling very weak. Don, that day, had pulled him up every pitch on a tight rope.

We settled down for the night. Hamish had elected to stay by himself on a minute ledge about fifty feet above us.

"I'm not going to loose any height," he said. "It's been hard enough gaining it. Anyway, I'll get a good night's sleep away from you lot. See you tomorrow." He always was an individualist.

I shared Don's plastic bivouac-sack. There was just room on the ledge to sit down, backs to the wall, feet over the edge, or knees drawn up to the chin. Either choice was uncomfortable and we both constantly shifted our positions to avoid getting cramp. We dropped the sack, a large plastic bag, over our heads. Inside it we generated a surprising amount of warmth, though at times I wondered if we were going to suffocate since there was no ventilation and Don smoked continuously all night.

"It'd be a good way to die, anyway," Don remarked stoically. "Better than freezing to bloody death."

The night passed more quickly than the previous one. We talked in a desultory fashion, occasionally dropping off into a doze. I dreamt of foaming tankards of beer, for we had not had anything to drink since the previous morning. We were so thirsty we were unable to eat what little food we still had.

In the morning we were impatient to start, but it was so cold that it took time to sort out tangled ropes, repack rucksacks, force feet into frozen boots. We nibbled an oatmeal block for breakfast and were ready.

"You go first, Walter. It's going to take Hamish a bit of time to climb the overhang," said Don. I was impressed by his refusal of the lead. He had found the right way the previous evening and had climbed the roof. Making the route out in front is by far the most satisfying part of any climb, but he was content to concentrate on his exacting task of nursing Hamish up the Pillar, and to let the Austrians press on in front.

Paul and I were to remain at the back with the job of taking out the pegs the front pair had hammered in. We had a long wait while the others climbed the overhang. I followed Hamish up, just a piton behind, swinging completely free in my étriers. Hamish had a desperate struggle for he could get no help from Don as the rope was running through so many karabiners. He sagged in his stirrups, panting hard: a desperate heave, and he lunged for the next peg at full arm's reach, clipped his étrier into it and dragged himself up. At times he went limp, hanging like a corpse chained to a gibbet. Only his raucous breathing showed that he was alive. Although I was just behind him there was nothing I could do to help but mutter the odd word of encouragement. I just followed from peg to peg, swinging in my étrier and breaking off the long icicles that hung down from the roof; but sucking them did little to alleviate my thirst. Paul, deep in the shadows below, had to wait patiently.

At last we reached the top of the roof. Another overhanging

groove stretched above, but its angle was easy compared to that we had just climbed. We were still in shadow and it was bitterly cold; I had, therefore, kept on my down jacket, but half-way up the groove I came into the sun. Suddenly I was sweating. What little strength I had left seemed to evaporate in the heat. By the time I had struggled, panting, to the next ledge, my clothes were soaked and my mouth even drier than it had been before. I stripped off my jacket and lay exhausted for about ten minutes before I could even start to bring Paul up. By the time he had reached me, having taken out as many pegs as he could, we had been left far behind. The bright, sunlit rock stretched as far and steep as ever above our heads: below, it shot into the deep shadows of the couloir. I felt horribly alone and longed to catch the others up. I was not even sure which way they had gone. I shouted and my voice echoed but there was no reply.

I left the stance and worked my way up a ramp, over a wall, to the start of a slab. It was smooth, featureless except for a peg transfixed in a crack half-way across. I could never reach it. My rope dropped out of sight behind me. I almost sobbed with loneliness and fear as I started to edge my way across the slab. I don't think it was particularly difficult but I had got close to breaking-point and only just managed to reach the peg. I clung to it, afraid to leave its safety. I shouted in despair and this time had a reply from just above. Hamish poked his head from round the corner.

"Let's have a top rope," I gasped. I have never been so glad to see a rope-end slide down towards me from above. I tied on, crossed the slab and climbed the last little wall before reaching the ledge. As I climbed it, I heard a steady purr and then, when I poked my head over the top, I saw, most wonderous of all sights, the stove with a pan-full of tea on top of it. They had found some ice in the back of a crack. There was gravel and sediment mixed in with the handful of tea leaves but it tasted like nectar: it was our first drink for over thirty-six hours. It required an effort of will to drink only a couple of mouthfuls, to leave Paul his fair share, but that drop of tea made all the difference.

I had come close to breakdown in the middle of the slab but now I had a new lease of strength. I still felt tired but for the rest of the climb I knew I could keep going. There were still many exacting pitches; the rock was more broken and this made the route-finding more difficult. On two occasions Walter had to come back and try another line. But at last, in late afternoon, the angle began to relent and we made rapid progress.

At last Walter shouted down: "I've reached the Shoulder. I can see the top." Just one more overhanging chimney barred the way but with success in sight we quickly stormed it. Easy rocks now led to the summit, but it was getting dark. There was no hope of getting down that night.

We had climbed the South-west Pillar but I felt no sense of exhilaration. I was much too tired and hungry; and too worried about our chances of getting down alive. Unnoticed by us, the weather had changed during the day. A cold wind was blowing, heavy clouds had crept across the sky, hiding the tops of Mont Blanc and the Grandes Jorasses, and a few flakes of snow swirled across the shattered rocks near the summit. I dreaded the thought of another cold, comfortless night.

Our only food was a packet of soup which we shared between the six of us: three mouthfuls each. I spent the night in a cradle of rope. Every time I dropped off into a doze, I slid down the steeply shelved ledge, to wake hanging on my safety rope, but I was so tired that I slept for most of the night, waking occasionally to hear the snow patter on the surface of my plastic bag and to feel the cold bite into my feet and legs.

It was an ominous grey dawn. Tattered clouds covered the glacier below us; a dull, grey ceiling pressed down on our heads, engulfing us by the time we were ready to start. The wind tore at our clothes, drove the snow with agonising force into our faces. We could see the dark shapes of rocks a few feet in front of us but everything else was white: cascades of snow down the mountain, snow piled high on ledges, snow driving through the air.

"Can you remember the way down, Walter?" asked Don.

"I think so," he replied. "We came down this side last year, but it is difficult to see anything now."

"Well, push on anyway. If we wait here we'll still be here next year, in the middle of blocks of ice," said Don.

The descent was a nightmare. The rocks, plastered with freshly fallen snow, plunged into grey cloud. The ropes were like wire hawsers, stiff and frozen to the touch, and yet seemed to have minds of their own, twisting themselves into impossible knots which had to be patiently untied with numb fingers.

There was no feeling in my feet nor in my hands, but I knew I could keep going. Hamish, also, had had a new lease of strength, but Riccardo, the youngest member of the party, was on the point of collapse: he could barely talk and just sat, slumped against the nearest rock.

We were abseiling down a series of grooves which we hoped would lead us to the ridge of the Flammes de Pierre, but after three rope-lengths, Walter admitted he was lost.

It was now that Don Whillans came into his own. He looked and behaved just the same way as he had at the beginning of the first day—a tough, self-contained, little man who would let no one or thing hurry him.

"Give us a rope, Chris," he commanded. "We're too far to the right. I'll have a look down here."

He shot out of sight. There was a long pause and then a shout: "Come on down. This is it."

Don had once again found the route and led us down towards safety. We still had a long way to go but the wind dropped and it stopped snowing. We caught a glimpse of the Flammes de Pierre through the clouds and knew for certain that we were going the right way. Suddenly, in spite of our fatigue, we felt light-hearted and started to talk of the mammoth feast we should have when we got back to civilisation. We were at the most dangerous stage of any descent. Unconsciously, we had all relaxed our attention in the moment of our elation. Walter dropped a sling over a razor-edged spike of rock, threaded the abseil rope through it and started down with a bold leap. There was a twang: the sling had been cut through on the sharp edge and he somersaulted downwards, hit a snow slope twenty feet below, rolled a few feet and came to rest on the brink.

No one commented on his narrow escape but I for one went on down with redoubled care. The glacier, far below, never seemed to come any closer. Abseil followed abseil. Slowly we crept down slopes of soft, wet snow, smooth rock slabs or hard ice. I longed for the safety of flat ground, to stride, unencumbered by the rope. At long last, almost unnoticed, a traverse brought us down to the glacier. More slushy snow, crevasses black and gaping below, an easy snow slope and the Charpoua Hut—and safety.

It was nearly dark, but we were determined to get back to Montenvers that night, to eat a hot meal, to change into dry clothes. We forced ourselves on, down to the Mer de Glace, across it and up the other side, slowly pulling our aching limbs up the steel ladders. They were only a couple of hundred feet high but they seemed to go on for ever.

That night we gorged ourselves in the Montenvers Hotel and then, happily bloated, tipsy with wine and exhaustion, rolled into our sleeping-bags. No meal had ever tasted so delicious. Our appreciation of every simple comfort was heightened by our experience of the last four days. A sleeping-bag on a hard floor was to us the very height of luxury. I slept solidly for twelve hours and then next morning, after a leisured breakfast, began to think of what I should do next.

There were many times in those last four days when I longed to be anywhere but on the South-west Pillar; when I swore that I should never again go on a route of its calibre, never again submit to such discomfort, cold and fatigue; and yet the morning after getting back to safety I was planning to risk repeating the experience. People who have never climbed, particularly those who have an instinctive aversion to heights, find it difficult to understand the motives of anyone who ventures on to a vertical rock face, let alone those who choose to undergo an orgy of discomfort and pain lasting several days. I shall try, anyway, to analyse my own reasons for tackling such routes.

I had been climbing our small rock faces in Britain for six years before visiting the Alps and have already described the pleasure I gained in doing this: the sheer physical enjoyment of climbing a stretch of rock. To gain this pleasure to the fullest degree, I had to climb to the limit of my ability. To strive always to coax my body up places that were ever steeper, that had fewer holds, and, in doing so, to discover new things about myself and the rock I climbed. The element of danger was an important factor: the knowledge that if I made a mistake I should fall, perhaps to my death. But I did not court danger and certainly did not relish it, for in many ways I am timid. I hate being afraid, hate getting into a situation where I have to fight for my life. This sounds contradictory but in undertaking a climb I do everything I can to make myself safe: by using carefully contrived running belays; by working out every move in my head before attempting it; by turning back if I think it is too hard. In doing this I am cheating the danger—reducing

The Petit Dru from Montenvers (*photo John Cleare of Gamma*).

End of the second day on the South-west Pillar. Hamish in background with a broken skull, Paul Ross in the foreground.

Climbing a Dolomite overhang.

what is inherently hazardous to something completely safe.

In the Alps it was the same but because it was all on a grander scale, one's every feeling was stronger. At first, I was afraid, for there were too many questions I could not answer. What would happen if we were caught by bad weather; if we lost our way on one of these huge, 2,000 foot faces; if one of the party were injured? I had little experience of snow and ice, even the glaciers held lurking threats of hidden crevasses and tottering seracs. Like most British climbers when they first go to the Alps, I was more worried about the descent down the easy side of a mountain than the difficult rock climb to its summit, which uses techniques with which I was more familiar.

It made no difference that I was with an experienced and competent mountaineer who did know the answers, for I had become used to taking the initiative and I could not feel happy unless I knew that I was capable of at least sharing in the decisions and judging the best course of action in any situation. When we went on the South-west Pillar, I was afraid before starting it, and even more so on the climb itself, when things started to go wrong, for it was all so new to me. I could not know just how serious our troubles were; whether I was capable of lasting out for several days on end; whether it was possible to get up the climb in bad weather. We got up alive because Don Whillans and Walter Phillip knew what they were doing. Their self-confidence encouraged me at the time and I also learnt a great deal from them. My experience on the Pillar taught me that however bad conditions become, whatever goes wrong, I could extricate myself. I never again suffered the blind fear of unknown dangers for, on all subsequent climbs, I was able to appreciate the extent of any danger that threatened, and find a way of avoiding it. I was still frightened at times but it was a fear that was quickly banished by action.

But why seek out situations that are frightening? Does one enjoy being cold at night; desperately thirsty; exhausted? I certainly don't. Sitting on a stance, taking in the rope, or during the long hours of the night when there is plenty of time for reflection, I long to get back to the comforts of civilization, but the moment I start to climb this is all forgotten and I am lost in the all-absorbing business of coaxing my body up the stretch of rock immediately in front. It is then that adverse conditions become a further exhilarating challenge: a problem to be overcome. And so it goes on. There are these moments of exhilaration and a few minutes later, waiting on the stance, there is time to notice parched lips, or, if the weather has broken, the trickle of icy water down the neck. But at the end of it all, back in Chamonix, the discomfort is forgotten; in retrospect it adds a piquant flavour to your memories and so you start planning the next climb. . . .

CHAPTER SEVEN

DIRETTISSIMA

"THAT's where they usually come off," murmured the German climber lying beside us.

We could just discern the arms and legs of the man spread-eagled on the yellow rock a thousand feet above. He was like a tiny black ant on the wall of a huge windowless warehouse. About fifty feet below him, stationary, was another minute figure. The rope joining them looked like gossamer thread, and the wall stretched above, below and to either side: grey, compact, yellow, featureless.

Suddenly the leading dot shot downwards. It was all over before the impact of the fall registered on my mind. The climber was dangling twenty feet from his original position, presumably held by a piton. He rested for a few minutes and then started up again, soon reaching the point from which he had fallen. A long pause, the faint thudding of a piton hammer and he was up.

I was sitting with a group of Austrian and German climbers on a boulder at the foot of the North Face of the Cima Grande in the Italian Dolomites. The two performers, far above, were on the "Direttissima", a route that had only been opened the previous year and which was reputed to be the hardest in the Dolomites.

A year had passed since my holiday in Chamonix and my ascent of the South-west Pillar of the Dru. I was climbing with Gunn Clark who was still a student, slightly younger than I, but with very similar mountaineering experience.

"It must be a good peg, anyway. What do you think, Gunn? Shall we have a crack at it?" I asked.

"Let's see how they get on at the traverse. It looks bloody terrifying to me," he replied.

We had been camped below the Tre Cime for a week and had done several of the easier climbs in the area, but from the start, the Direttissima had fascinated us. Four young Germans had made the first ascent, taking five days to complete it. They had used several special techniques. The wall was so continuously overhanging that it would have been impossible to retreat from it in the normal way, by abseiling: at the end of the rope they would have been swinging in mid-air several feet out from the rock. They therefore had to leave in place all their pitons, several hundred of them, so that if they had to turn back owing to a change in the weather, they would be able to climb down. This of course meant carrying heavy loads for they also had to carry water and food. To overcome the problem, they took with them a thousand-foot length of line* so that they could haul loads up from the bottom of the cliff. This was only possible because the face was so steep that the bundles nowhere touched rock on the way up.

It was much easier, of course, for the parties that followed, since all the pitons had been left in place, but even so the face maintained its reputation for difficulty. When we arrived that summer there had been a dozen ascents, mainly by German and Austrian parties. I was both attracted and frightened by the climb for I had done comparatively little artificial climbing and certainly nothing of the length or standard of the Direttissima. No other British party had done it and this made it seem even more formidable—there was no one with whom we could compare our own capabilities.

We heard any number of stories about the climb; there were plenty of other candidates camped around the Tre Cime waiting to go on it. They told us of the huge overhangs in the middle of the face and showed us various pieces of specialised equipment: drills for making holes in the rock where there were no cracks, expansion bolts to hammer into them, and even a hook for pulling up on pitons that were out of reach. But, more alarming, we heard that a member of the party that had last attempted the climb, had had a fall and had pulled out two expansion bolts. No one had been hurt but they had been unable to get up without the bolts in place and did not have any of their own. Since we did not have any either, we had decided to wait until another party did the climb. I think everyone was playing the same waiting game for no one went on to it for several days, until at last two Germans plucked up courage. We were watching their efforts that afternoon.

An hour went by and the two little dots slowly, almost imperceptibly, edged their way across the wall.

"They're on the traverse now," said the German who had already done the climb. "This is where the bolts came out."

* Thin rope—not used for climbing.

We watched with double interest. The leader stayed in the same place for a long time, went back, crept forward. We could hear faint shouts as he talked to his second. He moved again and there was a whoop of triumph: he was across.

We decided to go on to the climb the next morning and spent the rest of the day preparing our equipment, but that evening clouds began to build up and there was even a little rain in the air. That evening we drank late into the night in the Rifugio Laveredo, confident that the weather would be bad the follow-day, before tottering, very drunk, back to the tent.

Someone was shaking me; I kept my eyes closed and pre-tended to be asleep.

"Wake up, Chris. There's not a cloud in the sky. The Germans next door are getting ready. I think they must be going for the Direttissima," said the voice. I peered out of my sleeping-bag, hating to leave its pleasant warmth, and resenting Gunn's enthusiasm; but then I saw the thin blue of the sky and the two Germans bustling round their tent with last-minute preparations. The sight of them roused my competitive instinct.

We quickly cooked our breakfast, finished packing our sacks and set out for the face. It was only half an hour's walk from our campsite and along a good path all the way. It was eight in the morning when we reached the foot of the climb. There was no introduction to it, no glacier or snow couloir, not even the easy broken rocks that are found at the foot of most Dolo-mite walls.

It rose, sheer and uncompromising, straight from the path. Our way lay up a thin crack that was adorned with a solitary piton about thirty feet up. I have always hated climbs with difficult first pitches for there is no time to warm up, to find any kind of climbing rhythm. At the first step from the path I was hanging on my arms, thrust backwards by the steepness of the rock. I muttered to myself, cursed my rucksack which I had been too proud to leave at the bottom, fought the crack, cling-ing to it fearfully, until I reached the piton, clipped in and rested a moment. I was now more relaxed and felt my way up the rock, realising that it was not too difficult, just steep, and reached the stance. Gunn followed up quickly and I then set out on the next pitch, for we had decided that I should do all the leading. I was very happy with this arrangement—I love being out in front. (When second on the rope, I lose concentration, am aware of the danger of falling off, even though it would not matter if I did, and climb too quickly, without thinking out each move before making it.)

The first three hundred feet gave straightforward climbing to the top of a buttress that flanked the great, blank, yellow wall. The two Germans who had set out before us, were already a hundred feet ahead. It was reassuring to see them. The wall was so smooth and sheer that it was difficult to believe that any-one could climb it without pitons, and yet there were very few in sight, just one every twenty feet or so.

"What the hell do you do in between the pegs," I asked plaintively.

"You'll soon find out," the German replied.

Our route lay diagonally across the wall, so we were soon above unclimbable rock that dropped away to the path far below. The climbing was all-absorbing, the most airy and spectacular I had ever undertaken. Miraculously, the holds appeared: tiny, square-cut ledges that the toes of one's boots just rested on, that fingertips could curl over. There was no rest for the arms as nowhere did the angle relent. We were heading for a roof that jutted horizontally from the face. This gave me my first taste of $A3$—almost the top grade of artificial climbing. The pegs were anything but reassuring, hammered into tiny holes and blind cracks, at the most an inch of steel biting into the rock. I handled each peg with loving care, eased my weight on to the étrier step, pulled delicately on the next one, and tried to avoid swinging too much as I heaved over the lip of the roof.

I had hardly noticed that we had nearly caught up the Germans. Suddenly there was a yell from above. I glanced up to see a body, all arms and legs, rush down towards me. Instinctively I ducked, clung to the rock, but he never reached me. I looked up and saw him dangling on the end of the rope, about ten feet below the peg that had held his fall. He also had come off in the "usual" place. With hardly a pause he climbed back up, stepped cautiously into the top rung of his étrier and, precariously balanced, hammered in a piton above his head. The dull thud of the hammer inspired little confidence, but he clipped in his étrier and was soon standing on the ledge above. His second followed up quickly and all too soon it was my turn to start.

The rock was even more smooth and compact than it had

been before. There were no cracks for pitons and, from the stance, I could see no holds. About fifty feet above, at the foot of a shallow groove, I could just see a tiny black ring protruding from the blank wall, obviously an expansion bolt. I slowly edged my way up towards it. There were just sufficient holds but I had to weave my way from side to side, sometimes coming back a few moves when I had taken a blind alley. On reaching the groove I found some more pitons and a couple of expansion bolts. They were all at extreme reach: climbing on pegs might be compared to going up an iron ladder with rungs six feet apart and rotting away with rust.

Another twenty feet and I reached the point where the German and many of his predecessors had fallen off. There was an expansion bolt and then, a good eight feet above, the piton he had hammered in, a minute Cassin peg protruding downwards from a hole. I cautiously climbed the étrier until I was standing in the top rung, my left foot bridged out on a crease in the surface of the rock, my arms spreadeagled to keep me in balance for there was nothing to hold on to. My fingers crept up the rock towards the peg but they were still a couple of inches too low. I tried to stand on tiptoe on the étrier rung, it slipped and I was off.

Before I had had time to think, I found myself hanging a few feet below the expansion bolt which had bent over in a graceful curve. I felt no sensation of shock or fear for my entire concentration was devoted to that piton only a few feet above but seemingly out of reach. I went up again and this time placed my foot more carefully on the rung, stretched as far as I could but was losing my balance. My finger tips brushed the ring of the piton; another effort—the top joints of my fingers curled round it. My foot on the étrier scuffed round and I was hanging with all my weight on the two fingers. I now had to clip in a karabiner with my left hand and somehow extract the fingers of my right, which were trapped and extremely painful. My hands were tiring. All that existed in the world was a piton, a karabiner and a few inches of rock. A last struggle and my fingers were free: I was able to clip in my étrier and rest, panting, on it. Then a difficult move enabled me to pull up on to a narrow ledge.

Another pitch of free climbing, which was easy compared to the groove we had just climbed, led to the traverse where the expansion bolts had been pulled out. A line of pegs ran across a horizontal fault.

"It doesn't look too bad, Gunn," I shouted, for ever optimistic as I started out. But after twenty feet the pegs came to an end—the last one was a long channel peg, resting loosely in a crumbling hole, that held when pulled sideways but could be plucked straight out with a direct pull. A few feet farther to the left, and at a lower level, was a small peg jammed by a piece of paper into the hole left by the missing bolt. Farther still to the left a ring piton drooped from another hole. I did not feel like trusting my weight to any of them but there was no other way, for the wall was gently impending and completely holdless.

I am not often aware of the drop below me, and certainly am not worried by it, but here I was unpleasantly reminded of it as I leant down, hanging on the long channel peg, to place an étrier on the paper-plugged bolt—my eyes inevitably strayed down the giddy drop of the wall to the screes six hundred feet below. Stepping on the top rung of the étrier, held in balance only by the tension of my rope running back to Gunn, I breathlessly reached across to the next peg, clipped in my other étrier and stood on the rung, fully expecting the peg to plop out as I put my weight on it. Another tensed move and I was across on good rock holds that I could grasp and pull on. I felt a surge of relief and the rich satisfaction gained from completing a particularly thin piece of climbing.

I could hear voices just round the corner and a few minutes later we reached the bivouac ledge, the only one for eleven hundred feet. The two Germans had already settled down but there was plenty of room. There were two ledges each only two foot wide but to us they seemed as big as railway-station platforms. For the first time that day we were able to relax, to sit down. It was only four o'clock in the afternoon and there were still several hours of daylight, but the wall now reared over our heads in a series of jutting roofs and it was obvious we should never be able to get up through them before dark. It was pleasant anyway to sit in the afternoon sun and to eat for the first time that day—we had had no thought of anything but the climbing earlier on. We had two pints of water with us, and brewed tea, greatest luxury of all, over a solid fuel tablet. We spent the rest of the afternoon making our ledge more comfortable, shifting loose blocks and dropping them to the screes seven hundred feet below. A group of spectators, sitting near the foot of the cliff, quickly scattered as our bombardment crept towards them.

This was undoubtedly a four-star bivouac ledge: we could actually lie down, moored to the rock by a complicated system of belays. For the first time on a bivouac I slept really well, only waking with the dawn. There was no hurry, anyway, as we had to allow the two Germans to get away. We sat on the ledge watching them at work above us. Most of the time they were swinging clear of the rock in their étriers. Below we could see two tiny figures at the start of the climb. The German leader ran out a hundred feet of rope, and took a stance hanging in étriers immediately below the huge roof. His second followed up with surprising speed and, passing the stance, soon disappeared over the roof. We could hear him calling down from somewhere out of sight but the rope moved slowly and the pitch was obviously difficult.

Three hours went by and we were still sitting on the ledge. I was restless, wanting to get to grips with the problem, so finally started up the pitch. The previous day most of the climbing had been on vertical rock but now it was all overhanging and one relied entirely on the pitons that were already in place. I arrived below the German and made myself a cradle of rope to sit in. I had to stay there for a further hour, immediately above me the German's backside, below—space. I pulled loose a stone. Without touching anything, it dropped to the ground eight hundred feet below.

At last the German moved on and I was able to bring Gunn up to my belay. Changing stances was a nightmare of dangling bodies and tangled ropes that tried my patience to breaking point. This type of artificial climbing was something that neither of us had ever met before: it demanded a machine-like methodical approach. The ropes were threaded through anything up to forty karabiners and it meant concentrating the whole time on which rope to use, how to thread it, whether it was likely to cross the other or get jammed in a crack. I was for ever haunted by the fear of the rope jamming immovably when I was half-way up a pitch so that I could move neither up nor down.

After traversing a few feet to the right, away from Gunn, I had to pull up over the first roof. My view was immediately constricted to a few feet of rock. Below I could only see the scree, the entire face being cut off by the overhang, and above, the rock jutted out once again, hiding the sky. I felt utterly alone, frightened by the immensity of the face. Swinging in my étriers, feet well clear of the rock, I pulled into an overhanging chimney whose back was lined with loose blocks. I was already running short of karabiners, and the rope was beginning to drag—tugging remorselessly at my waist—but there was still no sign of a stance or even a piton on which I would dare to belay.

It never seemed to end; then at last, when I had used up all my karabiners and most of my strength, I reached a foothold and three expansion bolts* which were obviously used for belaying. Gunn now had to come up. It was just as hard for him as it had been for me: the rope passed through so many karabiners that he got little help from it. There were long periods when there was no movement at all and I boiled with impatience, though in fact he was taking no longer than I had done.

The change-over on the stance was even more awkward than on the previous one, and the pitch above every bit as long and tiring, but it did lead to a ledge of sorts, about nine inches wide, on which I could just stand in balance. By the time I had brought Gunn up, it was nearly dark and it was obvious that we would be able to get no further that night. It had taken us an entire day to climb three hundred feet. There was just room for both of us to sit on the ledge with legs dangling over the void. It was impossible to lean back for the wall behind us was gently impending. But our worst trial was thirst: we had only half a pint of water left and this did not begin to satisfy us. There were some drips falling from the overhangs above and we spent much of the night trying to catch them in a mess tin. It was a frustrating game for no drip fell in the same place twice, and the chances of one landing in the waiting pan were slight. Still, it helped to pass the time and we knew that we were now nearly up the steep section of the cliff, that we should be able to get out the following morning.

We started as soon as it was light—there was no temptation to linger. It was surprising how refreshed we felt after our uncomfortable night, especially since both of us had been exhausted at the end of the previous day. The overhangs above were not as severe as the ones we had already climbed and we soon reached a large ledge where we could have spent the night in luxury. Resting on it was a small lead case holding a book in which everyone who had climbed the "Direct" had signed their

* Where there are no cracks for pitons, a hole may be drilled into the rock, and a bolt tapped in.

names. We could not help feeling some pride as we added ours
to the list.

The angle now relented—it was merely vertical—and our
way lay up a deep-cut chimney that cleaved the face. The rock
was grey and firm to the touch, offering cracks in which to jam
our hands, and ledges and pockets. It was a delight to put away
the étriers, to climb on rock, once more obeying the natural
instincts of our muscles instead of the complex rope engineering
of the previous day. Pitch followed pitch, through deep
chimneys and over great boulders jammed in the bed of the
gully. We were now climbing with real enjoyment, carefree in
our confidence that we would soon be at the top.

Another hundred feet and we were there, lying in the sun
below the great cross that marks the summit of the Cima
Grande, but we did not linger long. The pile of empty tins
that littered the summit rock reminded us of our own hunger.
We coiled our ropes, packed away all the ironmongery and
raced down the broken rocks of the descent, our mouths water-
ing at the thought of Spaghetti Bolognese and bottles of
Chianti.

CHAPTER EIGHT

OUTWARD BOUND

B ACK in Germany, I was browsing through Routine Orders one day in the Squadron Office, when I noticed a paragraph advertising for instructors to the Army Outward Bound School. I had never before heard of it but it immediately caught my imagination. I knew something of the civilian Outward Bound Schools and this presumably was much the same. The thought of working in the mountains, of teaching climbing, was immensely attractive. I immediately made inquiries about the school—I was determined to get myself posted there—but equally quickly met with opposition.

"You know, it won't be good for your career," my colonel told me. "You would be much better off with a few more years in the Regiment and then a junior staff job or perhaps a secondment to the Trucial Oman Scouts."

But I could think of nothing worse than spending any longer with my regiment. I detested paper-work, and even the thought of adventure in the Oman was not over-attractive: there would be no climbing, the company of only a few other regular officers with whom I was unlikely to have much in common, and a complete dearth of women. So I persevered, and fortunately my Commanding Officer, who was a sympathetic man, agreed to let me go.

I left the regiment at the end of January 1959. I had few regrets, and though I wasn't prepared to admit it at the time, knew I would not return. After a few days leave in London, I caught the train up to Towyn in Central Wales to start my new job. By the time the train had reached Shrewsbury there were plenty of other young soldiers on board, all bound for the same destination as I.

At Towyn, a short, thickly-built sergeant, in the uniform of the 17/21st Lancers, was waiting for us on the platform. We all trooped out of the train, but there was none of the shouting I had become accustomed to in the army.

"Go over the bridge, lads, and form up in the station yard," said the sergeant in a pleasantly normal voice and herded them

Half-way up the Direct on the Cima Grande on our first day.

Gunn Clark coming up through the overhangs. The two figures at the bottom of the picture are sitting on the ledge where we spent the night.

good-humouredly but effectively off the platform. I just tagged on behind.

Outside the station was another man in uniform. He wore a kilt and had a short bristling moustache; on his shoulders were the insignia of a lieutenant-colonel and under his arm he carried a pair of bagpipes. I guessed that this must be Colonel Churchill, the Commanding Officer of the School.

"Ah, you must be Bonington," he greeted me. "I've got to see to this lot first. I'll see you later on in the mess."

By this time the young soldiers, looking a bit sheepish and very unmilitary, had been formed into three ranks. The colonel marched to the head of the column and to the skirl of bagpipes we set off down the road.

After a few hundred yards we turned into a typical army camp, a collection of drab brick huts with corrugated iron roofs, on a disused airfield. The column came to a halt, the bagpipes gave a last wail and another course of the Army Outward Bound School had begun.

I was not sure what to make of it all and I don't suppose the other newcomers were either; after all, when you attend a course in the army you are not often welcomed by the commanding officer playing the bagpipes, but I soon began to see what a good introduction this had been, for everything about the school was different—outside the run of normal army life.

The other instructors were waiting for the new course in a small laughing group; there were seven of them, one subaltern of about the same age as myself, and six sergeants. I was quickly introduced and told that for the first course I should be with Sergeant Cooper, after which I should have my own patrol. He was the youngest of the instructors, quite small but well-built, with a look of dedicated determination on his face; I winced inwardly and wondered how hard a time I should have trying to keep up with him.

Names were called out and the lads were divided out, ten to twelve in each patrol; they collected some extra equipment from the store and were then shown their huts—badly in need of decoration, with battered iron bedsteads and concrete floors.

"This is your home for the next three weeks," Sergeant Cooper told his charges, "I'll be down after supper to tell you something about the course. Come and have a drink in our mess," he added, turning to me.

D

In the mess, I immediately noticed the friendly, easy relations between the officer and sergeant instructors; they were all on Christian name terms, something unheard of in the army as a whole. When one thought about it, however, it was quite logical, as we were all doing exactly the same job.

The school had been in existence for just over a year, and had been built with close co-operation from the entire staff. Typically of the army, neither the Commandant nor the chief instructor had had any experience of Outward Bound training or even of elementary mountaineering before being told to form the school. The only man on the original staff with any knowledge of either subject was Sergeant Mick Quinn, who had spent some years with the Royal Marines Cliff Assault Wing. He was a brilliant talker, fixed you with a pair of bright blue eyes that carried absolute conviction, and could prove to most people that two and two made five, but it was his enthusiasm and knowledge that made the school a going concern. The fact that everyone had joined together, had often had fierce arguments over policy, and had finally got the school on its feet, had built this strong feeling of unity without any of the normal inhibitions that must exist between officer and NCO in other branches of the army. I recognised that this division must exist in the normal unit, but at the same time my experience of the freedom that existed in the school made me all the more loth to return to my regiment.

That night I went down to the patrol's hut to hear Ian Cooper tell the boys about the course.

"You've all heard a lot of tall stories about the school from other boys in your units who have done the course. I suggest you forget them, and I'll tell you what I shall expect of you for the next three weeks.

"For a start, after tomorrow morning's assembly, you don't wear uniform again until the end of the course." Loud cheers from the lads.

"In the next three weeks you will be doing a lot of things you haven't done before. This first week we'll concentrate on teaching you how to look after yourself in the hills and we'll tone up your muscles. In the class-room, we'll brush up on your map-reading, do a bit of first-aid and teach you what to do in the event of an accident. You'll have plenty of practice on the assault course, a few runs, a morning on a small rock face just near the camp and some canoeing. At the end of the week we go into the hills for thirty-six hours, to do some walking and map reading and have a night out in tents.

"Next week we shall go to Snowdon, where you will all have a chance to do some real rock-climbing and a lot of walking. Then in the third week is the final scheme. This is the climax of the course, when you will be able to put into practice all you have learnt. You will be out on your own, in groups of three, for three days and will try to complete a route we set you across about forty miles of hill country.

"Well, that's what you will be doing in the next three weeks. You might well ask what it's all in aid of. Some of you, no doubt, have heard that Outward Bound builds character; well, I wouldn't try to build any of your characters in just three weeks, but what you can do is find out something about yourselves. You will do things that you never thought you could. On the final scheme you might think you can go no further, but with some determination, you can force yourself on. There won't be anyone to drive you on, as there is back in your units, it will be up to you, on the final scheme and, for that matter, throughout the course. It's up to you to do your best at everything we show you, and provided you do, you will pass the course.

"This all sounds a bit grim, but in fact, I can assure you that you will all enjoy the course and the harder you throw yourselves into it, the more you will get out of it in the end.

"Well, that's enough for one night. I'll see you tomorrow morning at seven and we shall go for a dip in the sea." Loud but cheerful groans from the audience. "It's not nearly as bad as they all make out," added Ian with a laugh. I felt my hackles rise. There seemed to be something unpleasantly hearty about early morning dips in the sea at the beginning of February; but next morning, in the cold dawn, it was not nearly as bad as I had feared and I even had to admit to myself that it did wake me up.

That first morning, at breakfast, it was pleasant to look out of the window of the mess, over to the guard-room and see the sergeant-major hold his early-morning parade of a dozen cooks and drivers. It was a reminder of the army, of which I was now delightfully free. The sergeant-major was in the Welsh Guards, he was just over five feet tall, and as dapper as any guardsman could be. He wore his black peaked cap with immense pride. I was only too happy to forget that I was a soldier and plunged into my new role of Outward Bound instructor.

The days passed quickly, periods in the class-room teaching map-reading, racing round the assault course, climbing on the sea-cliff a mile or so from the school, and then days in the hills, walking with the boys or, having sent them off on their own, wandering alone from top to top. This I enjoyed most of all, and much more than the climbing—I quickly discovered that I was too interested in my own climbing to become a good teacher. I found it frustrating to take learners up the same easy climbs over and over again, and longed to escape on to harder routes which would tax my ability to the full, but for most of the boys the climbing was the highlight of the course, probably because it was exciting without being physically too arduous.

I soon became involved and found myself working harder than I had ever done in my regiment. Although the syllabus of each course was the same, no group of boys was identical and each required a different approach. Our students were from Junior Leaders' Regiments and Army Apprentice Schools; they had joined the army at the age of sixteen or so, planning to make it their career. Our best students were usually from the apprentice schools. They had a much higher degree of intelligence, and I suspect a more stimulating course of training, than the boys from the Regiments, the band boys and the lads from the Guards' boys' company, most of whom were right out of their depth in the hills. Some were practically illiterate, and a map merely a confusing pattern of lines and colours to them. You could spend hours teaching a simple knot, say the bowline, and at the end they would still be unable to tie it. Fortunately there was rarely more than one such boy in each patrol.

The final scheme was a really exacting test. The boys were on their own for its three days' duration, except when passing through instructors' check-points. They all went round a course that took in Cader Idris and the Arans in Central Wales, about forty miles across country with over 11,000 feet of climbing. In bad weather, when the cloud was down, it called for a high standard of map-reading to avoid getting lost, and a great deal of determination to keep going, particularly after a wet night, when sleeping-bags, tents and clothing were soaked. The ones that did keep going and managed to finish their route all agreed afterwards that it had been well worth while, whereas the comparative few who had given up when only half-way round suffered disappointment.

I have often had doubts about some aspects of Outward

Bound training and have heard the criticism that in making the mountains a place of harsh testing, the students are put off them for life and would never want to return, that they struggle through their three weeks, breathe a sigh of relief and return to normal life in much the same state as when they started the course. I think this is the danger in Outward Bound or in any form of training, and that the final impact on the student will depend on the methods of the instructor. We were given a free hand in our interpretation of the syllabus, and each instructor had his own method. A sergeant like Spike Jones, who was in his late thirties and had several children, took his patrol at a much steadier rate than younger men, like Ian Cooper or myself, though the final result, as far as the boy was concerned, was probably very much the same. I believed in setting the boys tasks that extended them, but which were well within their physical capabilities, whatever they themselves might think: whether they went for a walk over rough country, or got up before dawn to take full advantage of the day's length. I tried to make it exciting and enjoyable. Mixed in with the hardship was plenty of sheer fun: the rock-climbing, that nearly all the boys enjoyed; canoeing; even a grindingly long walk, a race down scree or some hilarious boulder-hopping down the course of a mountain stream. It all added up to three weeks that were different from the normal run of their training or anything they had ever done before.

Beyond this, some students got a long-term benefit from the course. Often the boy who was shy and retiring in his unit, because he was good neither at games nor drill but was intelligent, gained a good deal in self-confidence when he found that he could walk as well as if not better than the brilliant games-player and could take an active, even vital, part in the control of a group in the hills: he might be the only one capable of reading a map and navigating the party to its goal. Surprisingly, too, outstanding performers on the course were often habitual trouble-makers in their units: their uncurbed spirits had rebelled against military discipline; but in the hills, finding something that was both challenging and interesting, they entered into everything with enthusiasm and had the force of personality to carry with them their less volatile fellows. I very much doubt if we ever changed anyone's character but students often discovered things about themselves that either they had not known or were not prepared to admit—from the boy who gained self-confidence on the one side, to the one who tried to free-wheel the course, but was caught out, on the other.

During my two years at the Army Outward Bound School I returned to the British climbing scene. I felt rather like Rip van Winkle: there were new faces in the climbing huts and pubs, the hills were very much more crowded, but above all there was a different atmosphere.

In 1955 the routes put up by Joe Brown inspired a super-stitious respect; only a handful of climbers were venturing on to even the easiest ones. I could remember gazing up at the smooth cleft of Cenotaph Corner in the summer of '55, tentatively trying the bottom few feet, but without any real conviction, and at the first hard move, coming scuttling down. At that time it had not had a second ascent, but now in the summer of 1959 any number of people had climbed it. I can remember hearing above the babble of voices, one night in the bar of the Pen y Gwryd Hotel:

"Did Cenotaph today."

"What was it like?"

"Piece of duff, nothing to it. I don't know what they were making all the fuss about. You can put a runner on every six feet, all the way up."

The climbs that only a few years before had been thought impossible for all but men of superhuman strength were now being done by the run of competent climbers, many of them in their 'teens. The barrier that had stopped us in '55 had there-fore been largely psychological, a fear of the unknown.

On Clogwyn dur Arddu, for instance, eleven major routes had been made before 1951 and then, between '51 and '59, Brown, Whillans and Ron Mosely put up another twenty-five climbs, all of which were considerably harder than anything done before. During this period only one other person, outside the Rock and Ice Club, put up a route of similar calibre. This was John Streetly, a man of much the same physical propor-tions as Whillans and Brown, even shorter than either of them and superbly built—but from a very different background. He was at Cambridge University—the stamping ground of many traditional mountaineers. A brilliant athlete, holding three blues, he erupted on to the climbing scene, repeated many of the Brown routes, and then made his own contribution, the Red Slab on Clogwyn dur Arddu, before returning to his native Trinidad. It was only in 1959 that any other climbers began putting up such routes. Hugh Banner, a wiry, almost delicate-looking Liverpudlian, put two more routes on Cloggy, the Troach and Ghekko Groove; the former up a sheer, seemingly featureless wall. He was the forerunner of many more young climbers who that summer were gaining confidence on existing routes.

I, too, was content to tick off the Brown routes: there seemed no point in trying to do new ones before catching up on this great breakthrough and gaining confidence in the new standards. I went climbing on every available weekend and even in the long summer evenings after a day's work. On one such night I did Cenotaph Corner: only a few years before, the Corner had seemed impossibly huge, as smooth as the corner of a giant concrete building, but now, confident in the knowledge that many others had climbed it, and in my own experience on other climbs in the new idiom, it seemed to bristle with hand-jamming cracks and small holds. I was climbing no better than I had done earlier, but now had the reassurance that many others had also found it easy; there was no longer any mystery. Even on climbs that had not yet been repeated, that still had a reputation for great difficulty, the barriers were down. Setting out to attempt routes like the Woubits, a savage-looking groove, high on the Far East Buttress of Clogwyn dur Arddu, you felt that this was just one more difficult problem, perhaps harder than anything you had done before, but in th same kind of class. The very fact that the rest of the cliffs were criss-crossed with the ropes of climbers, that there was a subdued babble of voices, that you could see a group of girls sunbathing on the shores of Llyn dur Arddu, made the undertaking seem less serious.

Our equipment had improved. In the old days my running belay technique had been rudimentary: I had carried a few line-slings that I draped over the odd spike of rock; and if I had fallen the chances were that they would either have slipped off or been cut through. But now I carried a dozen or more slings and a pocket full of pebbles. A sling could be threaded round a pebble forced into a crack, and would then give protection for climbing to the very limit of ability with a fair margin of safety. With ingenuity, running belays could be contrived even where there were no spikes available, thereby reducing the risk of damage in a fall; this technique of inserting

chockstones was one at which Joe Brown excelled and even if
he did not invent it, he did much to develop it. On the one
occasion I climbed with him I was amazed by his patience and
skill in slotting stones into a seemingly featureless crack.

Footwear had also improved. In 1955 we had all climbed in
skin-tight gym shoes, but that summer I bought my first pair of
P.A.'s, a tightly fitting boot with a very thin but rigid sole of
smooth rubber, which adhered to wrinkles in the rock that a
gym shoe would have just rolled off. To achieve maximum
adhesion a great deal of comfort had to be sacrificed, for a
really tight fit was needed with toes bunched into the pointed
front of the shoe. At the end of each pitch it was a relief to take
off the shoes, and walking down hill at the end of the climb was
sheer agony; but, like a woman enduring the discomfort of
smart, high-heeled shoes, it was worth it.

My first summer at the Army Outward Bound School was
wonderful. I enjoyed the work, was fitter than I had ever been
before or since, and felt I was once more in the climbing world.
I now realised how much I had missed it when stationed in
Germany. True I had had my long Alpine holidays but that
left me with the greater part of the year away from the company of climbers. The thought of returning to my regiment,
now transferred to Libya, clouded the future: I began to realise
just how out of place I had been, how alien I had felt amongst
my fellow officers. As a result I began seriously to think of
leaving the Army. But it was a difficult decision to take, for I
am lazy at heart, and in many ways the army encourages
inertia: everything is done for you; you live at a high and
extremely comfortable standard and the future holds no real
worries. It was all too easy to drift along, and, anyway,
what could I do if I left the Army? Almost immediately I dismissed the thought of becoming a climbing instructor at an
Outward Bound School or similar establishment—I enjoyed
my climbing too much. Once you start teaching climbing, you
are not climbing to your own standard, but at that of your
pupils; to be a good instructor, one's vocation for teaching must
outweigh one's love of climbing, and in my case this was certainly not so. At the Army Outward Bound School, I even felt
some frustration because I could only escape to go climbing at
odd occasions: one weekend in three, and for the occasional
evening at the end of a day's work—though, even then, I

should probably have stayed with my patrol of boys if I had been giving absolutely everything to my job.

I therefore began to think of going into commerce, for I was used to the idea of security, and felt that I should aim for a high salary. At least in an office job I should have my weekends free and would be able to choose my own circle of friends and lead the kind of life I enjoyed.

My mind yo-yoed from one plan to another in my indecision and then, in the summer of 1959, it was temporarily put at rest: I was invited to join a Services expedition to the Himalaya. Its objective was Annapurna II, a 26,041 foot peak in Central Nepal, some ten miles east of the highest summit of the group which was climbed by a French party in 1950—the first peak of over 8,000 metres to fall. For the next nine months I had no time to think of anything else but the expedition; dreams of the Himalaya entirely filled my mind and, on a practical level, I was up till three o'clock most mornings doing my share of the work in putting it on its feet.

CHAPTER NINE

ANNAPURNA II—THE BUILD-UP

THERE was a smell of woodsmoke in the air and the rounded forms of the hills blurred into the evening haze. My body tingled with a feeling of love for the sounds and shapes around me—a feeling of voluptuous excitement that just wanted to absorb everything so new and strange. I was sitting on the top of a bank above the path, a few minutes from our camp. It was our first day out of Katmandu; the expedition was really under way.

A few of our porters straggled past. They walked with a hurried jerky motion, legs perpetually bent under their sixty pound loads—scrawny stunted men, their necks knotted with muscle from the strain of their head-bands, which took the entire weight of the loads. They came from the valley of Katmandu; you could tell from their dress—dirty, once-white shirts, with tails flying over ragged, cotton trousers. More colourful were a couple of hill men from West Nepal. They were in their early teens, their limbs smoothly rounded, covered by a short tunic of sack-cloth material, but their ears were gay with gold rings and they wore necklaces of beads and brightly coloured bangles. Their hair was shoulder length, but there was nothing effeminate about them; they had a look of devil-may-care virility, and carried wicked kukris stuffed into their waistbands.

The porters dropped their loads in a pile at the end of a narrow terraced field on which we had made our camp, and hurried off into the gathering dark to find lodgings for the night. I could just see the first houses of the village at the end of the path, squat buildings with reddish-brown walls and thatched roofs, dwarfed by the stately spread of a Banyan tree. Someone started singing, a high pitched wail, that was strangely beautiful in the dusk. A girl walked past me, very pretty with long black hair in plaits, a gold star pierced into one nostril, a brass water jar tucked into her hip. She had an easy, graceful stride. For a few moments I felt I was part of the land, and then there was a shout from the camp.

"Grub up—come and get it."

I walked over diffidently, feeling shy and withdrawn from the others. Wrenched away from the night and sounds around me, this was reality, the expedition of which I was a member—though we hardly knew each other and perhaps had little in common.

There were nine of us from three different countries, Britain, India and Nepal. None of us had met before the inception of the expedition and we had been brought together more by political expedience than on a basis of friendship or even climbing ability. Amongst the British, each of the three services had its nominee; then the Indians had been brought in for the sake of Commonwealth solidarity and the Nepalese to make things easier for us in Nepal.

I could see Jimmy Roberts, our leader, his face lit by the fire—a cross between that of a wrinkled boy and a petulant monkey. His voice was highly-pitched, particularly when he was excited, and one felt he was essentially shy, in spite of his job as military attaché in Katmandu. He had at first seemed reserved and rather distant, but one couldn't help liking and respecting him—a feeling that grew ever stronger in the course of the expedition. That night, he had good reason for seeming reserved: here he was, leading a group of complete strangers, with a dubious set of qualifications as mountaineers, on an expedition to a 26,000-foot unclimbed, Himalayan giant. Only one of the British party, Dick Grant, had been in the Himalayas before. Stewart Ward and Bill Crawshaw had only limited Alpine experience, whilst I was young for Himalayan climbing —only twenty-five—and was primarily a rock climber. Of the Indians, Jagjit Singh had been to the Himalayas several times, but had tackled nothing of great height. The two Nepalese, Prabaka and Gadul were so slightly built, that it was difficult to imagine them on a mountain.

That night, Jimmy's main consolation must have been the Sherpas he had selected: nine of the most experienced in the business, all of whom he knew and trusted. Their previous expeditions covered every major peak in Nepal—Everest, Kangchenjunga, Makalu and a dozen others. As they served our dinner one noticed their affection for Jimmy, as they joked and chatted with him. There was no subservience, just a friendly respect. Urkein, the cook, went round asking every one if they liked the meal, obviously getting pleasure from our approval. His enthusiasm was so great that even when the porridge was burnt or the tea tasted of Yak-dung smoke, one did not like to complain.

After the meal I was glad to crawl into my sleeping-bag, though it was a long time before I dropped off to sleep. I was wakened with a cheerful "Char Sahib" and looked up to see a grinning Sherpa leaning through the sleeve entrance of the tent with a mug of steaming tea in his hand. It was a wonderfully clear morning, and now from the tent door I could see the rolling green and brown hills merge into a rampart of snow peaks across the entire Northern horizon. I scrambled out of the tent and joined Jimmy Roberts, who was gazing at the line of mountains with an expression of ownership—they were so familiar to him.

"That's Himul Chuli over there," he told me, pointing to a distant, shapely pyramid of snow, "and that must be Annapurna II, though you can hardly see it."

You couldn't—it was little more than a pimple to the far west, a hundred miles away, but that moment was one of the most exciting of the expedition. Suddenly the whole thing became real. This first sight of your goal is even more exhilarating than the moment when you reach the top: then there is the sense of anticlimax—it's all over—you've just got to get back down in one piece and go home. Looking across to our objective, we still had before us all the interest and pleasure of the approach march. There were still any number of unknown problems to solve. There was the same element of excitement and self-doubt that I had had when I hitch-hiked up to Wales and saw Snowdon for the first time in my teens, the whole world of mountaineering before me. I wondered how I should perform, whether I should acclimatise well and above all, should I get to the top. Even though I told myself that all that mattered was that the expedition should be successful, and that someone should climb the mountain, I wanted desperately to go there myself.

For the next fortnight we made our way across the foothills of the great peaks, and then up the Marsyandi Khola, a precipitous gorge leading round the back of Annapurna II to its northern side—on the south, its defences seemed impregnable. Himalayan approach marches have been described many times over in expedition books and ours was probably much the same as any of them. But for me it had all the joy of a new

Annapurna II from the north.

Sherpas ferrying loads above the Dome on Annapurna II. The
mountains in the far background are in Tibet (*photo Major R. Grant*).

experience—the easy tempo of walking a dozen miles a day, the constant change of scenery, of different people and customs, and the steadily increasing size of the mountains as we drew closer to them. The luxuriant sub-tropical vegetation of the foothills, the rich red earth, mud-walled thatched houses; it all changed almost imperceptibly to harsher surroundings—forests of pine and larch, dry stony earth, stone walls and stone villages of flat-roofed windowless houses, terraced into the hillsides. Even the people became more rugged, coarser, more Mongolian of aspect, than the people of the lower foothills.

Our destination was the valley of Manangbhot, a desolate place of stones and windswept scrub. It lies close to the Tibetan Border, which is separated from it by a range of low mountains to the north, while to the south, it is barred from Nepal by the sprawling mass of the Annapurna range. To the west of the massif, hidden by a curtain of lesser peaks, is the main summit of the group, Annapurna I, climbed by the French in 1950. One of their greatest problems had been to find their way to the foot of the peak, so effectively was it hidden. Our own objective, Annapurna II, lies at the eastern end of the range. We had no problem in finding this mountain, for it towered above the valley in a clean sweep of glaciers and buttresses of snow.

The summit was a wedge of rock at least 2,000 feet high, perched on the end of a great whale-back snow ridge which seemed to offer the only feasible line of approach, but it was a long one—five miles in all—over a shoulder of 24,000 feet.

We were not going to an unknown mountain; five expeditions had already attempted it. Jimmy Roberts had been there in 1950, with a party led by Bill Tilman; they had got to a point shortly below the Shoulder, but were dogged by bad weather, having come out much too late in the season, when the monsoon had already started.

A German expedition in 1956 had reached the Shoulder but had been too small to tackle the long, undulating ridge to the final pyramid; they had snatched Annapurna IV, a shapely little peak just off the Shoulder, as a consolation prize. The following year another small expedition came out to the mountain, Charles Evans and Dennis Davis with three Sherpas, but they also, on reaching the Shoulder, felt they had insufficient in reserve to tackle the long ridge. Our party was certainly large enough and in addition had oxygen sets for the final

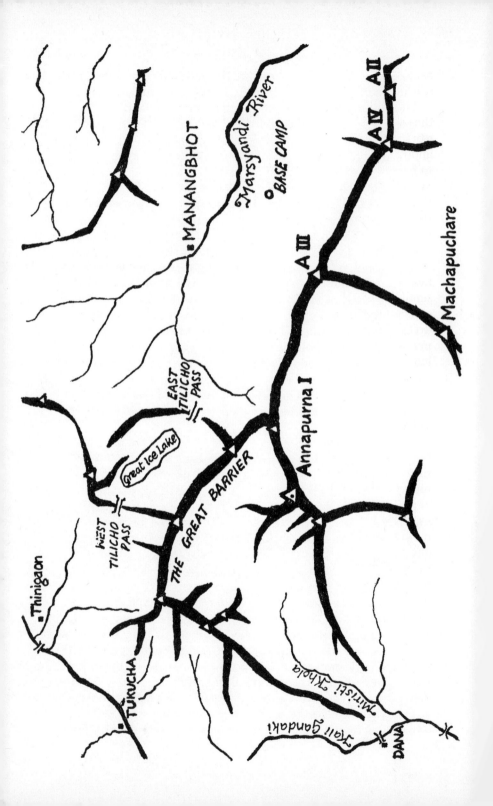

assault. Even so, at the end of three weeks hard work we were still below the Shoulder, as the weather was so bad.

The going was not particularly difficult; our enemies were the wind and thigh-deep snow—it was monotonous, grinding work rather than exciting and one day was much the same as another. But at least I was out in front the whole time helping to break the trail with Dick Grant and two of our best Sherpas. We always had the spur of anticipating what was round the next corner; of each day forcing the route a bit farther, while the rest of the party had the dreary, but very necessary job of ferrying loads in our wake up the mountain.

I woke to hear the steady purr of the Primus. I had got my head inside my sleeping-bag, with only my nose sticking out of a small gap at the top. It was uncomfortable with the wet of condensation from my breath, but I just lay still for a time, dreading the start of yet another day. Finally I looked out of my bag, and could see Tachei crouched over the Primus. He looked up, smiling.

"Tea ready soon, Sahib."

"What's it like outside, Tachei?" I asked.

"Some wind, some snow. Very cold," he replied cheerfully. It had been like that for the past fortnight, but somehow I felt encouraged by his optimism. He was in his mid-fifties, had been on some of the pre-war Everest expeditions and on many since. In the weeks we had spent together I had come to love him; "like" is too weak a word for the feeling of warm respect and affection both Dick and I felt for him. He had looked after us, indeed spoilt us for the entire time we had been on the mountain. At the end of a long day, when we had slumped into our sleeping-bags, he had struggled with the Primus and made the supper; this is something that any of our Sherpas would have done, but it was the warmth of his friendship and his never-failing loyalty that we valued so specially.

I glanced around our snow hole—it was about six foot high and ten long. The temperature was a degree or so below freezing, but compared with a tent it was sheer luxury. For a start there was no sound of wind—after a time the constant hammering of canvas drives you berserk. There was also space to move around, to stand up. We had carved shelves in the walls for our food and other equipment. In the passage we had even dug a small hole to use as a lavatory—basic, but it's no joke going out into the cold wind in the middle of the night. It had taken a day of hard work to build the cave on the crest of the ridge, but it was amply worth while. This was to be our jumping-off point for the summit, still five miles away.

Ang Nyima, lying in his sleeping-bag like a long grey slug, broke into a fit of coughing that seemed to tear deep into his chest. He had suffered from a bad chest cough for the entire time we had been on the mountain, and yet had always insisted on going out with us, even though his face was grey with fatigue. He had been on the successful Everest expedition and had carried a load to the top camp. Since then, he had joined the British Army and had been serving as a mess waiter in Malaya. The transition from the tropics to the Himalaya must have been particularly hard, but he was determined to keep going, I think largely because he realised he had a good chance of being in the summit party, owing to his position in the Services. We never got as close to him, however, as we did to Tachei; there was something aloof, almost disdainful, in his manner; I couldn't help feeling that he despised us.

Living in a cave, it was easy to get organised for the day—you could even put on your crampons before going out. Once out, we found the weather was the same as it had been for the past fortnight—clouds building up in the south, and a bitter wind blasting across the ridge. We hoped to establish a camp half-way up to the Shoulder, so that the next day, Dick and I could press on over the crest, and see the ridge that links the Shoulder with Annapurna II for the first time. We would then be poised for the final phase of our assault.

First we had to cross a knife-edged section of the ridge. Ang Nyima and I had reconnoitred it the previous day: to the north the slope dropped away steeply to the Marsyandi Valley, while to the south, we looked down into a plunging gorge that ran right to the foothills of Nepal. On the other side of the gorge was one of the most beautiful mountains of the Himalaya, Machapuchare. Embraced by the cirque of the Annapurna Range, it tapered into a fluted fish-tail of ice.

We pressed on, slowly but steadily, as the slope began to steepen.

"I'll take a go in front," I muttered to Dick, and plodded past him. I was panting hard, but felt I was going well, glanced up and saw the top of the slope only fifty feet above—we could have a rest there. Suddenly, like stepping through an invisible barrier, my strength, my very will to keep going seemed to ooze out of me.

The rest of the day was a nightmare—it never seemed to end. I was now bringing up the rear of the party. The rope, linking me to Dick, tugged at my waist whenever I paused for a rest. I repeated to myself, over and over again, "I mustn't give in. I mustn't give in." The only thing, I think, that kept me going, was the thought that if I did pack in, I obviously would not deserve to go to the summit. If Dick slipped there would have been no chance of my holding him, for my entire strength and concentration were directed to just putting one foot in front of the other.

At last we came out on to a shoulder.

"We'll make camp at the end of this," said Dick. "We can't go much farther today."

"Thank God," I told myself.

The ground stretched out in front of us in a level plateau, an antarctic waste of frozen snow.

"We can take the rope off here," Dick said. "You just follow on in your own time."

The others quickly drew ahead, while I stumbled on, a few paces at a time. At this stage I was getting some slight, rather twisted satisfaction from my performance, dramatising to myself the efforts I was making, basking in a feeling of heroism in face of supreme effort, for my mind seemed partly detached from my body. I had spent many hours as a child telling myself stories of heroic endeavour, with myself in the principal part, fighting against limitless odds. As I plodded across the plateau I was back in those childhood days, in a dream world, that at the same time was true; my mind alternated between euphoria and despair. As I stopped for the twentieth time in a hundred yards, I began to wonder about my chances of ever reaching the summit. I asked myself if I had reached my height ceiling—perhaps I just would not acclimatise to higher altitudes, and anyway what right had I to be with the trail-breaking party out in front —perhaps one of the others could go more strongly.

By the time I had caught up the others they had nearly finished pitching the tent. The canvas was flapping in the wind with a demoniac force. It took all our strength to pin it down.

Once the tent was pitched the two Sherpas turned away to return to the lower camp. We felt very small and lonely as we watched them disappear into the swirling clouds of wind-blown snow. We were now at a height of about 23,000 feet; above us the ridge stretched endlessly, in a graceful sweep, to the Shoulder immediately below Annapurna IV. It was a discouraging thought that our summit was another three miles beyond that. But now my only thought was to escape from the wind, to rest and find a little warmth. I struggled with my crampon straps—they were like steel hawsers—and then waited while Dick brushed the loose snow off his clothing before he dived into the tent. I shouted silent curses into the wind. At last it was my turn, and I wriggled through the sleeve entrance. Even though we had been careful there was snow everywhere inside. For a few minutes we just lay down, then we had to force ourselves into further activity.

"Come on, Chris, let's get this lot sorted out," Dick said at last.

Everything at that altitude seemed an insurmountable problem—even unpacking a rucksack or getting out a sleeping-bag.

"Well, we can't complain," grinned Dick. "This is the first night on the expedition we've had to cook our own supper. If you like, I'll do it tonight and you can do breakfast. You seem to be more lively in the mornings."

"That's fine with me," I agreed with relief.

I lay back in my sleeping-bag, while Dick struggled with the Primus—the more tired you are, the more trouble they give. He cursed, pumped wildly, and yellow flames gushed around him, only to die away to nothing.

"Where's the bloody pricker?"

I searched amongst the heap of frozen clothing and food tins and at last found it. He pricked the infernal machine, pumped like a maniac and lit it once again. The thing once more burst into flames. After several more attempts he got it burning with a steady roar, reached out of the tent to gather some snow, and we settled down to wait for our brew of tea. One learns to be patient in the Himalaya—everything takes such a long time, and a panful of snow slowly melts down to only a few spoonfuls of water. We added more snow, until we had enough. At this stage Dick succeeded in upsetting the Primus and our precious water went over my sleeping-bag. I could only laugh—it was just one more thing in an appalling day.

At last we had our tea and even some stew, but though I felt ravenously hungry, the taste of the tinned meat turned my stomach, and I could only manage a few mouthfuls. I longed for tinned fruit, for baked beans, for tuna fish, for things that we didn't have with us.

By the time it was dark, we had eaten. I was too tired to read and just dropped into an uneasy doze, but that night we never really went to sleep—the wind was too violent.

"We'll be lucky if the tent stands up through the night," said Dick. "Make sure your rucksack is packed before you go to sleep. We might have to move into the nearest crevasse at this rate."

We just lay and listened to the mad hammer of wind on canvas, watched it flap with an uncontrollable force. It seemed impossible that the tent would last the night. The hoar frost that formed on the walls, the condensation of our breath, was immediately shaken off on to our sleeping-bags where it melted and then, later in the night, froze.

Somehow the tent stood up to the wind. When morning came it was my turn to cook breakfast. I promptly evened up the score by spilling the porridge over Dick. It said something for our friendship, that neither of us lost his temper. In fact, in the five weeks that we were together, sharing a small tent, I don't think we ever got on each other's nerves. We never said very much, but felt a real bond of sympathy—or at least I did for Dick: he was the kind of person who could get on with any-one: he had an evenly balanced temperament and was com-pletely unselfish—I couldn't say the same for myself.

Breakfast was even worse than supper. Washing greasy pans is just about impossible at altitude—there is never enough water and the exertion is too tiring. As a result all food soon assumes a neutral flavour: the morning tea, a muddy grey liquid with icebergs of undissolved milk powder floating in it, tastes of yesterday's stew.

"Well, I suppose we had better try to get up to the Shoulder now that we have come this far," said Dick.

I agreed without enthusiasm, wondering how I should perform today. I had to force myself on, somehow, if I was to remain in the trail-breaking party and eventually go to the summit. Getting ready to start was even worse than settling in the night before. Our outer clothes were frozen into suits of armour, boots, which were made of rubber, were stiff and cold to the touch, and once out, it took ten minutes to put on crampons.

The wind was as savage as ever, blowing in a constant blast

across the ridge. We slowly stumbled towards the start of the
slope—I felt as listless as the day before, wanted only to get
back into the shelter of our snow cave at the start of the ridge. I
silently prayed that Dick would turn back, but did not dare to
suggest it. Even Dick was going slowly. After only a hundred
yards, which seemed as many miles, he turned round.

"We'll go back. It's bloody hopeless against this wind," he
yelled into my ear.

I hardly replied, just turned and bolted for the tent. We
dragged our gear out, and pulled it down, poles and all—we
could never have folded it up in the high wind—and then
started back for Camp III. Walking downhill seemed effortless
after our struggle of the previous day. It felt like a return to real
safety, and the snow cave a luxury hotel compared to our tent.
Bill Crawshaw and Stewart Ward were there with half a dozen
Sherpas; everyone was packing rucksacks.

"Jimmy Roberts has called us down for a rest until the
weather improves," shouted Bill.

I felt a wave of relief; I suddenly realised just how much I
wanted to escape from this world of discomfort, perpetual glare
and blasting wind. We wasted no time: having had the order
to retreat Dick and I decided to get back down that same day
—we could not have stood another night on the mountain. It
had taken us three weeks of hard effort to reach the site of
Camp IV; it now took us a mere eight hours to get down to
Base Camp, 12,000 feet below.

When we had walked up the long wooded valley from our
base camp at the beginning of April, the ground had been
covered in snow, but now, on our return, Spring was bursting
through the warm earth. The feel of young grass underfoot, the
smell of pine needles, the sight of soft browns and greens was
inexpressibly delicious.

We spent a week down at base camp and for the first day or
so it was a delight just to do nothing, to have a bath or lie in the
sun, but soon I became impatient to return to the mountain.
The moment we left the mountain the weather began to
improve—there was hardly a cloud in the sky and, more
important, none of those tell-tale plumes of wind-blown snow
on the ridge far above us. Jimmy stuck to his guns, however;
having brought us down, he was determined to give us a good
rest before returning for the final assault.

Sherpas resting on the Shoulder: the Summit Pyramid of Annapurna II in the background (*photo Major R. Grant*).

Chris Bonington, using oxygen, on the ridge leading to the Summit Pyramid of Annapurna II (*photo Major R. Grant*).

It must have been a hard decision, and one that showed his quality as a leader. He admitted afterwards to having been gnawed by doubts lest he had sacrificed our only chance of good weather. But we were all in desperate need of a rest.

I also had my own doubts—I could not forget how badly I had performed on our last day on the mountain. Had I reached my height ceiling at 22,000 feet? Would I be chosen for the summit party? I was on tenterhooks until Jimmy gave us our final briefing for the assault.

CHAPTER TEN

ANNAPURNA II—THE SUMMIT

It was like an "O" Group on a military exercise. We were
sitting in a half-circle round Jimmy Roberts, pencils and note-
books in our hands; we might just as well have been attending a
briefing on a company attack against Redland, as one for the
final assault on Annapurna II. It brought home the similarity
between planning a campaign in war and on a mountain.

"Dick, Chris and Ang Nyima will go for the summit,"
Jimmy told us, and I felt a tremendous feeling of relief and
elation. "They will be supported by six of the Sherpas, right up
to the top camp. Bill, Stew, Prabaka and Jagjit, you will go as
far as Camp III and help ferry loads to Camp IV. You can
then wait at Camp III until they have got to the top. Once
they have done this, you can have a go at Annapurna IV.

"I want to streamline the assault as much as possible. This
spell of good weather can't last for ever. You can move up to
Camp III in two groups, on successive days. Stop at Camp II
on the first night and then press straight on to III. You should
all be at III on the 11th May. On the 12th you can ferry loads
up to IV, and then on the 13th the assault party with the six
Sherpas can move in there. The next day they can ferry loads
up to the Shoulder, and on the 15th establish Camp V there.
On the 16th you should be able to push your top camp to the
end of the ridge below the final pyramid, and on the 17th, with
a bit of luck, make your assault.

"You two," pointing to Dick and me, "can start using
oxygen at Camp IV. Ang Nyima should only need it for the
final assault."

"I wish I could come with you, but with my stomach in its
present state, I should only be in the way. You'll be in charge,
Dick, and you can alter the plan as circumstances dictate. Are
there any questions?"

For the first six days we moved up the mountain with a
machine-like precision. The weather was perfect, not a cloud
in the sky or a breath of wind. I was delighted to find that the

oxygen-set brought my own performance to sea-level standard.
The strength-giving flow amply made up for the extra weight:
the set and cylinder alone weighed thirty pounds, and by the
time one had added some equipment or one's personal belongings it weighed a good fifty. Without oxygen-sets the Sherpas
were going nearly as strongly as we were. I couldn't help feeling
a twinge of guilt that we had this aid and they didn't.

We made our camp on the Shoulder according to time-table,

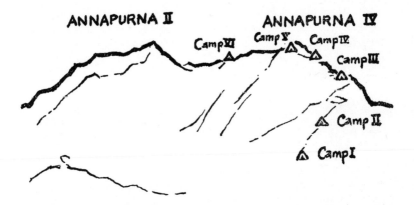

but that night clouds were building up in the south, and by
the morning a full-blown storm was raging outside.

"We'll go out on to the ridge, anyway," Dick decided. "We
can always dump the loads for Camp VI and come back if it
doesn't clear up."

I thoroughly enjoyed that day. At last we were venturing on
to ground that had never been touched by man—not that we
could see much, for we were in dense cloud all day. We just felt
our way along the south side of the ridge, crossing a snow slope
of about 45°. We didn't dare get too close to the crest of the
ridge for there were huge cornices on the northern side.

After a few hundred yards we came to a sheer drop, a step
in the ridge that had stopped Charles Evans in 1957. In the
cloud we couldn't even see the bottom, but managed to work
our way down it, slithering in treacherously soft snow. We
must have been a strange sight, Dick and I in front, like two
men from outer space with our goggles and oxygen masks, and
the six Sherpas strung out behind, all tied on one rope.

A further few hundred yards and we came to yet another
step. We were now several hundred feet below the Shoulder. It

was late in the afternoon and the weather seemed to be deteriorating. The Sherpas were grey with fatigue—they had no oxygen to help them on. Dick was in a bad way, as well. There was something wrong with his set so that he was only getting a trickle that barely made up for the weight he was carrying.

"We'll dump everything here," he shouted, "It's no good staying here. This might last for days and we should only be using up rations. Let's get back to the Shoulder."

On the return we were going uphill for most of the way, into the full blast of the storm. The Sherpas were stumbling like drunken men, exhausted by their efforts. But for the bamboo wands we had left every hundred yards or so, we would have had great difficulty in finding the camp at all.

That night we all felt near defeat.

"I think we've had our spell of good weather. We should have come up earlier," I said to Dick.

He was crouched over the Primus, trying to thaw out the regulating valve of his oxygen-set. There was probably some ice in it that had reduced the flow.

"It's not that bad," he replied. "We've got plenty of food and fuel up here. I'll send some of the Sherpas back tomorrow. We can sit it out for another couple of days, and then if it doesn't improve we'll have to go back as well."

"Do you think your oxygen set is going to be all right? Why not send down for a spare?"

"I shall. But I'll manage somehow," he replied. He had never complained during the day, though I could see that it had taken all his endurance to keep going—I knew that I could never have kept on in similar circumstances.

That night we slept well. There was none of the usual tension before going on a big climb—we were just looking forward to a day in our sleeping-bags, waiting out the storm.

It was daylight when I woke. At altitude, one's reactions are slowed down to a snail's pace. I had been lying awake for some time before I realised that there was no wind drumming against the tent. I poked my head through the sleeve entrance.

"What's it like?" asked Dick.

"There's a lot of high cloud coming from the north," I replied. "It looks as if it might brew up later on."

"Where did you say it was coming from?" he asked excitedly.

"The north."

"Do you realise, man, this is the first time since we've been here that it's come from that direction? It might mean a change."

"I hadn't thought of that. We might as well push on to Camp VI today."

"Bugger that, we'll go for the bloody summit. The Sherpas can follow on and put up the camp for us."

Having made the decision, we wasted no further time, had a quick breakfast, and by 7.30 had set out. The route that had seemed so forbidding in the storm the previous day, was straightforward in the bright sunlight. The three of us plodded steadily on, along the ridge, just below the crest; it dropped away below our feet, in a clean sweep of snow to the jigsaw of a hanging glacier several thousand feet below.

Although his set was still not working, Dick insisted on taking his turn in the lead. Whenever we paused he could hardly speak for panting, he was getting so little oxygen.

It took us only a couple of hours to reach the place where we had dumped our loads the previous day. It was a sobering thought that we still had over a mile to go, and a good 2,500 feet to climb. As we approached the final pyramid, it seemed to loom above us: it looked frighteningly steep.

"You can take a go in front," gasped Dick, and I moved into the lead.

Huge cumulo-nimbus clouds were building up to the south and from the north poured a flood of low grey cloud, washing against the ridge that we had just crossed; none of us said anything, but we were all secretly worried about a change in the weather. It never occurred to us to turn back—on those last stages of climbing a high mountain you are prepared to take any risk to reach the top.

The angle now steepened. A few hundred feet of hard snow led to a rock band, all hideously loose like the tiles of a roof on a derelict house. There was no time to take belays; we just eased our way over on loose flakes, careful not to touch the huge poised blocks above: Beyond, a fragile ribbon of snow clung to the crest of the ridge. A slash of the axe, step up, pant, another slash of the axe. It went on endlessly.

Again the angle steepened, the snow was all soft, slipping away under my feet; my hands burrowed frantically but found nothing. I glanced behind me; Dick was trying to find a belay, but could never have held me if I had come off. Somehow, I floundered on to firm ground, the blood pounding in my head, heart beating a mad tattoo.

"You bloody fool," Dick muttered. "You could have killed us all. There's an easy way just round the corner."

I pressed on, round a small gendarme and up another ribbon of firm snow. With the oxygen, I felt I had plenty in reserve—I even enjoyed climbing over a boulder that barred our way on the crest of the ridge. I no longer glanced over my shoulder at the boiling clouds, but just kept my eyes on the snow in front. I thought we were coming to the summit, only to find the ridge stretching on beyond to a higher point. It was a surprise when I realised that the slope dropped away beyond a small cone of snow just in front of me.

"We're there," I shouted to Dick, who was stumbling behind, head down—he had somehow kept going on a bare trickle of oxygen. We both stopped to allow Ang Nyima to catch up, and then, without thinking, thrust him up on to the summit. It was a tremendously moving movement, and the only time I have been so moved at the end of a climb—perhaps because this was my first big unclimbed peak, but more, I think, because we had worked closely and well together for such a long time. At that moment I was not aware of the other members of the expedition, whose efforts had, in fact, enabled us to reach the top— there were just the three of us on a small cone of snow with boundless space around us. We were cut off from the rest of the expedition—from the rest of humanity, for that matter—by the swirling flood of cloud that now filled the valleys to the north and south. Slowly it crept up the causeway running back to the Shoulder below Annapurna IV. To the south towered great mountains of cumulo-nimbus, dwarfing those snow peaks that had not been engulfed by it.

"Down going, Sahibs." Ang Nyima, for ever practical, brought us to our senses. It was now past four o'clock and we had a long way to get back.

The moment we started down, all my elation left me. I just wanted to get down in one piece, moved cautiously, afraid the steps might break under me, that rock would come away. On the way up there had been no room for such fear; nothing had mattered except reaching the summit, and at that last stage, we would have taken practically any risk to reach it. Our oxygen was now nearly exhausted and we were getting only the smallest trickle. It was all I could do to climb down myself, let alone watch the rope leading down to Dick.

Suddenly he was falling; before I could do anything I was tugged off my feet, and shot down the steep snow. Automatically, I used the pick of my axe as a brake, but it was no good, for it just cut through the snow. There was no time to think—I was past thinking anyway. I was going faster, suddenly shot past Dick, and the rope came taut with a violent tug. He had somehow managed to brake himself and had then held me. We stumbled to our feet, and continued down. No one said anything about the fall—I didn't even feel a sense of shock, I was too tired.

Once we got off the summit pyramid, the ridge seemed endless: we had to cross a couple of waves before reaching the site of our tents which Urkein and Mingma had brought along the ridge earlier that day. It was sheer heaven to collapse into sleeping-bags, eat a can of fruit (melted over the Primus), and drink tea. This had been the finest day's climbing I had ever had, more than compensating for all the sweat and the grind of the last few weeks; but now there was a feeling of anticlimax, and my one ambition was to get off the mountain as soon as possible. I was horribly aware of the physical discomfort I had previously ignored, my sore throat and hacking cough. That night, I even succeeded in convincing myself that I was in the last stages of pneumonia and about to die—I woke Dick up, so that he could share my last hours, but he was singularly unsympathetic and assured me that I would survive the night.

Three days later, back in base camp, I had the same feeling of anticlimax: my nerves felt raw with the prolonged proximity of the rest of the party and I longed to escape, if only for a few days. Jimmy Roberts' plans for our return gave me the opportunity.

"We'll have a change of scenery on the way back," he told us. "I'll send the porters back the way we came, while we, with a few Sherpas, can travel light over the pass to Muktinath, and then down the other side of Annapurna past Tukche to Pokara."

"Could I take Tachei with me, and go across the Tilicho Pass?" I asked. "We could meet you at the other side."

"All right," he agreed, "but don't get lost; there aren't any accurate maps of that area."

"That would be grand," chipped in Bill Crawshaw, "I'd like to come, too."

My heart dropped—I wanted at all costs to get away from the others; fortunately he changed his mind and decided to go with the main party.

A walk across a Himalayan pass probably sounds an anti-climax compared to the ascent of a major peak, and yet the three days I spent crossing the Tilicho Pass, in many ways meant much more to me than our ascent of Annapurna II. This was the pass that Maurice Herzog had crossed in 1950 in his search for Annapurna I. Its position, marked on the Indian Ordnance Survey map, bore no relation to the actual configuration of the ground. The Grande Barrière, a chain of 20,000 foot peaks, barred the way, and the Tilicho Pass was to the north of these. There was no path over it and it had never been used by the local people. The only map I had was the sketch-map in the back of Maurice Herzog's book.

It was three days before I could tear Tachei away from Base Camp: the Sherpas had settled down to a celebratory binge, consuming huge quantities of rakshi, a potent spirit distilled from barley or rice. They deserved it; their untiring efforts on the mountain had made our success possible. Two of them, Urkein and Mingma, were even celebrating the first all-Sherpa ascent of a Himalayan peak: while we were climbing Annapurna II they had slipped up Annapurna IV, leaving a dirty handkerchief tied to a bamboo wand as token of their achievement.

It was a delight to escape at last from the confusion of base camp, from the too-familiar sounds and voices. Tachei was looking decidedly the worse for wear as we walked up the wide, stony valley towards the village of Mananbhot. However slowly I walked I pulled a long way ahead of him after a few minutes, and would then settle down to read by the side of the track until he caught up.

"Sorry, sorry, Sahib. Very bad head. Rakshi, no good," he would mutter as he staggered up to me. Each time I took something from him until I looked like the Sherpa and he the Sahib; but it didn't matter—the sun was shining, we were leaving the expedition, and an unknown world was ahead of us. It was late afternoon when we reached the head of the valley and stopped in a village. The houses, with dry stone walls and flat roofs, were terraced into the hillside. There were no windows, not even chimneys, and smoke from the cooking fires found its way through the doors. The village street, not much wider than a footpath, wound its way through blank walls broken only by the occasional door.

We were soon followed by a troop of grubby, barefoot children, who nevertheless looked happy and well fed. They directed us to a house where we could buy rice and eggs. I sipped a cup of rakshi, while Tashei bargained and gossiped with the woman of the house, a plump matron with a ready twinkle in her eye. But we departed with bare hands; she claimed that there was hardly any food left in the village and that their hens were no longer laying.

That evening we walked up to the Yak pastures, about a thousand feet above. Two boys, who were looking after the herd, collected wood for us in return for a Mars Bar. They also brought back half-a-dozen eggs, green speckled with brown. They were the same size as European hen eggs, much bigger than anything you get in Nepal.

"What are they?" I asked Tachei.

"Rham Chicaw eggs, Sahib. Very good to eat."

We bought these with another Mars Bar. I insisted on cooking the supper that night—an omelette from the eggs of the Rham Chicaw and thick, creamy milk straight from one of the Yaks—it was wonderfully rich in flavour. You could imagine it on the menu of an exclusive London restaurant at thirty-five shillings a portion. The two lads crouched by the fire and watched our every movement—I don't suppose much ever happened up there at the head of the valley and I was probably the first European they had seen.

We didn't bother to put up the tent, but lay in our sleeping-bags by the fire. We talked a little, though conversation was very restricted as Tachei could only speak a few words of English and I a little Hindu. A great deal of our conversation took the form of mutual adulation:

"Sahib, very, very good Sahib," Tachei would assure me.

"Ah, but Tachei a very, very good Sherpa," I would reply. I certainly missed a great deal, not talking the language, for Tachei was constantly telling me about the country and people around us in a strange mixture of Hindi, Sherpa and English that was almost totally incomprehensible. I just answered with the occasional non-committal grunt, which kept the conversation going.

The next morning we set off for the pass. I had decided to

avoid the gorge leading straight to it, where the going was obviously going to be difficult; so we kept to the high ground and headed for a col over the ridge, running down to it. This was straightforward walking, but we had the interest of picking our route through unmapped ground. To reach the col we had to climb a treadmill of scree—two paces up, one back down. At its crest, we looked across to the huge ice wall of the Grande Barrière. It was a strange, desolate place, a wide basin of undulating, stony ground surrounding a huge frozen lake, whose surface was a jigsaw of dark cracks. We took a last look at Annapurna II, now partly hidden in cloud, and started down the other side across the snout of a dying glacier. It was nearly dark when we reached the shores of the lake and put up our tent. We were now a dozen miles from the nearest human habitation, not much really, compared even to the North of Scotland, but there was a sense of remoteness about the place that was emphasised by the size of the peaks around us.

The next morning we followed the shores of the lake to a line of cliffs. Herzog in 1950 had crossed the lake, but now the ice did not seem strong enough. We ended up by climbing the cliff though we had no rope, and it was a good five hundred feet high. Tachei was not very impressed by his introduction to the sport of rock climbing—the rock was unpleasantly loose and we had forty-pound rucksacks on our backs. Another few hours hard walking brought us to the head of the pass.

I felt sorry to leave the mountain solitude, but had already begun to dream of the chicken we would buy that evening. We were now above the Kali Gandaki, the valley running between Dhaulagiri and Annapurna. In violent contrast to the land of grey-brown rock that we were leaving, the fields formed a patchwork of brilliant green in the valley bottom. For the rest of the afternoon we picked our way down towards the valley, across high pasture land and then through dense scrub, losing ourselves in a maze of earthy gorges. That night we stayed in the village of Thinigaon. The houses were flat-roofed like those of Manangbhot, but they were much more spacious and clean, and built round a courtyard, with verandas looking into the centre.

We were given a room on the first floor; it was impeccably clean and well, though sparsely, furnished, with carved chests round the walls and ironware pots on the shelves. In the centre of one wall was a dried mud hearth for the cooking fire, and the smoke found its way out through a hole in the roof.

That night we feasted on chicken curry, washed down by quantities of chang, a beer, white in colour, made from fermented rice. Happily drowsy, I listened to Tachei talk with our host, and felt sad that on the morrow I had promised to rejoin the expedition, that once again I should become part of an alien group in a strange land.

CHAPTER ELEVEN

NUPTSE

BEFORE setting out for Annapurna II, I had been invited to join another expedition—to Dhaulagiri, then the highest un-climbed peak in the world. It was civilian, organised by Joe Walmsley, a well-known climber from Manchester, who had already led one expedition to the Himalaya. I had been tempted, but it seemed unlikely that the army would release me two years running; then I heard that a Swiss expedition had been attempting Dhaulagiri at the same time that we were on Annapurna. They succeeded in reaching the top and I put all thought of Joe Walmsley's expedition out of my mind.

On my return to England, I had only a few more months left at the Army Outward Bound School before it was time to return to my regiment. As the weeks went by, I became more and more unsettled, hating the thought of returning to regi-mental soldiering, but not seeing clearly what I could do in the future; then, in early October, at a dinner of the Climbers' Club in North Wales, I met Joe Walmsley once again.

"We've now got permission for Nuptse," he told me. "It's the third peak of Everest—25,850 feet high—and it looks as if it'll give some hard climbing."

"Have you got everyone you want?" I asked tentatively.

"Why, do you want to come along?" he replied.

I hardly thought, but made up my mind on the spur of the moment—to hell with the army!

"Yes, if you've got room for me."

"I can't say straight away. I'll have a word with the others and let you know next week."

Having made my decision, I was on tenterhooks as to whether I should be invited. The letter arrived at the end of the week—I was in the party.

I suppose I could have tried to get permission from the army to join the expedition, but somehow the idea never occurred to me. I started to hunt for a civilian job. I was so used to being in a large organisation—to the absolute security of the army—

Tachei.

Village at the end of our walk across Tilicho Pass.

Back to the "Main Road" after our walk across the Tilicho Pass: goats carrying loads down valley.

that it never occurred to me that I could do anything but go into another large organisation.

I wrote round to Shell, I.C.I., Unilever and B.P. One of my first interviews was with Unilever. I passed the initial one with flying colours—ego pleasantly boosted, for only a small proportion of applicants even survived this—and went on to their selection board. This was a more intellectual version of those of the army and air force, though instead of crossing alligator-infested rivers, we played with an imaginary soap-manufacturing company, had discussion groups and even psychological tests. I surmounted this hurdle, and the next thing was an interview with my future employer—the managing director of Van den Berghs Limited, an associate company of Unilever, that markets margarine.

I was confronted by the managing director flanked by two other directors.

"You know, you strike me as being a drifter," said one of my inquisitors. "First you tried the air force, then the army, now us. What makes you think you are going to settle down here?"

"I have only changed my career once," I replied hotly. "It wasn't my fault that I couldn't fly. The army was a straight alternative to the air force. As for my change now, it's all too easy to make a mistake in your choice of career in your early twenties. Surely the important thing is to recognise it, and then do something about it."

"Yes, but why choose marketing?"

"I'm interested in selling things, and the whole process of marketing. For instance, my job in getting the equipment for the Annapurna expedition was a form of counter-marketing—persuading the manufacturers to give us their goods free of charge. I thoroughly enjoyed this and the planning it involved."

"Sounds more like begging to me. But anyway, how do we know that you are not going shooting off on another expedition in a couple of years time."

"No, Nuptse will be my last expedition. I realize that I can't base my career on climbing all my life. I want to get stuck into a worth-while job with a future."

And so it went on. I don't know how far I succeeded in convincing them, but I certainly succeeded with myself. I was determined to settle down into a commercial career once I got back from Nuptse. I had taken the precaution, however, of giving myself a long climbing swan-song: I was not going to

E

join Unilever until the September of '61, which would mean I could have a couple of months in the Alps on my return from Nuptse.

We were due to set out in early February, some by road, travelling in two Standard Vanguards, and the rest by sea or air. I was lucky enough to go out by sea—one of the best parts of the trip—but was to return overland with the car party, and planned to stop off in the Alps.

The entire party, nine of us, assembled in Katmandu at the end of February. Three weeks later we had established our base camp below the South Face of Nuptse, and two of us were out in front, making the route up the lower slopes.

"We're wasting our time, Dennis. My feet are frozen solid. It's no good going on in this weather."

"I think we should, at least, get round this bluff and see what it's like on the other side. I won't be long now." And he continued chopping steps in the hard ice. I cursed him with everything I could think of—imagined the satisfaction of smashing a fist in his face.

"You can bloody well carry on by yourself then; I'm going back down," I shouted up after him. He returned slowly.

"If we don't keep pushing on, we'll never get up this arête," he reasoned. I realised I was in the wrong, but was infuriated, not so much by the cold, as by the man himself. We had been cooped up in a small tent for nearly a week now; had worked each day, foot by foot through tottering seracs and knife-edged arêtes; up ice that was like the skin of a rotting banana, ready to peel off its rocky flesh at the least touch. A blow of the axe opened gaping holes, and even a hundred feet below the crest of the ridge, you could, in places, look straight through a hole to the other side. The work was nerve-racking: this would not have mattered if we had been well attuned, but we were too different in temperament to climb together happily.

Dennis Davis was a wiry man of average height in his mid-thirties. His face was seamed by perpetual worry, emphasised somehow by his military moustache. He had a passion for hard work, driving himself perpetually to the limit, whether he was climbing a mountain or doing his job as a site engineer. Even at night in the tent he never relaxed, but had everything in apple-pie order. These, of course, are all commendable qualities. If you don't share them, however, they can quickly become maddening, especially when they are rammed down your throat. I am sure Dennis didn't mean to do this, but he always succeeded in giving me an uncomfortable guilt-complex when I was with him.

I am the very reverse, slightly lazy, often indolent, happy to do the minimum to keep things going. Not a matter of doing less than my share, but preferring to lie in the comfortable squalor of an untidy tent at the end of a long day, rather than spend the evening putting it in order, and preferring to eat off a dirty plate to avoid the trouble of washing up. Fortunately, many climbers are like-minded, but Dennis wasn't—hence my own guilt-complex bursting, under strain, into active conflict.

As we turned to go back, I felt a mixture of shame and anger. I changed my mind.

"Come on. I'll lead the bloody pitch; at least I won't take all day over it."

I hurled myself at the ice bulge. We were trying to get round a gendarme of ice barring the arête; there was a narrow shelf down its side that Dennis had been trying to cross. I slashed at the ice, getting rid of some of my frustration in the violence of my blows, and quickly passed the obstacle. Beyond, the angle was easier, though the ice was as hard as ever, dropping away to a glacier a couple of thousand feet below.

We pressed on in silence for another few hundred feet, taking turns to lead. It was a slow business: we had to cut steps all the way, and hammer in ice-pitons every few yards, to hold the ropes we had left in place for the entire length of the route. We had already used 2,000 feet, even though we had gained only 1,000 feet in vertical height above the start of the arête.

"This'd be all right in the Alps," Dennis muttered as he passed me, "but it's bloody ridiculous here. We'll have to fix-rope the whole mountain at this rate."

"It should be easier once we get into the middle of the face," I replied.

"For a bit, but what about that rock band. It's all very well for you rock gymnasts to dream of doing VS climbing at 24,000 feet, but I think you'll find it a bit different from the Pass when you get there."

"We'll see when we get there. Let's push off down."

This time Dennis agreed. We were both overwhelmed by the size of the problem and felt claustrophobic on the narrow confines of this flying buttress that leapt so crazily up the side of the

South Face of Nuptse. True, it opened out into a sweeping spur in the centre of the face, but that was somewhere above. Each time we reached a crest on the arête there was more beyond.

But at least that night we came closer together than we had at any other time that week. On the way down I apologised for my outburst. It was nearly dark when we got back to the tents. They were perched on a lip of ice that clung to a rock prow. For the first few nights I had lain awake wondering just how secure it was; the ice was honeycombed with holes—but soon we all just took it for granted. This was our third camp, though it was only at a height of 19,000 feet. The ground was so steep and difficult that we had found it necessary to keep the camps close together. Even so, finding sites was a desperate problem. There were few ledges large enough to take a tent and it would have meant hours of cutting to hack a platform out of the ice.

The rest of the party were ferrying loads across the glacier up on to the col at the foot of the arête. We could see the lights of Base Camp far below us; to the east was Makalu, black and massive in the gathering dark, while just opposite was the soaring spire of Ama Dablam, climbed only a few weeks before by Mike Ward and other members of Hillary's scientific expedition. They had wintered at a height of 20,000 feet and had slipped out to climb it in the early spring. They caused quite a furore, for they had not bothered to get the permission of the Nepalese authorities who inflicted a heavy fine on the expedition.

The next morning it dawned fine and we set out with renewed hope. Once the fixed ropes were established, ground that we had found terrifying when we first crossed it seemed easy. We didn't even rope up, just clipped karabiners, attached to our waist-loops, on to the fixed rope. In this way we were able to climb a stretch that had originally taken several days, in a matter of hours. We pressed on farther, and were now in urgent need of another camp-site but, if anything, the arête became even steeper. On our return, we found Les Brown. He was the youngest member of the party, tall and gangling, almost ungainly. He was an outstanding rock climber, having put up many hard, new routes in the Lake District. On the approach march, I had spent a great deal of time with him. Our attitude to and enthusiasm for climbing was very similar.

"John's coming up the day after tomorrow, and Joe says that you two can come down for a rest while we move through to the front."

"That suits us fine," replied Dennis. "We've been out in front quite long enough. I could do with a good wash."

"What about tomorrow, though. Someone should go out on the arête. I wouldn't mind going up with Les, and I can come down tomorrow night," I suggested.

"Suits me, provided you *do* come down," said Dennis. "It's no good sticking out in front the whole time."

Dennis went down that night, leaving Les and me in possession of Camp III. The next day was the best I had had on Nuptse. We quickly got on to new ground, and reached some rock gendarmes. Climbing on firm brown granite was a delight, but more than that, with no feeling of strain in our relationship, we enjoyed each other's company. It was just like an easy Alpine day. We came to a level part of the ridge and could see what we thought was the last barrier before reaching the centre of the face.

"You should be up that in a couple of days," I told Les, feeling a twinge of envy. Although I felt in need of a rest, I hated leaving the front. I longed to see over that barrier myself.

John Streetly was in his sleeping-bag when we got back—he was small, bubbling over with vitality. I have already mentioned him as the only climber outside the Rock and Ice circle to have climbed at their standard in the early fifties. Since then he had returned to his home in Trinidad, and had built up a prosperous engineering business. He was the kind of person who was successful at anything he attempted, yet his dynamism had nothing ruthless about it. He had a wry sense of humour and an unending fund of stories that really were funny, but he had a reserve that, I imagine, few people broke: in spite of his warmth and friendliness, I never felt I knew him.

"How did you get on?" he shouted.

"We got in sight of the top," replied Les. "There's just one more rise in the arête, but it's a big one."

"That's great! Did you see a decent camp-site?"

"There's bugger all. We were looking all the way."

"Oh well, we'll just have to cut one out tomorrow, and we can push through to the top next day."

"I'll give you a hand tomorrow," I told them—secretly loth to go down.

The next day I went with them, carrying some food, to the site of their camp and left them cutting manfully into the ice—there were no platforms anywhere. I should then have gone down to Base, but once again found a good reason for staying up. Two of our Sherpas were now at Camp III and had carried loads with me, that day, to the site of Camp IV. I decided to stay with them, ferrying loads behind Les and John. I enjoyed the company of the Sherpas, and anyway it meant being spoilt: I could lie back and wait to be fed.

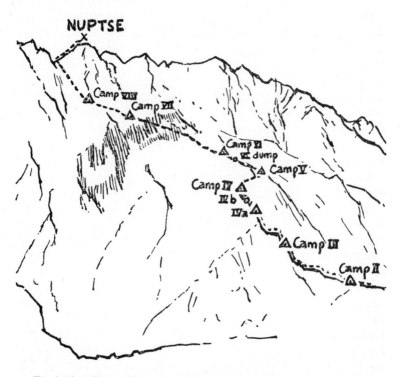

Each day I carried a load up the arête, but the two in front seemed to be making no progress. John had hardly acclimatised and had some kind of fibrositis in his back; Les and he, rather like Dennis and myself, seemed not to have been on the same wavelength—perhaps there was too great a difference in age and temperament.

After a couple of days they returned; Simon Clark and I moved up to take their place. I had already done some climbing with Simon in the Alps. Dark-haired, very intense, with pale face and horn-rimmed spectacles, he had done well at Cambridge, led an expedition to the Andes while still at university, and was now a management trainee with Shell.

By the time we reached the tent that Les and John had pitched, we were bubbling over with righteous indignation.

"It's a bloody shambles inside," shouted Simon. "What the hell have they been doing for the last three days?"

"Eating up the rations we carried up," I replied dourly. "Joe should never have let them out in front."

We settled down to a grumbling session, criticising the leadership of the expedition and everyone in it; no doubt, at that moment, someone else was giving us the same treatment. I don't think our expedition was unique in the amount of back-biting that went on. It can happen all too easily on a large mountain, when people are under heavy strain, and often working in small isolated units, dependent on others above or below, but without adequate communications with them. In these circumstances it is easy to imagine that your own little party is doing the vital and by far the most unpleasant job of the entire expedition—and that because supplies are slow in coming up, or the people in front are not pushing forward, they are slacking.

The following day Simon and I made the big breakthrough. It took us six hours to climb a few hundred feet, leaving fixed ropes behind us all the way. The expedition had now nearly run out of rope; we were using our climbing ropes, and had even bought, at an extortionate rate, some old hemp rope from the Thangboche monastery. On the arête alone we had put nearly 5,000 ft in position. We edged our way over blades of rock embedded in ice, conscious always of the steep drop below, now getting on for 3,000 feet, to the gaping crevasses of the Nuptse glacier. A last wall of ice, and the angle began to ease, the slope opened out before us and we were on the col—level, crunchy snow with room for a few tents. After the confines of the arête it felt like a football pitch.

For a moment we felt as if we had climbed the mountain; that it was all over. But then we glanced up at the snow slope stretching above us: a band of steep rock barred the way into the upper ice-fields and summit gully, and we realised just how far we had still to go.

Sobered, we returned to the camp-site. I had a feeling of flat anticlimax. I had put too much of my strength and enthusiasm into getting up the arête. Now that we were up it, I seemed to have lost the urge to press on. I was full of plans. Simon and I spent most of our time planning streamlined assaults on the summit, and grumbling about the slowness with which supplies were trickling up the arête, but when it came to action I was hopelessly lethargic. We had intended to move up to the col the following day, but instead stayed in our sleeping-bags. I became obsessed with my own health, was coughing a lot, and had a pain in my chest that Jim Swallow, our doctor, assured me was merely from strained muscles. I didn't believe him, however, and imagined diagnoses of pneumonia or the like. Finally, after a lot of dithering, I decided to go down to Base Camp for a few days rest. As I scrambled down the arête, I had a feeling of guilt, mixed with fear that I should miss the final assault altogether.

I spent the next three days in my sleeping-bag in Base Camp. It was a depressing spot, not a touch of green anywhere, only stones and glacier debris. John was down there, still recovering from his fibrositis. The only other occupant was Jim Lovelock. He was a free-lance journalist and had come out to look after Base Camp and write newspaper reports for the *Daily Telegraph*. He did much in those few days to bolster my morale by his unfailing cheerfulness and repertoire of bawdy stories.

It was agony watching the tiny black specks of the others creep ant-like up the shoulder on to the snow dome. I longed to be up with them. At this stage the weather began to break—it had been remarkably settled for the past three weeks—and the mountain was plastered in heavy cloud; snow fell every afternoon. Down at base we could only guess at the progress of the others as we caught glimpses of the upper slopes through rifts in the cloud. Dennis Davis and Jim Swallow were now out in front, at Camp V, about five hundred feet above the col. It was here that Dennis showed his dogged tenacity. Each day he went out in the storm to force the route a bit farther on, very often on his own, for Jim was not feeling too well. He didn't achieve very much, but the mere fact that he was up there and still trying, kept every one else going. Joe Walmsley and Les Brown, with a couple of Sherpas, were on the col, in Camp IV. In those few days enough supplies were ferried up to Camp V to make a summit bid possible.

After three days in Base Camp, I was still feeling weak and tired, but John decided to go back on to the mountain. I hated the thought of being left behind while everyone else was doing something, so I went with him. We stayed at the foot of the arête for the next few days. There seemed no point in going any nearer the front in bad weather, when it would just mean that more people were wasting rations without making any forward progress.

The weather had been bad for over a week and it was now well into May.

"It looks like an early monsoon to me," I said gloomily to John.

"Certainly looks like it. We'll be lucky to get up at all if it doesn't improve soon."

Already the arête was nearly impassable with freshly fallen snow. It certainly would have been if we hadn't fixed ropes all the way up it. John and I had the toughest but most enjoyable day of the expedition when we carried a couple of loads of food up it in a blizzard. We were out for ten hours, and got back in the dark after being swept away several times by avalanches of powder snow; we were saved by the fixed rope into which we had clipped.

The day after our epic ascent, when we were still trying to dry out our wet clothing, Simon Clark came down from Camp IV.

"It's bloody murder up there," he told us. "The wind just never stops; it's been hammering the tent, day and night for the last three days. I think you get a bit of shelter down here." Later that evening he dropped a real bombshell.

"I'm getting worried about my wedding," he told us—he was planning to get married on his return. "If I don't start for home soon, I'm not going to have time to make all the preparations. I must leave on the 12th May."

"You might as well start straight away, in that case, for we're certainly not going to climb the mountain in the next few days," I observed.

"You know, I think I might come with you," John added. "I've got a hell of a lot to do back home—I've been away too long already."

And so it was decided that they should set out in a few days time. I was sorry to see John go, as I had particularly enjoyed climbing with him; but they were not leaving us in the lurch— the mountain was overcrowded as it was.

Climbing a Himalayan peak requires a pyramid of effort, with plenty of people at first to help ferry loads to about half-way up the mountain; but there comes a time when the party needs to be thinned out, when more people high up, simply

means that more food and fuel are consumed, and that, therefore, more has to be brought up. Already there were four
climbers and two Sherpas at Camp IV and beyond: enough to
reach the top, if only the weather changed. Simon's and John's
departure was, however, symptomatic of the spirit of the
expedition. Somehow we had failed to forge any bonds of real
friendship and affection while climbing together. I didn't go
home with them, more because I personally wanted to reach
the top of Nuptse, than because I had any unselfish desire for
the eventual success of the expedition as a whole. I rather think
that was the feeling of nearly everyone else, with the exception
of Joe Walmsley, the leader, who devoted himself throughout
to the prosaic but absolutely essential task of ensuring that our
supplies were ferried up the mountain behind the party out in
front.

The morning after John and Simon had made their decision,
the weather showed signs of improvement and I decided to go
up to Camp IV, since it should now be possible once more to
make some real progress on the mountain. I wasn't made over-
welcome when I arrived.

"What do you think you're doing?" asked Les.

"I thought I'd come up and see what's happening up front.
Dennis has had a good spell up there."

"Yes, in the rough weather. Why not ferry some loads up
from III. We could do with some more food up here. You've
done bugger-all load-carrying."

I lost my temper.

"And you've done bugger-all in the last week except eat up
food. When you were out in front you made precious little
progress."

Fortunately Joe put a stop to our stupid quarrel, and agreed
that I should come up. There was a lot of justice in what Les
had said. Perhaps in going down for a rest I was motivated by
self-interest. Anyway at that moment I was determined to get
up to the front and knew I was now going strongly—certainly
as well as Les.

A couple of days later, Les and I went up to Camp VI just
below the rock-band that Simon and I had seen when we
reached the top of the arête. As far as we knew, Jim Swallow
and the Sherpa—Pemba—were at V; Dennis and Tachei at VI.
The previous evening we had seen the top pair go right to the
foot of the rock-band. As we plodded up, I prayed to myself

that they had found a way through it. If we could only surmount this last obstacle, we should be able to reach the summit.

Jim and Pemba were already ensconced at Camp VI when
we arrived, so we hacked out another platform and settled
down to wait for Dennis. It was a magnificent evening. We
were at last creeping above the surrounding mountains. Ama
Dablam's slender spire merged into the background peaks, as
we looked down on it; to the west the rounded dome of Cho
Oyu seemed not much higher than we were; and beyond
stretched the ragged skyline of the Rolwaling Himal.

It was after dark when Dennis got back to the tent. His face
was even thinner than when I had seen him last—haggard with
weariness—and yet there was a look of triumph in his eyes.

"We've got through the band," he announced. "It doesn't
look too bad beyond."

"What was it like?" I asked.

"Nothing like as hard as we thought it would be. You don't
have to go straight up it; there's an obvious traverse line with
just one hard pitch—a chimney bunged up with ice. That was
bloody thin. You know what Tachei's ropework is like. I might
as well have done it solo. I've left a fixed rope on it."

"How's Tachei going?"

"Really well. It makes all the difference having him with me;
anyway I was getting bloody tired of looking after myself; it's
great having someone who'll make the early morning tea."

"I reckon we're in a position to make a dash for the summit
now, don't you?" I suggested.

"I don't know about that; it's still a hell of a way to the top.
We're not much higher than 22,500 here. I was beginning to
wonder what had happened to the rest of you—nothing much
has been coming up for the last few days. I was thinking of
pressing on with Tachei. It looked as if we should have to do
the whole bloody lot ourselves."

I had an idea that this is what he would have liked most of all,
he seemed almost sorry to see us; but I felt warm respect for
him and the way he had kept battling on, all these days, in
appalling conditions with very little support from anyone.

"Well, now that we are here, don't you think we could get
things moving. If you like, Les and I could have a go out in
front," I said.

"All right. You two can go and stay at the top of the rock
band tomorrow and you could push on towards the foot of the

summit gully the day after. We'll go with you with a load, and come back here. We'll come up and join you the day after tomorrow."

"What about me?" asked Jim.

"Could you and Pemba ferry some loads up from below— we've got precious little up here in the way of food and fuel," replied Dennis.

The next morning, the four of us set out for the rock band.

It quickly became obvious that Dennis and Tachei were much more fit than we were. They pulled away from us steadily. Both Les and I were feeling lethargic and took rests every few yards. The rock band, which had looked such a formidable obstacle from below, proved to be quite straight-forward. Just above it, was the site of our camp—a small spur of snow on the end of the ice-field. It took us all afternoon to cut out a platform. We took it in turns to work: each cut for a few minutes and then collapsed exhausted while the other took over. Every now and then there was a deep-pitched whistle and a rock hurtled down from the huge black cliffs above us. We just had to hope that they would go to either side of our spur, but we felt hideously exposed.

We tried to put the tent up too soon, before we had cut a sufficiently large platform; we were so tired, we decided that it would have to do. It sagged crazily over the drop, poles askew, guy lines all at the wrong angle. That night, we felt that the least breath of wind would blow it away. In the morning, getting ready was sheer hell. The Primus wouldn't work and the inside of the tent was a sordid mess of dirty pans, spilt food and cloth-ing. Les was never at his best in the morning and lay in his sleeping-bag—a pallid corpse—as I struggled with the break-fast.

It was impossible for both of us to get dressed at the same time in the tent so I volunteered to do it first, and wait outside. Les seemed to take hours to get ready as I stamped around in the bitter cold, trying to get some warmth into my limbs. I could see Dennis and Tachei at the foot of the rock band and the last thing I wanted was to be caught in camp by them.

At last we were ready, and started across the ice-field. We had to cut steps all the way. I trended too high and got on to some awkward rock, cursed myself, and had to start cutting down the slope. Les was feeling the altitude even worse than I, therefore I had to do all the step cutting. It was back-breaking

Nuptse: ferrying loads on the arête leading into the upper part of the face (*photo Dennis Davis*).

Les Brown on a gendarme on the arête between Camps III and IV on Nuptse.

work in an uncomfortable position; our progress was desperately slow. The slope seemed endless, until we could actually look up into the summit gully of Nuptse and see, far above, where it joined the summit ridge.

"I reckon we've done enough for one day. Let's get back," I suggested to Les, and we started down. It was dark when we reached Camp VII, but very comforting to see the other tent up; to know that we weren't alone that night.

"Come in and have some tea," Dennis shouted. My heart warmed to him but, as so often happened, he added a barb.

"Why, on earth, did you go so high; you couldn't have chosen a worse line."

I knew we had gone too high, and that I had made a mistake, but we had put everything we had into making any progress at all. Over supper, we discussed plans for our assault.

"If you and Les could carry the tentage and food, Tachei and I could go up the gully tomorrow. I think we'll need at least a day's work cutting steps up there, before we can go for the summit and you can move up tomorrow. We can then all go for the summit together," Dennis suggested.

It seemed the best scheme. There was no doubt about it, Dennis and Tachei were going much better than we were, and as he observed, even the foot of the gully was a long way below the summit.

The next morning Les and I carried about forty pounds each up into the gully, and left Dennis hacking out a platform on a narrow rock ledge—it was an inhospitable spot. As we turned to go, I had an uneasy feeling that they would try for the summit the next day. I was tempted to stay there myself, bivouac, and go up with them; but in doing this there would be little chance of a second attempt if we all failed. My commonsense told me it would be better to go back. After all, if they succeeded, we could always follow up the next day, and if they didn't, we should be fresh for the second assault. It was the old battle between being unselfish, thinking only of the success of the expedition, and my own personal ambition to reach the top. Not just to be the first on top, but also to enjoy the full climax of weeks of effort—the day when you force your way to the summit, see the top slowly get closer, and finally stand on it. Being the second party up could never be the same.

That night I lay awake thinking of how Dennis must now feel in the top camp, and wishing I were there. I half prayed

that they wouldn't try for the summit, but was ashamed of
myself for doing so, knowing full well, that in their position, I
should go. There were now four of us at Camp VII, for Jim
Swallow and Pemba had come up the previous night. I must
confess, we were not over-glad to see them—the top camp
would be a squash with four, let alone six people.

On 16th May, we all went up into the gully and spent most
of the afternoon hacking out a platform barely large enough for
two tents. By the time we had finished, it was nearly dark; still
no sign of Dennis.

"The bastard's gone for the top," I told Les. "They'll have
a bivouac if they don't hurry up."

It was past eight o'clock when we heard shouts in the gully.
A few minutes later they staggered down to their tent.

"Did you do it?"

"Yes."

"Bloody well done, you deserved it," and I really meant it.
I should have loved to have been with them, but in face of
Dennis's greater determination and fitness, he so obviously
deserved to get there.

"How did it go?"

"The gully was the worst part of it. We started at six and
didn't get any sun all the way up. It took us six hours to get up
it cutting steps all the way. Old Tachei went great guns, did
his full share of step-cutting—you'll be able to tell the ones he
cut, they're enormous. We wanted to cut them big enough to
get down easily; bloody glad we did, or we'd have never got
back in the dark. The summit ridge is quite easy. We reached
the top at three-thirty. Never thought it was coming; there were
several false summits."

None of us slept that night; a combination of excitement and
acute discomfort kept us awake. I was on the outside berth of an
Italian assault tent that seemed to have been designed for one
small person. I spent most of the night having a pushing match
with Jim to avoid being thrust over the abyss. He had a definite
advantage, for he had a large lilo that filled most of the space,
while I was lying on a small sheet of foam rubber.

Combined with my excitement at the thought of going to the
summit, were some sneaking doubts about the safety of our
situation. We knew there was no one else on the mountain
above Camp IV, but worse, that there was hardly a scrap of
food or fuel on any of the Camps. With us we had just enough

for a meagre breakfast. If the weather turned, it would have been impossible to get back across the long ice-field to the rock band for it would be swept by avalanches from the rocks above.

When we set out in the morning, we found the line of steps, cut by Dennis and Tachei, so good that we were able to take off the ropes and climb solo. I soon pulled ahead of the others, with Pemba on my heels. The gully seemed interminable, and was deep in shade. Far above, at its top I could see a tiny triangle of sunlight, but it never seemed to get any closer. My feet had long lost any sense of feeling and I wondered if I had frostbite.

It was sheer delight when I eventually got into the sun; a few minutes later I could see over the top of the ridge. This was a bigger moment than actually reaching the top. For six weeks we had only been able to look south, had been enclosed by the great Wall of Nuptse, but now I was looking straight down into the Western Cwm; Everest—massive and black—was just the other side, its summit only 3,000 feet higher. But most impressive of all was a rolling sea of brown hills broken by the occasional snow cap. It was utterly desolate and yet inexpressibly beautiful.

Pemba and I turned to the final ridge leading to the summit. As Dennis had told us, it was set at quite an easy angle. We were able to move comparatively quickly, though every hundred feet or so I found that I had to lie down, my heart rattling like an old car-engine whose big-end had gone.

We were on the top by midday, but there was no real feeling of emotion; we had just followed in someone else's footsteps. more than anything else, I had a sense of relief—it's all over, let's get the hell out of it.

By all appearances, we had been completely successful on Nuptse—six of us had reached the top. But at the finish of the expedition, I had a feeling of personal inadequacy, not because I had failed to be first on the summit, rather because I had lacked determination, had gone down to Base Camp thinking myself sick. I spent many hours in painful self-analysis, going back over events, hating my weakness. I also became very aware of my own failure to forget individual ambition and prejudice for the good of the party as a whole.

No one could have described us as a happy expedition—there was too much backbiting for that—but at the end of it none of us was an enemy for life, as has happened after quite a few Himalayan expeditions. Similarly, few friendships were cemented. We had remained throughout, nine individuals—at best several small groups—but never a complete team.

Immediately after the expedition I longed to go back to the Himalaya, just to prove to myself that I could do better, both physically and morally; the memory of the hardship and boredom of it all was too close to think of Himalayan climbing as pleasant. But when, after a year or so, as one always does, I had forgotten the unpleasant part of it, or at any rate, no longer rated it important, I longed to go out again for the sheer excitement of finding my way up a great unclimbed mountain.

CHAPTER TWELVE

EIGERWATCHING

I HAD been stuck in the same position for nearly ten minutes. My arms felt weak, my legs were shaking; my body seemed heavy and useless, and I was frightened by the steep rock above and below.

"You're climbing like a bloody nana," came from my second, fifty feet below. "At this rate we'll have a bivouac."

We were on the Menagaux Face of the Aiguille de l'M, a standard little training climb, popular with all the British.

I had arrived in Chamonix the previous afternoon, at the end of the 7,000-mile journey from Katmandu. The trip was a vague blur of dusty roads, flies and punctures. I suppose it should have been a highlight of the expedition, but we were all too tired of travelling, too tired of each other, to absorb anything of the countries we had passed through.

I had arranged to meet Don Whillans in Chamonix at the beginning of July. We planned to spend the summer in the Alps, our main objective being the North Wall of the Eiger. It said something for our timing that we arrived below Mont Blanc within twenty-four hours of each other. Don had hitch-hiked out from Manchester, taking three days to do it—his rucksack was nearly as tall as he himself.

It was I who had insisted on going on the North Face of the Aiguille de l'M; I wanted to find out just how unfit I was. When eventually we reached the top I told him.

"I don't think I've ever been so unfit; I'll never get up the Eiger at this rate."

"You'll be all right. When Joe got back from Kanch he was nearly as bad," he replied.

"How about doing a few more training climbs before going over to Grindelwald? Sitting in a car for five weeks is no training for the Eiger."

"You can do your training on the face. By the time you get to the top you'll be fit—or dead! Anyway, we haven't enough money to hang around. How much have you got?"

"Ten quid, but John Streetley has promised to send me another twenty."

"That won't go far. You'll just have to tighten your belt— anyway, it'll get you used to civvy street. You don't know how soft you had it in the army."

We left Chamonix early the next morning. We were lucky enough to scrounge a couple of return halves of tickets to Grindelwald from Geoff Oliver, a climber from Newcastle, who had just come back after an abortive skirmish with the bottom few feet of the Eiger. Grindelwald was the same as it had been four years before, spotlessly clean and smug, frowning on penniless climbers.

"Don't want to stay in this place longer than we have to," Don remarked. "They charge you even to breathe round here."

To save money, I walked up to Alpiglen, while Don caught the train with all our gear. We had decided to camp there, since it was not as crowded as Kleine Scheidegg at the end of the line, and the walk down to Grindelwald to get food was rela- tively easy. It was an hour's walk up, and I found Don sitting in the forecourt of a small, wood-built hotel, the Hotel des Alpes. From a distance I could see he was fuming.

"Even the ticket collectors think they're God Almighty round here. One of the bastards tried to throw me off the train. I got into a first-class compartment by mistake. I wouldn't have minded if he had asked me civil like, but he started shouting his head off, and then grabbed my shoulder—I just gave the bugger a push—that was enough. The sooner we climb the face and get out of here the better."

We pitched our tent a hundred yards from the hotel and settled down to wait. If you want to climb the North Wall of the Eiger, it's not just a question of going straight on to the face and up. You are lucky if it comes into the right condition more than once in a season. You need settled weather, and the Wall should be clear of freshly fallen snow, but being a north face it takes several days to get into condition. That summer the weather followed a regular pattern—one day of stormy weather with heavy falls of snow, next day the clouds would slowly clear, the next would be beautifully fine and our hopes would begin to rise, but just as we began to prepare our equipment it would cloud over once again.

A couple of weeks went by, but the pattern never changed

and we dropped into a pleasant, if monotonous routine. We were equally lazy, and who should do the cooking often became a real test of will power that I usually lost.

"The trouble is, Chris, you're too greedy. You'll always crack before I do."

This was at four o'clock one afternoon, when we hadn't cooked anything all day and I had just started to peel some potatoes.

"What's on the menu, today?" asked Don.

"I'll curry them for a change," I replied.

Our diet consisted of potatoes and vegetables—you could boil them, fry them or curry them for variety. We couldn't afford meat, but had the occasional egg and plenty of cheese. Each night we sat in the Hotel des Alpes, eking out a bottle of beer between us. Funnily enough, though, I found all this enjoyable and could feel my strength, drained by the climb on Nuptse and the long car journey, slowly come back. We didn't do any climbs—the weather was too unsettled to do anything serious, and anyway, Don wasn't prepared to go on a snow slog, just to get fit.

"I'll only do a climb if I'm really interested in it," he observed. "It's got to be a good line—not just hard—but one that catches my imagination."

This summed up his entire attitude to climbing—all the routes he had put up in England and Scotland had been superbly direct, uncompromising lines—ones that hit you in the eye as obvious, but at the same time were too difficult, or more often too frightening, to have been done by anyone else. To this day, some of his climbs rank among the most formidable in Britain.

His attitude to climbing in the Alps was much the same—he made up his mind about what he wanted to do, and then stuck to it.

In fact, this summed up his attitude to life. He had a rigid code of his own, that no one could make him budge from. He always thought carefully before committing himself, and then once committed could be relied upon absolutely. He was intensely aware of his own rights, perhaps because he had to fight hard for them, and was bitterly aware of the limitations that his primary school education and upbringing in Salford, had imposed upon him.

"I'll meet any bugger half-way," he often told me, "but I

won't go any further. I'm not going to be imposed on by any-one."

This chip on the shoulder often made my relationship with him hard work; it meant that I had constantly to go more than half-way to find any point of contact. We couldn't have been more different in personality—where he was cautious, I tended to be impetuous, all too often undertaking something that, on mature thought I found I could not fulfil. In the mountains I enjoyed making last minute changes of plan, dashing off to climb this route or that, was restless if there was no climbing to be done. Don, on the other hand, decided the routes that he wanted to do, and was then quite happy to wait for them to come into condition, and was not prepared to fill in with any-thing second best.

Yet once we got on to a mountain we became a complete team, a single smooth-functioning machine. We never talked much, never seemed to waste any time, built up a rhythm of smooth, steady movement that, to me, is the height of pleasure in climbing. I have certainly never enjoyed climbing with any-one as much as I do with Don.

After sitting below the Eiger for a couple of weeks, we were both getting restless.

"I could do with a change," said Don, "anything to get away from this dump."

"How about doing a climb round here?" I suggested, with-out much hope.

"No, it's not worth the effort; I'd rather fester here."

"Well, let's get a change of air, anyway. We could hitch to Lucerne and see Max Eiselin. I met him when he came to Manchester to lecture on Dhaulagiri. He said I should call in on him. He might be good for a decent meal."

Don took the bait and we set off for Lucerne; we never got there and very nearly didn't get any farther than Grindel-wald. We had been sitting by the roadside for two hours trying to hitch a lift.

"I'll give it four more cars and I'm going back to Alpiglen," announced Don. "At this rate, we'll take ten days to reach Lucerne."

But our luck changed and we got a lift down to Interlaken. We were just walking across the bridge, not even bothering to hitch, when a Volkswagen pulled up beside us.

"Do you want a lift?"

Tachei reaching the summit of Nuptse (*photo Dennis Davis*).

Everest from the summit of Nuptse.

"Yes, please," and we piled in; it couldn't have been better; the driver was a girl; what's more she was attractive, American, and on her own.

I had managed to seize the strategic seat beside her.

"Where are you going?" I asked.

"Only a couple of miles up the road, I'm afraid. Where do you want to get to?"

"Lucerne," I replied, "but let's have a coffee before we press on."

Over coffee, we tried to persuade her to come with us to Lucerne, but ended by staying with her—she slept that night in the Youth Hostel, and we, under the stars. The following day, after a swim in the lake, she took us back to Grindelwald and spent the rest of the weekend in Alpiglen.

Things were looking up—Anne had to go back to Geneva after the weekend, but she promised to return, and for the rest of the holiday was our faithful chauffeuse, as well as being a good friend. She had only been in Europe for a few months, having come over to study French. She was a big girl, not conventionally pretty, dark-haired, but with a strength and warmth in her face that was attractive. From our first few words in her car I felt happy and at ease in her company; we could talk of anything and everything.

A couple of days after Anne had returned to Geneva, we acquired new neighbours: four Poles, also bent on climbing the Eiger. At first we regarded them with suspicion, resenting the fact that they might be on the face at the same time as ourselves, fearful that they might hold us up, that we could be involved with them in an accident. Their arrival acted as a spur for us to go and have a look at the face, to see just what was involved.

"Let's go up on the next fine day," suggested Don, "I think we'll have to come back down again, but at least we'll then know a bit more about what we're up against."

A couple of mornings later, we were plodding up the grassy slopes above Alpiglen—it was still pitch dark, but we hoped to get on to the face just as it became light. I felt none of the fear I had experienced that first time I went on it with Hamish, as I had a better understanding of the difficulty and more confidence in my own ability, and, equally important, complete trust in Don.

We scrambled, silent grey shapes in the half light of the dawn,

up the lower rocks. We soon had to put on crampons because
every ledge was covered with iron-hard snow, and the rock was
smeared with verglas. Nevertheless, we made quick progress up
to the top of the first Pillar, a hundred feet or so higher than I
had been in 1957.

"I reckon we must have got higher than any other British," I
suggested to Don.

"Doesn't say much for us," was his matter-of-fact reply.

Beyond the Pillar there was even more snow—we were using
the front points of our crampons the whole time. It was a wonderfully exhilarating feeling to stand poised on just two points
which bit into the snow for only an inch, while a clean sweep
of white dropped away to the dark shadows of the valley below.

We had climbed more than a thousand feet, though we had
been going for only a couple of hours. Our way was blocked by
the occasional short wall, plastered in verglas, but we still
climbed solo to save time. We only paused to put on the rope
when we reached the foot of a band of steep, overhanging rock
that stretched across the face—we had reached the start of the
serious climbing.

I found myself leading the first pitch, a traverse below the
wall; it was all covered in smooth, hard water-ice. You could
see the dark-stained rock through its transparent shield. I
chipped away at it with my axe—it was about half an inch
thick and absorbed my blows as if it were treacle. I placed a
crampon point in the nick I had carved out fearful that it
would peel away under my weight. There was no protection,
no feeling of security; by the time I was half-way across the
pitch, I was wishing I was anywhere else but on the North Wall
of the Eiger.

I reached a ledge, and was able to belay.

"There's a rope been left here," I shouted to Don. "This
must be the Difficult Crack; it looks bloody awful, it's completely plastered."

Don left his rucksack with me, and started up the wall. It
took him over an hour to climb eighty feet—it was like a vertical
skating rink. The rope, left, I imagine, by the party that made
the first winter ascent earlier that year, was no use to him—it
carried an inch-thick sheath of ice. He had to clear each tiny
handhold with his peg-hammer. The whole pitch was vertical
so he had to hang on with the frozen fingers of one hand, while
he hammered away with the other. When it was finally my turn

to come up on a very tight rope, I couldn't help marvelling
how he had led it, and feeling grateful that it hadn't been my
turn to go first.

The angle eased as we traversed across a snow-field below the
huge, blank face of the Rote Fluh—it was as big as most Dolo-
mite walls, but here it was just one small feature on the North
Wall of the Eiger. We reached another steep chimney piled
with powder snow and an impossibly steep wall of snow.

"You know," said Don slowly, with a dry grin, "you and I
are wasting our time; you could almost say that the face isn't
in perfect condition. That's the Hinterstoisser Traverse."

"Let's push off down," I replied. "You can't even see the
fixed rope across it. I wonder how long it'll take to clear."

"It'll be some days yet, if at all. Let's get back before the
stones start coming down."

We turned tail, abseiled down the steep sections and scrambled unroped down the rest. Just below the Difficult Crack, we
saw four figures coming up towards us.

"Here come our Polish friends," remarked Don. "I wonder
how high they'll get."

We started down towards them when I noticed a cave in the
face about fifty feet to our left—it was the Stollenloch, an
entrance to the railway tunnel that pierces the Eiger leading
up to the Jungfraujoch. Every day hundreds of tourists travel
in this tube-train, happily unaware of the climbers clinging to
the face outside.

We scrambled over to it, pushed open a solid wooden door
and walked into the railway tunnel. The contrast was bizarre:
one moment we had been on the dreaded North Wall of the
Eiger, a place of rock and ice, a thousand-foot drop below our
feet, and the next we were in the man-made safety of the
tunnel. A train clanked slowly past—white gawping faces
pressing against its windows stared down at us; a guard shouted
and gesticulated, wordless, and the train ablaze with light
rattled on up the tunnel leaving us in the dark.

"The buggers'll only make us pay, if they catch us," said Don.

"I can imagine them chucking us back down the face, even
in a blizzard, if we hadn't got the fare," I agreed. "Anyway, it
won't take us long to get down outside."

By the time we got back into the sun, the four Poles had
reached us. Two of them were already starting to climb the
Difficult Crack, while the other two sat at its foot, disconsolate.

"We've dropped our rucksack," one of them told us. "The other two will go on, but we must return."

"You're not missing anything," replied Don. "Even the Hinterstoisser is plastered. The conditions couldn't be much worse."

"All the same, we should like to have a look," shouted down the men out in front, and continued to climb up the Difficult Crack. The ice had now melted, but nearly as bad, a waterfall was pouring down it.

We went down with the other two Poles. Somehow, meeting them on the face had brought us together. That night we cooked a communal meal and wondered how the other two had fared on the wall. Looking up we could see the glimmer of their light below the dark shield of the Rote Fluh.

Next morning the two Poles returned—they were a pathetic sight, their clothes still sodden, their equipment hanging in disarray around them. The temperature had not dropped below freezing; as a result they had spent the night sitting in the direct line of a waterfall on the only ledge they could find. That morning, being numb with cold, they also had gone through the Stollenloch, determined to walk straight down the line. They were picked up by the first train going up and were taken to the Eiger station where they had to wait for the next train going down. They were then made to pay the full fare up to the Jungfraujoch, and, because they hadn't any money with them, had to leave their cameras behind. Such treatment was probably correct on the part of the railway officials, but their complete lack of sympathy with the two Poles and their downright discourtesy, were less excusable.

After this little débâcle, we joined forces with the Poles—it certainly did a lot to raise our standard of living, for they had brought plentiful supplies from their home country. Tinned ham and sauerkraut were a welcome change from a diet of potatoes. Cheswav, the only married man in their party, was appointed cook. He had a vivid imagination: we dined off villainous looking mushrooms collected from the woods, and one day he even brought back a tinful of snails—I don't know who it was who let them escape before he could try them out.

As soon as we returned from our reconnaissance, we had our first taste of the publicity anything to do with the Eigerwand seems to arouse. We were summoned to the telephone in the Hotel des Alpes that same afternoon.

"Were you on the Eiger this morning?" an excitable voice shouted down the other end. "I'm from the *Daily Mail*."

"Yes," I replied, guardedly.

"Why did you come back—was one of you injured?—the weather seems very settled."

"Yes, but the face isn't in condition. We just went to have a look."

"When are you going back?"

"Depends on conditions. We might not be able to go on it at all."

And so it went on. The next morning a Swiss freelance journalist arrived. He looked like a smoother version of Spencer Tracy—rugged good looks and grey hair outside, but in Don's words "soft as shit" inside. He was dressed in the most immaculate climbing breeches I have ever seen—they had never been messed up on a mountain. He wanted to help us, develop our films for us, become our father confessor. I'm afraid we regarded him with the deepest suspicion.

"They all seem to want to get a story for nothing," observed Don. "I wonder how much they make out of it."

"I don't see why we shouldn't make something out of it ourselves. If we get up let's sell the story to the highest bidder. The papers will make a story up even if we don't tell them anything —and God knows we need the money. There's only six pounds left in the kitty."

Don hated having anything to do with everyday money transactions and I had therefore been appointed treasurer and chief buyer—I did all the shopping.

"Well, let's climb it first; we can then think about selling stories," was Don's down-to-earth opinion.

Another fortnight went by, but the weather was no better; there were never more than a couple of fine days in succession. Towards the end of August, the snowline dropped below Kleine Scheidegg: it didn't look as if the Eiger would be in condition that summer.

"I think we're wasting our time here," decided Don. "Let's push off to Chamonix. Do you know anything about that Central Pillar of Frêney?"

"Robin Smith went to have a look at it in '59. It sounds as if it could be really good. Shall we have a go at it?"

"Aye, we could do that. If we got up, it'd be better than doing the Eiger. I fancy doing a good new route. It faces South so it should come into condition very quickly."

The four Poles also decided to abandon the Eiger. Cheswav was going to return home to his family—Stanny and Jan Mostovski wanted to go to Zermatt to try the North Face of the Matterhorn, and Jan Djuglosz, who spoke the best English of these three, asked if he could join us on the Central Pillar. We had become very close to the Poles and were delighted. Jan was a professional mountaineer, making a living as an instructor and writer in his native Tatras. He was strongly built, and looked very purposeful with heavy horn-rimmed glasses and a jutting jaw.

A few days later, driven by Anne, we left Grindelwald for Chamonix and the Central Pillar.

CHAPTER THIRTEEN

THE CENTRAL PILLAR OF FRÊNEY

THE refuge bivouac on the Col de la Fourche is a tiny cor-
rugated-iron Nissen hut designed to hold eight people; it clings
to a small ledge just below the crest of the ridge and from its
door you get a giddy view of the great Brenva Face of Mont
Blanc. In early July of 1961 Walter Bonatti, with two companions, Andrea Oggioni and Roberto Gallieni, arrived at the
hut. They were on their way to the Central Pillar of Frêney, an
unclimbed rock buttress high on the south face of Mont Blanc.
At first glance this seems an unlikely approach, for the Central
Pillar is at the head of the Frêney Glacier, and from the Col de
Fourche they would have to cross below the Brenva Face and
then ascend the couloir leading up to the Col de Peuterey, a
new route and major ascent in its own right. Only then would
they be able to start climbing on the Pillar, the most remote and
highest Grade VI climb in Europe. The more direct approach
up the Frêney glacier was even more difficult, for the glacier is
seamed by crevasses and threatened by tottering seracs.

To their surprise, the three Italians found the hut occupied
by four Frenchmen. Bonatti recognised one of them as Robert
Guillaume, a young climber who had already put up several
important first ascents. The others were Pierre Mazeaud, an
extremely experienced mountaineer, Antoine Vieille and Pierre
Kohlman. There could be no doubt where they planned to go.
Bonatti must have been bitterly disappointed to find them
there: he had had his eye on the Central Pillar for nine years
and had already made one attempt on it, but it is an indication
of his character that he immediately offered to go on to another
climb since the French were there first. They rejected this offer,
however, insisting that the Italians should join them.

They set out in the middle of the night, and in cold, clear
conditions crossed the head of the Brenva Glacier, over the
Col Moore and up the Peuterey Couloir, reaching the Col de
Peuterey just after dawn. That day they managed to climb
about two-fifths of the way up the Pillar; so early in the season
the cracks were still heavily iced, making progress slow.

The Central Pillar has a smooth rock obelisk about four hundred feet high, that rests on a 2,000-foot plinth of broken granite. They reached the foot of the obelisk on their second day, but during the afternoon, wisps of cloud had been forming, and suddenly the storm broke around their heads—an inferno of snow, thunder and lightning. Kohlman was struck by one of the flashes and was badly shocked.

They settled down for the night, confident that a storm of such violence could last only a few hours and that they would then be able to scale the few hundred feet of steep rock that were between them and safety. But the next morning the storm was as furious as ever, and they resolved to stick it out. Retreat in those conditions didn't bear thinking about, especially down the icy chaos of the Frêney Glacier.

They sat it out on the ledge for three days and nights, and still the storm showed no sign of letting up. In this type of bivouac it is impossible to stay dry—snow inevitably seeps into the bivouac tent, condensation from the breath soaks everything. They could eat only limited quantities for it was practically impossible to light their cooker in the storm. The French were even worse off than the Italians for they had no bivouac tent but relied on plastic sheets which they wrapped around themselves. Quite apart from the mutual warmth you gain in a tent, it is much easier to maintain morale when huddled close together, able to talk to each other.

Bonatti very quickly emerged as the natural leader of the party, closely supported by Pierre Mazeaud. On the fourth day, their fifth out from the Col de la Fourche, he decided that they must retreat, while they still had the strength to do so.

The snow was falling as thickly as ever, as they abseiled, rope length after rope length, down the Pillar—the ropes must have been like hawsers, their clothes frozen into armour plating. Once off the Pillar, however, it was even worse; they were up to their chests in powder snow and could only see a few feet in front. Bonatti, with an uncanny sense of direction, guided them to the Col de Peuterey, but by that time it was nearly dark, and they had to resign themselves to another bivouac in the bowels of a crevasse.

There was no question of getting back the way that they had come; the couloir leading down to the Brenva Glacier was a death trap, continuously swept by avalanches. They made for the Rochers Gruber, a rock rib running down into the lower basin of the Frêney Glacier. Near the top of the rib, Vieille, the youngest member of the party, was unable to go any farther —they tried to haul him along, but he died in front of their eyes from exhaustion and exposure. Down on the glacier, Guillaume collapsed—they were unable to carry him for they were all near the end of their tether; their only hope was to reach the Gamba Hut and send back a rescue party. Without Bonatti it is unlikely that they would ever have picked their way through the crevasses of the Frêney Glacier, but eventually, when it was already getting dark, they reached the couloir leading up to the Col de l'Innominata. Oggioni, who had taken up the hardest position of all throughout the retreat, at the rear of the column where he had retrieved all the abseil ropes and had helped on the others, was now able to go no farther. Mazeaud stayed with him at the foot of the couloir.

From the top of the Col de l'Innominata they had 2,000 feet of steep descent to the Gamba Hut. Kohlman was now showing signs of delirium, threatening to take Bonatti and Gallieni, tied to him on the same rope, down with him. They tried to drag him along, but eventually, when he actually attacked them, were forced to untie from the rope and flee down to the Hut.

When the rescue party went out to pick up those who had been left behind only Mazeaud was left alive. So ended one of the most long drawn out and at the same time heroic tragedies in Alpine history. It was a miracle that anyone survived at all; this was largely a tribute to the determination and skill of Walter Bonatti.

Only a month later another party set out for the Pillar— Pierre Julien, an instructor at the École Nationale in Chamonix, and Ignazio Piussi, a leading Italian climber who was attending an international meet at the school. They caused some criticism by using a helicopter to reach the top of Mont Blanc and then just descending the Peuterey Ridge to the foot of the Pillar. That same day they climbed as far as the smooth section near the top, but dropped a rucksack containing their gear; as, anyway, the weather was beginning to look threatening, they made a quick retreat.

When we set out to try the Pillar for ourselves we knew no more than the bare outlines of the stories of the previous attempts and had only seen a photograph of it, taken from a distance. On reaching Chamonix, our first problem was to find a fourth member for our party—three is an awkward number on a long rock climb.

"How about asking Julien?" suggested Jan. "I know him quite well from a course at the École I attended last year."

"Might as well ask him," agreed Don, "we might get a bit of information from him, if nothing else."

We walked over to the School that afternoon and asked for Julien. He wasn't much taller than Don, but was more heavily built—dark glasses, a smooth V-neck sweater and immaculate breeches; he oozed an aggressive, bouncy self-confidence.

After the preliminary introductions, Jan told him of our interest in the Central Pillar and asked if he would like to join us.

"It is impossible," he replied. "I have too much guiding to do, but I should be happy to give you any help I can."

"What is it like where you turned back?" asked Don.

"There are some cracks out to the left. You need plenty of big wedges," he told us.

On the way back to the camp site we met Ian Clough. He had just arrived from the Dolomites. Neither Don nor I had climbed with him, but we knew him by reputation. Although only in his mid-twenties, he had done as much hard climbing in the Alps as anyone in Britain. He came from Baildon, in Yorkshire, had served three years in the R.A.F. Mountain-rescue Team at Kinross, and had then decided to devote his entire time to climbing. For the last few years he had eked out a precarious living as an instructor for the Mountaineering Association. He had just climbed the North Face of the Cima Ovest di Lavaredo by the French Direttissima route. It was continuously overhanging for seven hundred feet and he had spent two nights sitting in his étriers—we decided that this was ample qualification for a place on our team.

A few days later, the weather seemed settled and we caught the last téléphérique up to the top of the Aiguille du Midi. Just as the doors were about to close, three heavily laden climbers piled in. I immediately recognised Pierre Julien.

"The others are René Desmaison and Poulet Villard," Jan muttered to us.

"I don't think there's any doubt where they're going," said Don.

For a few minutes we pretended to ignore each other, glancing across occasionally with lowered eyes; then Julien walked over to us.

"You go to Frêney?" he asked.

"Perhaps, and you?"

"Perhaps."

At the top of the Midi the three Frenchmen took one of the tele-cabins going across to the Torino Hut. I couldn't understand this, for the obvious way to the Col de la Fourche is to walk down on to the Vallée Blanche from the Midi.

"I wonder what they're up to?" asked Ian.

"They've probably got a helicopter waiting for them," suggested Don. "Anyway, there's nothing we can do about it. Let's get to the hut before it's dark. We'll only have a couple of hours' rest as it is."

On the way across the Vallée Blanche, just below the dark spire of the Grand Capucin, we noticed a solitary tent, but at that stage were unaware of its significance. The hut, when we reached it, was crammed to bursting: there were already a dozen people packed on to the two-tiered bunk that almost entirely filled its interior. As we cooked our meal in the open doorway, I kept glancing across the expanse of the Brenva Glacier to the vast bulk of the Brenva Face and across it to the sheer silhouette of the Eckfeiler Buttress, climbed only a few years before by Walter Bonatti. You couldn't see the Pillar from here; it was hidden by the upper part of the face, but the sight of the ground we had to cover that night was frightening enough. Behind the Eckfeiler Buttress I could just see the Couloir leading up to the Col de Peuterey; it looked impossibly steep and long—a major climb in its own right and we had to get up it in the dark.

As I looked, my eye caught a puff of smoke high up on the face of the Eckfeiler Buttress; it quickly spread into a plunging torrent of swirling brown cloud that completely enveloped the face; almost at the same time came the noise, a deep pitched thunder that hammered at our ears, filling me with an instinctive fear. I have never seen such a rock-fall—it seemed to stretch into minutes, though in fact it could have only lasted a few seconds, but even when the sound had vanished into the stillness of the night a heavy sulphurous smell lingered on, though we were nearly a mile away from the Buttress. Later that night we intended to pass below the very same place.

To me it seemed an omen; before a big climb I have always felt some fear, but that night my imagination was working overtime as I thought of our prospects of survival should the weather break when we were high on the Pillar. There was little chance of sleep, anyway, for we were packed together like the inmates of a concentration-camp barracks; you couldn't possibly turn round, or even lie on your back, there was so little room.

But the evening's excitement was not over. At about eleven-thirty, the door swung open, and in strode a big, handsome-looking man wearing a domed crash hat. He had an air of absolute self-confidence as if he owned, not only the hut, but the entire mountain. He went straight to the hut book, which we had filled in a few hours before (Frêney Pillar with a big question mark), glanced at it, wrote his own entry and walked out. As the door closed we dived for the book—there it was—Walter Bonatti. He was with a client on his way to the Brenva Face.

"Well, at least he can't get up on to the Pillar for a while," observed Ian.

"Put yer heads down. Let's get some kip," said Don. "We'll have to start in an hour."

I don't think any of us slept, we just lay and waited for the alarm. At last it was time to get up; the other occupants were also stirring. We had a quick brew of coffee, loaded our rucksacks and set out. A couple of parties had already left. We could see their lights slowly move across the glacier below. We put on crampons straight away, and scrambled down steep snow and rocky steps to the glacier. High up on the Brenva Face we could see tiny pinpoints of light—Walter Bonatti and his client.

The sky was a deep black, glistening with a myriad of stars; there wasn't a breath of wind and yet I felt there was something wrong; subconsciously, I think, wanting any excuse to avoid going on to the Pillar. I heard a trickle of water running down the rock.

"You know, it can't be very cold. There's some running water over there. That could mean that the weather's changing. I wonder if we should just go up the Major."

"It's as settled as it ever will be," replied Don. "We've come this far, let's go on."

We crossed the Col Moore, and then left the beaten track to the Brenva Face and dropped down to the other fork of the Glacier. Now that we were committed, my fears seemed to vanish and I began to enjoy myself; we came to a bergshrund at the bottom of the slope. Don jumped across without hesitation, rolled a couple of times on the other side and stopped

Central Pillar of Frêney from the Col de Peuterey. Clough, Whillans
and Djuglosz in the foreground.

The Central Pillar of Frêney in profile. The snow arête in the foreground is the Peuterey Ridge. The broken buttress on its immediate left is the Right-hand Pillar. The crux of the Central Pillar is the steep candle of rock on the sky-line (*photo Philippe Gaussot of* La Dauphine).

himself with his axe. I paused on the edge for a minute—I have always hated jumping—and then for fear of seeming a coward launched myself into the dark, bounced and rolled down the slope.

We roped up for fear of hidden crevasses, and were soon picking our way across the glacier. As we approached the dark bulk of the Eckfeiler Buttress we could still detect a heavy smell of sulphur in the air: we had to clamber over the debris of the rock-fall a full hundred yards out from the face.

The couloir now stretched above us. An awkward ice-bulge at the bottom fell to Don's axe, and we were then able to make our own way up the firm snow, climbing quickly and silently in pools of light from the head-torches. It was a good 2,000 feet long, but we reached the top well before dawn. For its last few feet it reared up steeply, a wall of mouldering rock held together by bonds of clear ice. It was my turn to lead; a boulder rattled away under my foot, narrowly missed Don fifty feet below, and bounded out of sight into the deep shadows of the couloir. I jerked my head, and my head-torch went out—I must have disconnected the battery. In complete darkness I felt my way up the rock—it was unpleasant, as dangerous as anything we were to find on the Central Pillar, but not unenjoyable. A few more feet and I was standing on the Col.

We had taken only four hours to reach the Col de Peuterey, and it was still dark. There was now no question of it being too warm—we were all chilled to the marrow.

"There's no point going to the foot of the Pillar before it's in the sun," decided Don. "Let's have a brew."

We crouched around the gas stove, trying to capture a little of its warmth, and stamped up and down the level plateau of the Col. We were there for over an hour before the line of dazzling sunlight slowly crept down the length of the Pillar to its foot. The rock, a rich brown in the sun, looked warm and inviting.

"Someone's coming up the couloir," shouted Ian.

"It must be the French," said Don. "How many of them are there?"

"Just two."

"That's odd, I wonder what's happened to the other. Anyway, we'd better get started before they arrive."

We quickly crossed the snow slope of the Upper Frêney Glacier, found a way through the big bergschrund at the foot of the Pillar, and started up the rock. Don and I went first, followed by Ian and Jan. It was some of the best climbing I have ever done. The rock was superbly sound, warm to the touch, and we had all the excitement and interest of being on new ground. There were no signs of our predecessors and we just picked our own route, winding our way through thrutchy chimneys, up jamming cracks, over steep walls.

The shattered tooth of the Aiguille Noire had been far below us at the base of the Pillar; soon we could look over the corniced summit of the Aiguille Blanche to the haze-covered foothills of Italy. The couple we had seen in the couloir had now reached the Col; about an hour later another pair arrived. They made no move to follow us, but put up tents and seemed to be waiting to see how we fared. We assumed that these must be the French, and that somewhere they had picked up a fourth person. We were wrong, however. The first pair had been two Americans, Garry Hemming and John Harlin, complete outsiders to the Frêney stakes, but formidable climbers. They had spent the previous night in the small tent we had seen below the Capucin. The second pair were Desmaison and Poulet Villard. They had had a hard time of it: they had climbed the couloir after the sun had come on to it, when the snow was dangerously soft, and they were constantly bombarded by stones dislodged by the two Americans.

The three French climbers had gone over to the Torino Hut the previous night, hoping to find there Ignatio Piussi who had been summoned by telegram to join the team. He had hired a car and raced across North Italy from his home near Trieste, but had been delayed on the way and missed the last téléphérique up from the valley. Julien had therefore stayed behind while the other two pressed on. Piussi and he set out first thing that morning but only reached the couloir in the late afternoon. So, late that evening there were six camped on the Col de Peuterey.

By that time we didn't worry about them; we were fifteen hundred feet up the climb, and it seemed a fair lead. At four o'clock we had reached the foot of the final tower. The Pillar now slimmed down from a broad, crack-seamed buttress to a slender, monolithic candle of rock, girdled at half height with a belt of overhangs. There were few cracks up it, and what there were all petered out. Gazing up at it, we each had a twinge of doubt—we had no drills or expansion bolts with us—if there were no cracks, no holds, we should be defeated.

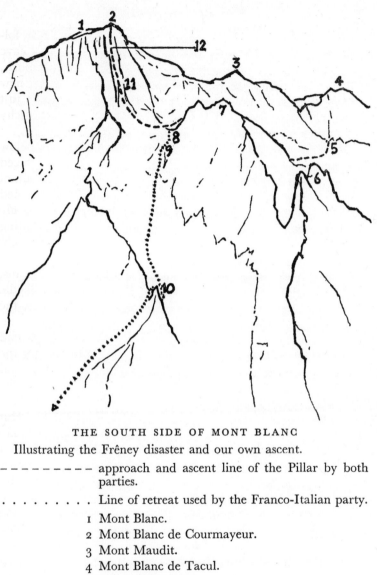

THE SOUTH SIDE OF MONT BLANC

Illustrating the Frêney disaster and our own ascent.

— — — — — — — — approach and ascent line of the Pillar by both parties.

. . . . Line of retreat used by the Franco-Italian party.

  1 Mont Blanc.
  2 Mont Blanc de Courmayeur.
  3 Mont Maudit.
  4 Mont Blanc de Tacul.
  5 Col de la Fourche.
  6 Aiguille Noire de Peuterey.
  7 Aiguille Blanche de Peuterey.
  8 Col de Peuterey.
  9 Rochers Grubers.
 10 Col de l'Innominata.
 11 Central Pillar of Frêney.
 12 Highest point reached by Bonatti and his party.

Resting against the Pillar was a rock pedestal some fifty feet high. Bonatti and his party had sat out the storm on top of it. There were a few sad relics of their ordeal, an empty gas cylinder, a cooking pot and some wooden wedges.

"We've time to have a look up there before it's dark," said Don. "Hold the rope."

The rock was smooth and sheer, but up to the line of overhangs there were some cracks, and Don made good progress, hammering in his own pegs and using a few left by our predecessors. On reaching the overhang, he edged his way to the left.

"I reckon this is as far as the others got," he shouted down. He disappeared out of sight and the rope lay still in my hand for nearly twenty minutes. At last he reappeared. "There's bugger all round here," he shouted.

"What about Julien's wide cracks?" I asked.

"Not a sign of them—the cracks are all blind and just vanish above the overhang—you'd never get up her without bolts. What's it like to the right—can you see round the corner?"

"Can't see much—there seems to be a chimney up through the roof and there's a corner leading up to it. There might be some cracks in it, but it looks as if it'd be bloody hard getting into it."

"I'll have a look."

Don worked his way back and was soon directly over me, spreadeagled, crucified on an overhanging prow of rock. There were no cracks for pegs and he seemed to spend hours on end in the same position before inching forward imperceptibly. I longed for him to come down, so that we could put on duvets* and settle down for the night. The sun had dropped out of sight round the side of the Innominata Ridge and it was bitterly cold —we were now at a height of over 14,000 ft.

"I think it'll go," at last shouted Don.

"Well, come on down, I'm bloody freezing."

Ian and Jan had caught us up and were sorting out their equipment on a ledge to the side of ours. The gas stove was purring steadily. Don threaded a rope through his top piton and abseiled down in the fast-gathering dark.

We settled down for the night—Ian, as the youngest and most easy-going member of the party, was appointed chief brew-maker; every hour or so during the night he made us some tea or

* Eiderdown jackets.

Clough and Djuglosz on our first bivouac—the site of the disastrous bivouac of Bonatti and his party.

Don Whillans on the
Central Pillar—
Matterhorn in far
background.

soup. None of us slept much, it was too cold for that—our legs, unprotected by down clothing, were numb. From time to time I had attacks of the shivers when my teeth chattered with the speed of castanets. I couldn't help thinking of the isolation of our position, of the difficulty of retreat if we should be unable to climb the sheer tower above our heads. I could imagine how Bonatti and his party, seated on this same ledge only a couple of months earlier, must have felt—with safety so near, and yet so unattainable.

After a bivouac you are so chilled that it is difficult to start moving before the sun warms your bones. Fortunately, high up on the south side of Mont Blanc, we caught the sun early.

This time I went up the first pitch, using the pegs Don had hammered in the night before. I took a stance on a small foot-hold just below the overhangs, sitting in a sling. I felt I was poised immediately above the great ice-falls of the Frêney Glacier 3,000 feet below. Don moved up past me and was soon thrust out of balance on the overhanging prow. The time crept slowly by and it was all I could do to stay awake in the warmth of the morning sun. A hundred feet below, Jan and Ian basked on the bivouac ledge, while, on the Col de Peuterey, the campers were showing signs of life. Two tiny figures set off down towards the Rochers Grubers and the other four started out for the foot of the Pillar.

Don was now out of sight round the corner of the Pillar. I could hear the dull thud of his peg hammer—the cracks were all blind—and the hoarse pant of his breath. He was two hours on the prow: there was nowhere on it to rest; nowhere was it less than vertical.

"Give me some tension."

My grasp tightened on the rope. Out of sight, poised, alone over the steep ice gully, he leant across the blank wall—there was nothing for his hands or feet, no crack in which to hammer a peg. His fingers latched round a wrinkle; he was held in precarious balance by the tight rope stretched horizontally from round the corner. The farther he moved across, the more it tried to pull him back, to send him swinging, helpless, into mid-air far out from the overhanging wall. The corner, with a reassuring crack in it, was only six feet away, but it might just as well have been a hundred, the rock seemed utterly impreg-nable. He searched for a crack—relaxed, somehow, even though he had now been hanging on his fingers for nearly an hour. He found one low down to the right—little more than a score on the surface of the granite. He probed it with a tiny ace-of-hearts peg, tried to make the point stick in, for he could only spare one hand; then, oh-so-carefully, reached for his hammer, just tapped at the head to lodge it in the crack. The peg skewed to one side and shot down out of sight—hands getting tired, muscles aching, Don patiently tried to place another peg. This time it stayed in the crack—went in a good half-inch. Holding it gingerly, he edged his way across the wall into the corner.

He had said nothing for over an hour, but I could feel the tension transmitted through the rope by the imperceptible slowness with which it had run through my hands. The pegs now had a good resonant ring to them. There was obviously a useful crack in the corner. Another hour crept by—you need a lot of patience to be a climber.

"You'd better come on up to me," came a muffled shout. "The rope's dragging and I think I'll have to do the next bit free. The crack's too wide for the channels and too narrow for wedges."

As I crossed the prow, I wondered how on earth Don had managed to lead it—it was all I could do to cling on. It was difficult to conceive how he had managed to place the pegs.

I found him ensconced half way up the corner, sitting in his étriers.

"You'd better stop down there. There's a bit of a ledge for you to stand on. There's sweet bugger-all up here."

As soon as I was belayed, he started on the last stretch up to the roof. The crack in the corner was just wide enough for his fingers. The roof jutted out above him a good twelve feet, but in the corner of the roof the crack widened into a chimney actually cutting through its ceiling.

We were in heavy shade, and it was bitterly cold on the belay. The rope ran swiftly through my fingers—thank God he's nearly up—but then there was a long pause. I gripped the rope more firmly. He was now a good fifty feet above me—his shoulders jammed in the chimney, his feet pawing ineffectively on the smooth rock below. There was a crack sufficiently small to take one of his pegs, right in front of his nose, but he was unable to let go with either hand to grab a peg and thrust it in. He struggled to get higher into the chimney, but could get no purchase with his boots.

"I'm coming off, Chris."

There was a long pause—not even a man as hard as Don resigns himself to falling. I hunched my belay, wondering what the impact would be, whether his pegs would stay in. A mass of flailing arms and legs shot down towards me, the rope came tight with a sudden, but not over-violent jerk and I found myself looking up into Don's face. He was hanging upside down a few feet above me, suspended from one of his pegs. He had fallen just over fifty feet.

"I've lost me 'at!" he stated.

"Are you all right?"

"Aye."

"Shall I have a go at it?" Quickly. I was tired of standing in the cold, anxious to seize the opportunity to get out in front while Don was still stunned.

We changed over—that took a long time—and I started up the crack. I had no illusions about it. If Don couldn't climb it free, I certainly couldn't, but I hoped I might be able to engineer myself some kind of aid. There was nothing, however —as Don had said, the crack was too wide for our pegs, too narrow for the wedges.

I returned. "Let's see if the others have anything," I suggested, and shouted down to Ian and Jan. But it was no good, we had the entire stock of ironmongery with us.

Meanwhile, the other party had just arrived below the steep section, having climbed most of the way up the gully at the side.

"Ask the French if they have anything," I shouted.

There was a long pause. When the reply came I could only just hear it—we were a hundred and fifty feet from the others round the corner.

"They say we can have some gear in a minute. They want to look at the other side first," shouted Ian.

Another long pause—it was now late afternoon.

"Have they made up their bloody minds yet?" I asked.

"They say that we are on the wrong line—that it goes up the other side. They need all their gear for themselves."

"Well, bugger them in that case; we'll get up by our own means. Have you any slings down there?"

"Yes, what do you want them for?"

"I'll try chockstoning the crack—show the Frogs some Welsh technique," I replied.

It took us an hour to manœuvre the rope so that we could

haul up the slings. I then collected some small stones from the back of the crack, jammed them into it, and, threading the slings behind them, clipped in my étriers and tentatively trusted my weight to them.

In this way I was able to reach the ceiling; standing in a sling, I hammered in a good peg. From there I had some of the most awe inspiring climbing I have ever experienced. Above my head the chimney narrowed down to a dark slit, while below there was nothing but space, dropping away to the Frêney Glacier. If I had fallen I would have been dangling some ten feet out from the rock. At the end of the roof, the chimney thinned down to an ice-blocked crack; I had to arch myself out from its comforting confines and swing up on frighteningly small hand-holds. There was no time to pause—even to notice the fear that filled my body. I climbed those last few feet with a desperate speed, only conscious of the need to reach a resting place before my strength ran out.

I reached a ledge and let out a yell—we were over the main difficulties. Don followed me up quickly, and shot past round a ledge just above. It was now very nearly dark; we had climbed only two hundred feet in a complete day. Ian and Jan were still sitting on the ledge where we had spent the previous night. The French seemed to have made no progress round the corner and were preparing a bivouac site.

"You two had better prusik up," Don shouted down to the others. "It'll take too long if you try to climb. We'll drop a rope."

We dropped a single rope and Ian went first, spinning like a spider on the end of a thread, as he worked his way up on slings. Just as Jan prepared to follow him, Desmaison offered him some pegs and asked him to take their rope up, so that they could prusik up the next morning. Jan agreed to do this.

We found a small ledge on the other side of the Pillar. It was sloping and only just fitted the four of us, but that didn't matter—we were nearly up. Nothing could stop us now. My position was at the lower end of the ledge, and I spent most of the night fighting to maintain it as the others slowly slid on top of me—at any rate it helped to keep me warm.

Next morning we climbed the last two pitches. A couple of light planes were roaring round our heads, taking photographs. We all had a feeling of wild exhilaration and triumph, heightened by the struggle we had experienced the day before. The

Don Whillans and Chris Bonington on the top of Mont Blanc after climbing the Central Pillar—note the upturned bottle of wine brought up by a French journalist (*photo Leblanc of* La Dauphine).

Looking south from the southern flanks of Mont Blanc.

Pillar ended in a slender tower; thence a short abseil took us down to a snow slope leading to the top of the Brouillard Ridge of Mont Blanc de Courmayeur. Another hour's plod and we were on the top of Mont Blanc. A French reporter, dropped there by helicopter, was waiting for us. More important than his congratulations was a flagon of red wine and tins of fruit juice. Slightly tipsy, we staggered to the Vallot Hut and then on down to Chamonix.

CHAPTER FOURTEEN

EIGERWANDERING

ON our return we found Chamonix in a state of turmoil. That same day a jet fighter had struck one of the telecabin cables across the Vallée Blanche. The cabins nearest the break had fallen to the glacier several hundred feet below, killing the occupants, while the rest were stuck at intervals along the remaining cable. A major rescue operation was being launched to bring down the stranded passengers and as a result the town was buzzing with reporters.

The day after our return we had a celebratory champagne lunch with the three French climbers and Ignatio Piussi. After the lunch, when I had got over the initial excitement of doing a great climb, I began to think of what we could do next.

I was due to report at Van den Berghs in just four days time to start my new career as a margarine executive, but the weather was still miraculously perfect. Surely we could fit in one more climb before going back; but if we were to do this, I should have to fly, and I certainly couldn't afford the fare. I then began to think once more of the Eigerwand. It must be in condition after nearly a fortnight of perfect weather.

That night, in one of the bars, I met a reporter from the *Daily Mail*; he was a straight-speaking, cheerful Australian. Over a bottle of wine, I suggested they might like to finance our bid on the face and fly me home afterwards; he 'phoned Head Office and they agreed. Don and I were in the hands of the Press.

Time was vital, so next morning Anne ran us over to Grindelwald. By the time we reached Alpiglen, in the late afternoon, we were tired out but felt we must go straight on to the face. I had only three days left and, anyway, we wanted to use the good weather while it lasted. It was blazing hot as we tramped up in a cloud of buzzing flies; somehow it all seemed farcical and make-believe. Back at Alpiglen we had posed for photographs.

"Now let's have a picture of you and Anne together, saying good-bye—can't you make it a bit more personal than that?—come on, closer—they'll probably never use it—that's it—let's have a bit of real passion—lovely—just the thing."

Inevitably the picture appeared—on the front page—titled "A kiss before the Eiger".

"Can I say anything about you and Anne? Any romance in the air? You are just good friends? Well, I suppose that's better than nothing."

A photographer was following us up through the Alpine pastures, panting hard, cursing under his breath; he looked utterly out of place in a lightweight, Soho-style suit and winkle-picker shoes. Every hundred feet or so he collapsed, groaning.

"It's bad enough up this—how the hell you characters hope to get up there I just don't know. I wouldn't do this again for a hundred pounds."

"We'll take you a couple of hundred feet up the face, if you like," I offered, "just think of the name you'd make for yourself in Fleet Street."

"You know what you can do with that. This is as far as I'm going. Hold on a minute while I get my breath back—now turn round and give us a wave as you go up the slope—best of luck—bloody glad I'm not in your shoes."

The Face seemed strangely peaceful and real after the hectic rush of the last twenty-four hours. Bargaining for the right terms, posing for photographs, answering questions, were now all matters of the past. We were on a climb that we wanted to do; relief at escaping all the hullabaloo below completely drowned any feelings of doubt or fear that I might otherwise have had.

We scrambled up the bottom slopes over easy-angled slabs and steep little walls. It was completely different from three weeks before. We were sweating in the heat of the sun—the Face had hardly any snow on it at all. We intended that afternoon to reach the Swallow's Nest Bivouac, at the foot of the first ice-field. We should then be poised, ready to cross the ice-fields in the early hours of the morning before the daily stone-fall started. We now felt we knew the Wall, had given a great deal of thought to climbing it safely and, by doing this, were confident that we could keep the danger factor to an acceptable level.

We roped up at the foot of the Difficult Crack. This time it was clear of ice—warm dry rock in the afternoon sun. Don made short work of it. The Hinterstoisser Traverse was also clear—a steep holdless slab, with a rope stretched across it. It was my turn to lead. I treated the rope cautiously, for who could tell how long it had been there? Another pitch and we reached the Swallow's Nest, a ledge about eighteen inches wide, at the side of the first ice-field.

We cleared some ice from it and settled down for the night, full of confidence, as we now felt on peak form and the face seemed in perfect condition. We couldn't lie down on the ledge, but were fairly comfortable, sitting crouched, close together; from time to time we had a brew, chatted for a few minutes, dozed off. But at midnight Don asked me:

"Can you hear all the running water? Even the bloody stones are still falling. You know, it can't be freezing up there."

"It might do in the early hours of the morning," I suggested.

For the rest of the night we waited for it to start freezing, so that the stones in the upper part of the face would be held safely in position in the clasp of the ice, but the gentle trickle of falling water interspersed with the distant rattle of stones continued.

In the dawn there were a few wisps of cloud to the west.

"I don't like the look of the weather," said Don. "If we push on now we're going to get stone-fall all the way up the face. It's just not worth it. I've no desire to give the papers a sensational story."

"We could go up just a bit," I suggested. "The weather might improve."

"What's the point? That's how half the accidents occur on the Eiger, with people pushing on just a bit farther, not knowing when to go back. We can always come back next year."

Don's argument was conclusive, and a sign of his prudence as a mountaineer. We packed up our gear and started the long trek down. Although we had only been 1,500 feet up the Face, the reporters were waiting for us in force. We spent the night in Alpiglen, and the next day I booked an air passage back to England—I should get back with a night to spare. The weather now seemed to be more settled and I longed to wait out for just a little longer. I half envied Don his freedom, he was staying out for a few more weeks, but I was obsessed with the importance of starting my new job on time, of creating the right impression.

Just as we were ready to leave Alpiglen, a tourist rushed into the Hotel.

"I have seen someone fall from the mountain!" he shouted, incoherently. At first we didn't believe him, but felt we had to go and just make sure, so plodded back towards the foot of the Eiger; we saw someone wave and walked over to a self-important German tourist.

"The body is over there," he announced proudly. We walked hesitantly, averting our eyes—neither of us wanted to look—as we held the blanket we had brought up with us, ready to cover the corpse. We had a vague impression of blood and naked limbs twisted into grotesque shapes—the clothes had been torn to shreds in the fall, but skin is a tough covering—and then dropped the blanket over it. The German was hovering at our side; he lifted the blanket with the flourish of a showman, to show us how the head had been bashed in. I could have killed him at that moment—I couldn't help feeling that here was the fascination of the Eigerwand, the thing that makes the crowds gaze through the telescopes when someone is in trouble on the Face, the thing that makes the Eiger front-page news.

We went in search of the dead man's companion, but could only find the odd trace of blood—he could not possibly have survived, anyway, for he must have fallen from the crest of the Mitellegi Ridge, 5,000 feet above. We decided to leave it to the guides, and returned to Alpiglen.

I had now missed my plane. I booked another for the early hours of the morning and drove through the night to Geneva, giving Anne a hurried farewell; we made plans to meet again, but somehow it seemed the end of the line. Those six weeks had been idyllic in their complete lack of any form of responsibility, in the tension of doing an exacting climb and the absolute relaxation of lazing in the valley; but now, that was all over. I was both excited and nervous at the prospect of my new career.

The pace at which I was moving was too great for me really to appreciate the change. Five hours after saying good-bye to Anne in the empty airport lounge, I was standing, scrubbed, shaved and dressed in a dark suit outside the doors of a huge skyscraper office block. It was nine o'clock, and a flood of men and women poured in around me through the doors. I went in hesitantly, found that I had lost the letter telling me to whom I had to report, so went up to the porter:

"I've come to work here—who do you think I should go and see? I'm afraid I've lost the letter telling me."

"Well, I don't know—I suppose it could be Mr. Smith. I'll try to find out."

Half an hour later he discovered the right man and I was welcomed into Van den Berghs.

The first six months as a management trainee were spent looking round the firm, tramping from department to department, sitting in front of innumerable desks and hearing about the occupants' jobs. Having listened for a couple of hours, you were expected to ask intelligent questions—I could rarely think of anything to say. In the Army I had detested office work and in civilian life there seemed to be little difference. Still, it was only for six months. Then I was given my first real job—as representative in Hampstead. I had to go round the grocers' shops taking orders for margarine, putting over the Company line, and persuading the grocer to accept display material. We had learned the process at training school. You walked through the door, brief-case in one hand, display material in the other, contrived to raise your hat and give the grocer a cheerful good-morning. He ignored you, being busy or naturally bad-tempered. It was part of the job to assess the margarine the grocer required, and make the order for him. Some of my clients were happy to let me do this, others were passionately possessive about their shops, trusting no one. In my case they were probably very sensible—working out the quantities you had to put in was very simple, but somehow I always got it wrong—the rage of the shopkeeper knew no bounds when he discovered that he had fifty or so boxes of surplus margarine, or conversely, that he ran out in the middle of the week.

The Company was not averse to the closing of accounts with some shops, provided new accounts were also gained in others. I was only too successful in the first venture, closing over a dozen in six months, but I never actually opened a new account. It was less work that way—by the end of my tour of duty I had only three calls to make on Fridays, which helped towards a long weekend.

As the winter drew to a close, I became increasingly restless. Although I told myself that I would only be a representative for a few months, that in a couple of years I should hold an interesting and responsible job as Brand Manager, or perhaps District Manager in charge of an area of South East England— I just couldn't see it; did not really like the work. With the coming of spring I began to fret over the idea of only three weeks' holiday in the Alps, and turned over the tempting thought of accepting an invitation to join an expedition to

South Patagonia—one that I had regretfully refused only that autumn when I was still fresh and keen in my new job.

Practically speaking, I should have settled down happily in Unilever, for I had just become engaged. I met Wendy at a party (very conventional) in the New Year. She was small and dark, wore a little black dress, and rubbed herself up against me when we danced with the ecstatic pleasure of a kitten being stroked. Fortunately, she wasn't in the least bit conventional, and was even more appalled by my future in the margarine business than I. The prospect of being a suburban housewife had little attraction for her. She was an illustrator of children's books, had never been out of the country, never even been north of Leicester, but had a powerful urge to see more of the world. When I met her she had just written off to answer one of those advertisements asking for crew members on a yacht sailing to the Far East, but had begun to have second thoughts when she was asked for a photograph and her vital statistics.

Soon after we were engaged, I bought her a pair of climbing boots and took her to the hills. We went on Gritstone: her first climb was to be on Froggatt Edge. She was full of enthusiasm, but looked a bit apprehensive when I tied the rope on.

"This is only a Diff," I assured her. "You'll find it a piece of duff."

"What's a Diff?" she asked, bemused.

"Difficult."

"Couldn't we do something easy to start with."

"Difficult is easy—I know it sounds contradictory, but beyond Diff there are four more grades—anything easier than this would be a walk. You won't have any trouble on this and we'll soon have you doing V.Ss."

I started up the slab.

"Now, watch how I do it—keep your body well out from the rock, just like walking upstairs—this is too easy; I'll just do a little variation—just step up on to this little hold here—that's more interesting—Right—I'm belayed; come on up, love."

Wendy started up the slab cautiously; almost immediately she looked tensed and frightened, and hugged the rock. Even so, she reached the scene of my variation without too much trouble. The rope was now at a slight angle and if she had slipped she would have swung across the face. I suddenly realised that my belay wasn't much good, my stance worse, and wondered if I could hold her, if she did fall.

"For God's sake don't slip, love—I'm not sure that I can hold you."

That was the last straw! The poor lass dissolved into tears, lunged across the slab and grabbed one of my boots—with a struggle I managed to pull her up.

That was the first and last time Wendy ever tried rock climbing. But she enjoyed being in the mountains and was quite happy to sit at the foot of a crag while I climbed. This suited me well—better, in fact, than if she had acquired a passion for the sport. If she had wanted to be taken climbing, she could probably not have followed me up the routes that I wanted to lead, and even if she could, I could never have felt certain that she could hold me if I came off. In the Alps, the difference in strength and endurance between a man and a woman becomes even more evident. I was pleased that we each had our own strong interests—Wendy's were painting and singing—that we could each follow to the full.

We got married in May, only five months after our first meeting, and shortly after this I made my decision to go to South Patagonia, knowing full well that my firm would probably refuse to let me go. I had taken ten years to make up my mind to put climbing first, rather than a conventional job, though during those years climbing had always been my first real love. I soon got my firm's reply—the letter that I have used to open this book. I had spent many hours of indecision before taking the final step. I was still not quite sure how we were to make a living but had a wonderful feeling of freedom as I wrote my letter of resignation. An Alpine season was before us and then an expedition to South Patagonia. I was even planning to take Wendy with me, though at this stage we had only fifty pounds in the bank, barely enough for me, let alone her.

That summer, Don and I planned to have another look at the North Wall of the Eiger. I now realised the potential value of the story of the first British ascent and intended to make the most of it. This sounds rather like doing the climb for money, something that leaves a slightly unpleasant taste in the mouth, particularly in mountaineering circles. But I was happy in my own mind that I wanted to do the climb for its own sake; if I could make sufficient money out of it to go to Patagonia, to take Wendy with me, to retain my freedom to climb, then so much the better.

I also thought of my responsibility to Wendy, not so much in the context of the Eigerwand, but as a mountaineer generally. As far as the Eiger was concerned, I felt, and I know Don did, that we could climb it relatively safely by going on it only in the most suitable conditions and then avoiding the stone-fall areas at the times when they were swept. We had already turned back twice because conditions had not been right. We didn't look at the Eiger as a unique climb, suggested to the public by the sheer weight of sensational publicity surrounding it, but rather as a potentially dangerous face that needed extra care and planning to negotiate safely.

As far as I was concerned, if I went on climbing at all now that I was married, I might just as well go on the Eiger. Wherever one climbs in the Alps, and at whatever standard, there is a certain degree of danger—much higher than on the rocks of this country—but the greatest danger is not so much on the difficult faces, when nerves are taut and concentration at a maximum, but on the easy stretches, where a momentary loss of concentration can cause a slip which can all too easily prove fatal. Comparatively few good mountaineers are killed on hard routes; they lose their lives on the easy ways down. Herman Buhl walked through a cornice; Robin Smith and Wilfred Noyce slipped on bad snow on the way down from a peak in the Pamirs; Toni Kinshofer, one of the four to make the first winter ascent of the Eiger, was killed on a tiny practice climb in Germany. There are many more examples.

When she married me, Wendy knew that I could never give up the mountains, they were too much a part of me. Nor could I start climbing at a lower standard, for, to me, the joy of climbing is to stretch my powers, my experience, my ability to the limit, and yet still have something in reserve. I don't enjoy danger for its own sake, certainly hate being afraid, as I inevitably am if things get out of control—if, say, I am out of condition on a climb that is too hard for me. But when on peak form, the exhilaration of climbing is at its greatest when I am in a potentially dangerous position yet feel in complete control.

It is difficult, probably impossible to equate this attitude with the full responsibilities of a married man, but I know I could never give up climbing. All I can do, is to take every possible precaution to keep the risk factor to a minimum. As July approached I made my preparations for another attempt on the Eiger.

CHAPTER FIFTEEN

RESCUE ON THE EIGER

THERE was water everywhere. It trickled down the slabs and walls, staining them a gleaming black in the afternoon sun, and poured down the cracks and chimneys in foaming white waterfalls. This time the Difficult Crack was swept by a torrent. Our waterproof mitts were of little avail: it poured down inside our sleeves, and thundered about our heads as we climbed. By the time we had reached the top of the Crack we were both soaked. It was the end of July and once again we were going up the lower slopes of the Eiger, planning to stop the night in the Swallow's Nest.

We reached the chimney leading up to the foot of the Hinter-stoisser Traverse. I was belaying Don, with the rope round my waist; I flicked it over my head as he reached me and it caught the head of my ice axe tucked into the shoulder-strap of my rucksack. Out of the corner of my eye I saw something flash down, glanced round and watched with a numb horror my axe cartwheel out of sight down the face.

After the first shock I felt a heavy shame. I had committed the cardinal sin, shown myself utterly incompetent.

"I've dropped my axe," I shouted.

"I know. I saw it. I was expecting something like that to happen. You've been with the fairies all afternoon. Are you feeling all right?"

"I'm O.K. The rope flicked it out. Shall we go back down for it?"

"We'd have to go down too far. Anyway, we'd probably never find it. I've had enough of trogging up and down the bottom of the Eiger. Whoever's out in front will have to use my axe. For Christ's sake, don't drop that or we really will be in the cart."

Neither of our peg hammers had picks, so that we were now relying completely on Don's axe. Perhaps we should have gone back, but we had been on the face too many times to contemplate that.

When we reached the Swallow's Nest, we found that water was even trickling down the overhang above it.

"Let's hope it freezes tonight," observed Don, "or we're going to have a wet bivouac."

We did—if anything, the flow of water increased in strength during the night. We dropped the bivouac-sack over our heads, but this didn't really improve matters: its inside was soon wet from the condensation of our breath. In the morning there were a few wisps of cloud—if anything it looked more threatening than it had done the previous September. We should have turned back straight away—stones were even bounding down the First Ice-field—but we had been on the Face too often, and hated the thought of another retreat, of having another night in the Swallow's Nest. We took our time in the morning—both thinking along the same lines but not voicing our doubts.

"We might as well start up the Ice-fields," I suggested, "and get a bit farther than last year."

"Aye," agreed Don. "It'll be easy enough to turn back."

We climbed up the side of the First Ice-field. It was set at an angle of about fifty degrees and was ice all the way. The front points of our crampons bit in about an eighth of an inch—just enough to hold our weights, but it felt precarious—one false step, a momentary loss of balance, and we'd be off. Even so, this was safer than cutting a grand staircase, because the time taken to cut large steps would increase the chances of being hit by falling stones.

At the top of the Ice-field, we reached the Ice Hose, a short gully joining the First and Second Ice-fields. It was jammed with near-vertical ice. I broke out on to rock on the right where the holds were all sloping, covered with a thin veneer of ice. Soon I was a hundred feet above Don, with no sign of a ledge, not even a peg crack—I had no runner, and if I had slipped, would almost certainly have taken him with me. A stone sliced past me with a high, thin-pitched whistle—we really were on the North Wall of the Eiger.

I had run out a full hundred and fifty feet before I reached the foot of the Second Ice-field and was able to put in an ice screw. Don came up to me quickly; we looked across the field— a grey expanse of steep ice—another stone whistled down—we felt small and helpless against its monstrous threat.

"I don't like it—I think the weather's brewing," I told Don.

"Aye—we've come far enough—let's push off down."

We turned to go down. We saw two climbers coming up towards us. The one in front shouted something in German—I couldn't understand what.

"We're English," we shouted.

"Two of your comrades are injured," he replied. "Will you help us to rescue them?"

Of course we agreed and turned back up the slope. At this stage we didn't know just what had happened. The previous day, through a telescope at Alpiglen, we had seen two climbers moving very slowly across the Second Ice-field; we didn't know who they were.

We only heard the full story when we got back down. The pair were Brian Nally and Barry Brewster, two climbers from Southern England. I had met Barry once before; he was a student at Bangor University—one of their tigers. I was impressed, and a little frightened, by his intense seriousness as he talked about climbing. He had done all the hardest routes in Wales, climbing many of them in tricounis just to improve his technique. His experience on ice was limited: he had had several seasons in Chamonix, but, like most British climbers, had tended to do rock routes. Brian Nally, a house painter from London, was the ice specialist of the party. The previous year he had made the first British ascent of the North Face of the Matterhorn with Tom Carruthers, a Glasgow climber. Before going on the face, they had agreed that Brewster should be the rock expert, while Nally should take the lead on the ice-fields. In Nally's words—"he was the brains of the team—I the navvy."

They set out just twenty-four hours before us, bivouacked in the Swallow's Nest and, like us, were soaked to the skin. That morning they started out up the side of the First Ice-field, but instead of going into the Ice Hose, they followed Heinrich Harrer's description from the back of his book, *The White Spider*, and attempted the wall, about a hundred feet to its left. In doing this they lost the route and wasted several hours. As a result it was getting on for midday when they reached the Second Ice-field. Here they decided to cut steps diagonally across it, and so their progress was slow.

It was four o'clock when they reached the end of the ice-field; the stone-fall was by now violent as the afternoon sun loosened the rock in the upper part of the face. Looking up at the Eiger, it is difficult to get any idea of scale, the top is so foreshortened, but the entire upper 2,000 feet of the Eigerwand are in the shape of a huge ampitheatre round the White Spider. Every stone that falls inevitably goes into the Spider, which then acts as a funnel, concentrating the bombardment down the centre of the face on to the Flat Iron. This place is a death trap after midday.

Barry Brewster took over the lead at the foot of a rock pitch —the start of the Flat Iron.

"There's a pitch of V Sup. up here," he remarked, as he took off his crampons.

He ran out about eighty feet of rope, and clipped into a couple of pegs. Nally, who was belayed to a ring peg at the top of the ice-field heard him shout—

"Stones!"

Brian ducked into the rock instinctively, for he was now hardened to the constant bombardment that they had experienced from the start of the Second Ice-field.

Suddenly, the dark shape of a body came hurtling down. Both peg runners were pulled out by the force of the fall, and Nally was only just able to hold the rope—the peg to which he was belayed bent to a frightening angle. The rope held, and Barry was lying suspended on the end of it on the steep ice a hundred feet below. When Nally reached him, having secured the rope to the peg, Barry was unconscious. Brian Nally then did everything that anyone could have done in the circumstances. He cut out a ledge for his friend—no easy matter in hard ice, with the stones continuously whistling down—gave the injured man his crash hat, wrapped him up in all the available spare clothes and then settled down for the night: his second in wet clothes.

The following morning we learnt of the accident, and turned back up the ice slope. Don led out the first pitch, slowly cutting steps—it was no good moving fast now, we had to have a line of large steps on which to retreat with an injured man.

"I think I can see someone," Don called down. "Look, at the top of the ice-field."

I could just discern a small red figure moving slowly along the top.

"Stop where you are," shouted Don. "We'll come up to you."

He didn't reply, but took no notice and continued for thirty feet or so; then he stopped on a small spur, and seemed to be lying down. This gave us some idea of the vast scale of the face, of the distance we had to cover to reach him—he was just a minute blob of colour in the dull grey of plunging rock and gleam of ice.

We were now getting used to the sound of falling stones which were coming down the whole time: a high-pitched whistle, then a thud as they hit the ice around us and bounded on down the face.

"It's as good as a bloody war film," remarked Don, after a particularly bad bombardment.

But then we heard a deeper sound—it seemed to fill the wall with its wild keen. I looked across and saw the tiny figure of a man shoot down the ice into space. It was like being hit hard in the stomach—I just hugged the ice and swore over and over again—then got a grip of myself—became aware of the danger we were in, of the man who was still alive at the end of the ice-field—the little red blob of colour was still there; it must have been the injured man who had fallen.

We shall never know exactly what happened, but probably Brewster had been swept from his perch by stonefall. Mercifully, he was dead when he fell, for Nally had been with him when he died early that morning.

If he hadn't died, I am not sure what we could have done to bring him down. Although fourteen Swiss Guides had come as far as the Gallery Window, it is doubtful if they would have crossed the ice-fields, and anyway, it would not have been justifiable. Nally told us that Brewster was paralysed below the waist, probably with a broken back; in trying to carry him back we should almost certainly have killed him. To carry him, we should have needed at least eight people, and with such a number and the time it would have all taken, someone else would inevitably have been hit by stones.

We could certainly rescue the remaining climber, however, so Don and I continued cutting across the ice-field. It wasn't so bad while you were actually moving—your attention was completely taken up with the job in hand—but it was a different matter on the stances; you then had sufficient time to wonder about the chances of being hit by stones, to notice that the weather was closing in. The sky was now completely overcast; wisps of grey mist were reaching round the side of the face. I pressed myself against the ice, tried to vanish under the protective cover of my crash hat, to present as small a target as possible; stones whistled and landed all round me: one bounced off my helmet, another hit my shoulder—is anything broken? I worked my arm up and down—it felt numb but I could move my fingers—just a bruise, nothing more. And so it went on—

"Come on, Chris."

I left the ice peg in place for our retreat, and hurried to join Don. I could see the line of the other party's steps just above us —they had been partly washed away by the streams of water pouring down the ice, and, anyway, seemed to wander haphazardly across the face.

"It's no good following their line," Don remarked. "It'd be too difficult getting back along it. We must cut across in a dead straight line."

Pitch followed pitch—it just never seemed to end; all this time Nally was lying inert on the small spur of rock. I wondered if he also was injured, whether he would be able to help himself on the way back. Don and I now felt very much on our own, for the two Swiss Guides had vanished—there was no one else on the face and I couldn't help wondering what would happen to us if we were hit by stones.

One last rope length and I found myself only a few feet from Nally; I had run out the full length of rope, so turned round to tell Don to come up so that he could lead the last few feet.

"It's all right," Nally called out. "I can come over to you."

I had never met Brian Nally before. At first glance he seemed unaffected by his ordeal. He was wearing a red duvet that clung wetly to him, and he moved slowly, methodically, as he cut steps across to me. Round his neck, in a tangle of knitting, was his climbing rope; an end of it trailed behind him. His features were heavy with fatigue. He had a look of simplicity, yet in his eyes there was a wildness.

"Are you going to the top? Can I tie on to you?" he asked.

My nerves, already stretched, exploded.

"We've come to get you down, you bloody fool."

"But why not go on up, now that you've come this far."

"Your friend is dead! Do you realise that? We're taking you down."

It was only then that I realised how shocked he was, how misplaced my anger. He was like an automaton, did what you told him, but was incapable of thinking.

"We'll have to put you in the middle, between us. We'll use your rope. Give it to me."

I spent the next twenty minutes untangling the rope—it was knotted as only three hundred feet of nylon can be. Each knot had to be undone separately, the rope was sodden, it numbed and cut my hands, but at least I was doing something. Don, a hundred and fifty feet below, was in the line of some of the worst stone-fall. All he could do was to wait patiently and watch the storm gather about our heads.

At last the rope was untangled. I tied Brian into the middle and he started back towards Don. Our progress was painfully slow—most of the steps had again been washed away by streams of water pouring down the ice—and stones were still coming down the whole time. Brian had given his crash hat to Brewster; a stone hit his head with a dull thud, he teetered backwards, and I grabbed his arm, pulling him back into the ice. He shook his head and seemed all right, or, at least, no more shocked than before.

At the end of the ice-field the storm broke: there was a deafening blast of thunder followed by a torrent of hail. Like a river in spate, it completely covered us, tore at us with steadily increasing force. We were all suspended from the same ice piton which was submitted to a seemingly impossible strain. Then, as suddenly as it started, the storm stopped.

"Let's get a move on," Don shouted, "before it starts again."

We abseiled carefully down the Ice Hose, and then Don demonstrated yet again his genius as a mountaineer. Instead of branching back right, the way we had come up, the way used as a line of retreat by countless parties in the past twenty years, he led down to the left, to the brink of a sheer drop. Just a hundred and fifty feet below was the end of the Hinterstoisser Traverse—if only Hinterstoisser and his companions, who discovered this line in 1936, and in doing so, the key to the Eiger, had found this way down they would have been alive today; instead they tried to get back across the traverse, having failed to leave a rope in place behind them to safeguard their retreat. Without it, the traverse was impassable and they lost their lives in trying to abseil straight down the sheer wall below it.

Once down by the side of the traverse, we began to feel more safe, though I didn't relax till we reached the Stollenloch Window, where a reception party was waiting. We were pulled through the window, blinded by the flash bulbs of press cameras, and the whole ghastly nightmare reached its climax.

Don and Chris setting out from Hampstead for the Eiger in the summer of 1962 (*photo Daily Express*).

Brian Nally at the top of the Second Ice-field, at the moment we reached him to bring him back to safety.

On the face, things had been very simple—a straight question of survival. Don and I had a job to do, and we did it. There was no time to feel afraid, no place for fear. I should imagine it was rather like soldiering in the First World War—after a time you become accustomed to being under fire, fatalistic about the chances of being hit. But now, back in safety, it was different; a couple of Swiss journalists had laid on the special train to take us down, just to make sure of getting the story first. Inexplicably, the train remained stationary in the tunnel for nearly an hour, in spite of the fact that we were soaked to the skin and near exhaustion. In that time they got the full story from Nally, taking advantage of his shocked condition.

A couple of days later he was presented with the bill for his rescue—one for several hundred pounds, covering the employment of fourteen guides, the hire of a special train and the loss or damage to the guides' climbing equipment. He didn't have the money; he could probably have sold his story for a large amount immediately after the accident but the Swiss journalists had already prised it from him, and, anyway, the very last thing he had thought of was to sell the story of his friend's death to the highest bidder.

The whole question of rescue on the Eiger is a difficult one and has caused endless controversy, from the early attempts before the war, right up to the present. In all Alpine Districts the local guides are responsible for mountain rescue and are obliged to go out if anyone is in trouble. The North Wall of the Eiger has been made an exception to this rule and the Grindelwald Guides are not obliged to go on to it. I can sympathise with their attitude. The North Wall is a dangerous face and any amateur venturing on it does so with this knowledge. It seems hardly fair to expect a man whose job it is to take tourists up the easy routes of the Oberland, who in all probability is not technically skilled on steep ice and rock, who has a wife and family dependent on him, to take the serious risks that an Eiger rescue would entail. Inevitably, however, many guides feel guilty in refusing to go on to the face, and this guilt leads to an aggressive attitude towards anyone else attempting the Eigerwand, or, as in 1957, even against the amateurs who organised the rescue attempt of Longhi and Corti. In this case, the chief of the Grindelward rescue section, Willi Balmer, refused to co-operate in any way with the rescue.

In the case of the Nally-Brewster rescue, the Guides had at

least set out, and two of them came as far as the foot of the First
Ice-field. Presumably, if they had not caught up with us, they
would have crossed the Second Ice-field, to the injured man. As
soon as Brewster fell, however, they all retreated, leaving us to
bring Nally down on our own. We should have been perfectly
happy if some of them had stayed in safety at the end of the
Second Ice-field—we should then, at least, have had some kind
of support if anything had gone wrong. Instead, they all went
down and then six of them picked up Brewster's body from the
bottom of the face. We couldn't help feeling that they were
putting their priorities in the wrong order.

In view of their behaviour, their bill seemed particularly
unreasonable—if they had actually joined us they would have
deserved every penny they took.

"I've had enough of the Eiger for this season," observed Don
that night in our hotel bedroom. "All this publicity and money-
grubbing is enough to make anyone sick. Let's push off to
Austria and do some real climbing."

I was only too happy to agree, and the next day we piled on
to the motor-bike and set off for Innsbruck.

CHAPTER SIXTEEN

THE WALKER SPUR

We spent three weeks around Innsbruck. Our two wives, who had come out from England separately and had been trailing behind us as we dashed from peak to peak, now caught us up. We climbed on the limestone faces of the Kaisergebirge and Karwendel—pleasant lighthearted routes on warm dry rock—and put all thought of the Eiger out of our minds.

Towards the end of August Don had to return home; by this time we had both nearly run out of money, and since we could not afford the girls' train fare, asked them to hitch-hike back to England while we travelled back on the bike.

"We might as well do a climb on the way," I suggested. "The girls are going to take longer than us to get back."

"Aye. I've always fancied the North Face of the Badile. We'll go and do that," agreed Don.

We sent most of our climbing equipment back in a friend's van, for the Badile is a rock route and we didn't expect to have to bivouac on it; we wanted to travel as light as possible on the bike. At this stage I had no thought of doing any more climbs before going home with Don.

We drove over to the Badile in a day. It is situated in the Bregalia—a soaring shield of smooth granite slabs. It was once rated as one of the great rock climbs of the Alps, but now, with the overall rising standard of rock climbing, it has almost become a "Voie Normale"—certainly among British climbers. It was in perfect condition when we arrived, without a spot of snow on it. We bivouacked below the face and climbed it the next morning in six hours. There was no doubt about it, we had both reached peak form—something that only comes at the end of a long season.

On the way back to England we decided to look in at Chamonix, and arrived there a couple of days after climbing the Badile. The town, now somnolent at the end of the season, basked under a heat haze; the Aiguilles, a rich brown in the afternoon sun, were blemished by only the odd streak of snow.

"Even the big stuff must be in condition. How about one more route?" I asked Don.

"No. I must be back in three days. Anyway, we haven't got any gear. You stay on if you like. I don't mind driving back alone."

"If I can find anyone to climb with, I think I shall."

There weren't many climbers left in the Camp Site, but that evening in the Bar National I met Ian Clough.

After doing the Frêney with us the previous year he had stayed on in Chamonix and had done the complete traverse of the Chamonix Aiguilles, had gone home to spend the winter working as a Student Teacher in metal-work, and intended that Autumn to go to Training College.

"It's high time I settled down," he told me. "You can't bum around all your life."

"Who are you with?" I asked.

"Geoff Grandison and Wilky," he replied. "We're going back in a couple of days."

"How about doing a route with me before you go?" I suggested.

"I'll have to ask the others. What are you thinking of doing?"

"The Walker Spur should be in condition. How about that?"

"I'll let you know in the morning."

I was now in a fever to go climbing. I had always wanted to do the Walker Spur of the Grandes Jorasses, ever since that first abortive attempt with Hamish in 1957. I also had a dream, that I tried to dismiss as impractical, to finish the climb by doing a traverse across the Jorasses and the Rochefort Ridge, all the way to the Torino Hut. It seemed an exciting finale to a great climb, better than just going down the easy way at the back. I had never mentioned this to anyone—didn't suggest it to Ian: it seemed too far-fetched, on the end of a 4,000 foot rock climb that ranked as one of the most serious in the Alps.

Next morning, Ian came over to our tent.

"The others have agreed to wait for three days, so I can come."

"Grand. Let's go up this afternoon. I'll try to borrow some gear from someone."

I spent the rest of the morning scrounging gear. Fortunately, nearly everyone was on their way home and by lunch time I was once again fully equipped with borrowed duvet, pied d'éléphant,* bivouac sac,† axe and crampons.

We caught the last train up to Montenvers and walked up

---

* Half-length down sleeping-bag.

† A large waterproof bag that can be dropped over the heads of two climbers, covering them like a tent.

The Grandes Jorasses and Rochefort Ridge from the north-west. The Walker Spur is the dark buttress going to the highest point of the Jorasses. Our day finished at the Torino Hut, well off the picture to the right. Photographed from the Aiguille du Plan.

Ian eating some spaghetti we found in the Jorasses bivouac hut, on the col between the Jorasses and the Rochefort.

the Mer de Glace in the gathering evening. Just as we came
through the moraine at the juncture of the Leschaux Glacier
with the Mer de Glace I saw a couple of figures also hurrying
towards the Jorasses.

"Come on, Ian. They must be going for the Walker. We'll
drop into this gully and try to get in front of them. I think we'd
better miss out the Leschaux Hut and bivouac at the foot of the
face to make sure of being first in the morning."

We hurried, almost ran, up a small valley in the glacier, and
pulled ahead of the other pair. I have always hated being
behind other parties on a long climb in the Alps.

We were just congratulating ourselves on being at the head
of the queue, when we reached the foot of the Walker Spur. A
couple of French climbers were sitting on a slab of ice, obviously
settled for the night; they already looked chilled and thoroughly
disconsolate. They waved up at the face, and said something
that we couldn't understand.

"We'd better climb a bit up the face," suggested Ian.

"It'll be a lot warmer than sitting on the glacier," I agreed.
"I've had one night like that already with Hamish."

We scrambled, unroped, up the first hundred feet of the
spur, up a short icy gully and then over slabs. Soon we discovered what the two Frenchmen had been talking about:
every single ledge on the lower slopes of the Walker was already
occupied by climbers; there were at least four parties out in
front of us. This is a mark of just how popular the hard climbs
are becoming: the Walker is so rarely in condition that, when it
is free of ice, literally dozens rush to it.

We spent an uncomfortable night seated in a slight depression
in the surface of the slab. It was impossible to relax, for we were
both constantly slipping off it. As soon as it was light, we started
up the climb, spurred on by the shouts coming from below—we
certainly weren't at the end of the queue.

We caught up quickly with the pair immediately in front of
us—three Parisians. On the stances we chatted together, discovered mutual acquaintances, discussed climbs we had both
done. The lower part of the Walker Spur offers a series of
vertical steps up steep grooves, divided by traverses across easy-
angled slabs. I found that we could overtake the climbers
immediately in front on these traverses. Perhaps this was con-
trary to climbing etiquette, but there is nothing more irritating
than to be held up by a slower party in front.

Our climb now began to resemble a car trip from London to Brighton on a Bank Holiday, as we slowly jumped the queue, overtaking whenever an opportunity offered. On the vertical steps we had to wait our turn, but even this was quite pleasant —there was someone new to talk to each time: on this ledge an Austrian who knew Don, on the next a Swiss whom I had met a couple of years before in Chamonix. In such an atmosphere you didn't feel that you were on a serious climb; the actual technical standard of the climbing was not very high, and the number of people on it made it feel more like Cloggy.

We had reached the foot of the first great landmark of the Walker, the famous point of no return—the Grey Tower. We had at last fought our way to the front, though, in our hurry, we had gone too high. We should have traversed across at a lower level, and then done a short *pendule** across a wall to reach the only line of weakness up the Tower. It was reputed that once across this you couldn't get back.

Unnoticed by us, a bank of grey cloud had been creeping over the sky from the north-west. Suddenly the sun was obscured; I noticed the cold wind, the dark threat of the clouds. We had grown used to the shouts of the other parties— it was like the Tower of Babel, with everyone yelling at the tops of their voices in several different languages—but now the sounds were receding. We were on our own; the rest, twenty other climbers, were all going down in face of the threatening weather.

It never occurred to me to retreat—I didn't reason it out— Ian and I didn't discuss it. We both instinctively felt that the weather would not break, and were so confident in each other that, even if it did, we felt we could cope with it. It wasn't a form of foolhardiness: we had merged into a single unit, think- ing almost as one person. This is something that I had never experienced before, not even with Don. In climbing with him, although we always shared the lead, I knew he was a better mountaineer—that in the final resort I should always defer to his decision. With Ian, I found an equality that made us, I think, a near perfect team.

The cloud now lapped around us, cut us off from the others, and enclosed us in a small world of our own—a world of grey cold rock dropping away into the grey swirls of mist. We

* Method of crossing a blank wall by swinging on the rope held from above by a piton.

climbed without a pause, without a word being said, leading
through on each pitch. Because we had come too high we had
to make a series of spectacular tension traverses, from pegs we
hammered in, across a blank wall to the foot of the Grey Tower.
Back on the route, we passed the odd piton, clipped into it,
worked our way up through the murk.

It was getting lighter—a break in the cloud appeared above,
a patch of blue. We had reached the foot of the Red Tower high
on the buttress. The rock was now more broken, and in places
covered by ice. We had established a steady rhythm of climbing
that made short work of each difficulty: it was impossible, later,
to remember one pitch from another, in retrospect they all
seemed the same. This is climbing at its best—a drug more
exhilarating than any purple heart or jab of cocaine and every
bit as addictive in its after-effects; once you've tasted this feeling
you can't live without it. An icy gully, broken rocks, the glimpse
of a cornice through a break in the cloud, and we were standing
on top of the Walker Spur. We had taken thirteen hours from
the foot, at least two of which had been wasted, waiting to pass
the parties in front of us.

With the drying up of new routes in recent years, an increasing importance has been placed on the times taken on different
climbs—people just can't resist the competitive element in the
sport however much they deplore competition in mountaineering. I certainly find a great deal of satisfaction in doing a fast
time up a climb, not so much for its own sake but because it is a
sign of competence; also it is safer, for the quicker you are, the
less likely you are to be caught out by bad weather. To me,
though, the greatest attraction of putting up fast times, is the
rhythm of movement that is built up: nothing exists but the
climber and the mountain. Once you start wasting time, losing
the route, getting the rope in a tangle, this feeling vanishes and
frustration sets in.

We paused on the top only for a few minutes—a cold wind
was blowing from the north, and there was still a great deal of
cloud about. I didn't mention to Ian my idea of a long traverse,
the weather was much too threatening, so we started down the
south face, now in Italy. We had got about fifteen hundred feet
down, to the foot of the Rochers Whymper, a rock spur running
down from the Pointe Whymper; the weather was looking
more encouraging, and, anyway, there was only half an hour
of daylight; I suggested to Ian:

"How about stopping here for the night. It's a hell of a slog right down to the valley and we'll then have to pay for the téléphérique to get back up to the Torino Hut. If it's fine tomorrow, we could have a crack at traversing the Jorasses and then going along the Rochefort Ridge. Hermann Buhl has done it as far as the Col de Grandes Jorasses, but I don't think anyone has done the whole traverse as a finish to the Walker."

"All right by me," he agreed, "how about going the whole hog and doing a traverse of the whole bloody range—finish on the top of Mont Blanc?"

"That'd be great. We can always have a day's rest at the Torino. We could then do the Major. I've always wanted to do it."

It was wonderful climbing with someone who could respond so spontaneously to an impromptu change of plan—who had exactly the same enthusiasm as I had. We settled down for our second bivouac on a comfortable ledge. We both felt pleasantly fresh, were warm in our duvets and pieds d'éléphant and had sufficient to eat—the greatest luxury of all, however, was that we could even lie down on our ledge.

Next morning dawned fine, and we decided to do the complete traverse—we had a pleasant feeling of madness as we plodded back up the arête we had descended the night before. There was nothing very difficult on the ridge—we only put the rope on for one short section—but there was some of the most enjoyable climbing I have ever had, over airy pinnacles, round tottering gendarmes, on tapered snow arêtes. To the south, in a heavy haze, stretched the brown hills of Italy; to the west, the rounded dome of Mont Blanc; while to the north the massive buttress of the Jorasses dropped away below our feet to the glacier, a crazy jigsaw of crevasses, four thousand feet below. On a face you spend all day, or even several days, with the same view, but here on the crest of a ridge, crossing summit after summit, the view was for ever changing, there was limitless space around us.

We had scrambled over the pinnacled summits of the Jorasses, and the ridge now dropped steeply towards the Col de Jorasses. A couple of abseils took us down. We found a pleasant surprise: on the col was a small, newly-built bivouac-hut roofed in gleaming metal. There was no question of spending the night in the hut—it was too early—but inside we found a packet of spaghetti which made a welcome lunch as we had now very

nearly run out of food. Above the Col, the Calotte de Rochefort
rose steeply in a rock buttress. Perhaps we lost the route here
for we found this short section harder than anything on the
Walker Spur. Once up, however, it was easy going once again
along a snow arête; we were able to put the rope away, and
climb solo.

I noticed that our speed was dropping—I began to feel I
had had a hard day.

"How's it going?" I asked Ian.

"I'm buggered," he replied.

"Me too," and we plodded on.

There were still two summits to cross—the snow was now soft
from the afternoon sun, and at every step we sank in to our
knees. On any long day there comes a point when you are
getting tired and your one ambition is to get to the end of it,
to have a good meal and lie down; it is always the same, but,
in retrospect, it is this very period that seems the most worth
while.

Our progress was no longer easy: each step required an effort
of will. We slogged on: one more summit, the Aiguille de
Rochefort; an awkward crevasse—to hell with it—jump and
hope for the best; some unpleasant wet snow over ice—not
worth putting on crampons—we slowly teetered across, rubber
soles sliding on the ice; we struggled over a small crest—will it
never end? Then the Dent du Géant, a blade of granite, rich
brown in the rays of the setting sun, was immediately above us.

"We can just nip up the South Face to show we're real hard
men," said Ian.

I managed the weakest of laughs.

"I couldn't walk up a bloody mole-hill, let alone climb.
Thank God we can get past it without climbing. Anyway, it's
not really on the ridge—it's just a subsidiary summit."

It was now downhill all the way—I led off, feeling a new
burst of energy with the end in sight, but skidded on a piece of
soft snow; I stopped myself with the axe just in time.

"Steady on," Ian murmured. "You don't want to go down
that fast. I reckon you're getting a bit bloody dangerous. This
is where Arthur Dolphin was killed."

Ian's warning brought me back to my senses; Arthur
Dolphin, one of the best climbers that the Lake District has
ever produced, had been killed on this same descent only a few

years before. With doubled caution we scrambled down the last slopes to the huge, flat snow-field leading to the Col du Géant and the Torino Hut. Darkness had fallen: we had been on the go, with hardly a pause, for sixteen hours.

The danger was over—it was just a matter of putting one foot in front of the other, heads down, each immersed in his own thoughts. The lights of the Torino glimmered warmly, but never seemed to get any closer. I dreamt of litres of watered Chianti, succulent spaghetti—great long coils of it, greasy with meat sauce—filling my mouth, of the clean flavour of a salad, above all of bed; just to lie in bed for days on end. Another glance up at the light showed it still no nearer. Time seemed to stop altogether—the walk was endless and would go on to the end of all time—yet only a month before, Don and I, on the way to climb the South Face of the Géant, had bounded across this same plateau, hardly noticing it.

The refuge finally took us by surprise—it was suddenly in front of us. Push the door open, stand blinded, confused in the light—people sitting at tables, eating, laughing. The Guardian jabbers at us in Italian—have we Alpine Club Cards?—can't find them—just want something to drink, lie down, go to sleep. A bottle of Chianti—can't eat anything—too tired—can't keep my eyes open. I stagger up to bed, pull off my boots, feel the rough embrace of old blankets, relax to the sound of the other occupants' snores. The best two days' climbing I have ever had were over.

CHAPTER SEVENTEEN

SUCCESS ON THE EIGER

My whole body ached with fatigue, yet I was at that state of exhaustion when I was too tired even to sleep. I lay awake in the darkened bunk room, my mind flitting from image to image—incidents of the last two days—had Wendy got home all right?—where was she now? And then I thought of the Eiger—I'm not sure how it started, but suddenly, with a dazzling clarity, I realised that we could do it. It must be in condition. The weather had now been perfect for over a fortnight, and we were both on peak form. All the grim associations of the Eigerwand had been washed away by the climb we had just done. I thought of it as the magnificent route that it is, and one that we were ready to tackle.

The rest of the night, waiting impatiently for the dawn when I could tell Ian, I turned over plans. As soon as there was a glimmer of light, I rolled out of the bunk and shook him—

"Ian, wake up—I've just had an idea."

He rolled over, burrowed under the bedclothes; I persevered.

"Come on, Ian—it's important; how about going for the Eiger?"

"Fuck off. Tell me about it later." And he burrowed down still further. I had to contain my enthusiasm and return to bed. A couple of hours later I had another try, and this time he was more receptive.

"Might as well have a go," he agreed. "I've always wanted to do it but never had the right partner."

That morning we walked down the Vallée Blanche to Chamonix, and the following day caught the train across to Grindelwald. Less than forty-eight hours after arriving exhausted at the Torino Hut, we were sorting out our gear at Alpiglen.

I had a feeling of foreboding—stronger than I had ever had before. There were a few high clouds in the sky—could this mean a change in the weather?—surely not, the weather forecast was excellent, but it had been wrong before now. Down in the village we had heard that only two days before Diether

Marchart, a brilliant young Austrian climber, had fallen from the Ramp when trying to climb the face solo. In the excitement of rushing across to Grindelwald, I had no time to think of Wendy, but suddenly I began to think of the dangers of the Eiger, and became convinced that our attempt was doomed; what if I were killed? But I had gone too far—I had talked Ian into coming with me—there was no turning back now.

We left Alpiglen at half past four in the afternoon—rather late, but we intended going only as far as the foot of the Difficult Crack: I had had quite enough of the Swallow's Nest bivouac and had noticed a good ledge protected by an over-hang at this lower level. As we scrambled up the lower rocks I noticed a trail of blood stains, a piece of flesh clinging to a small bone; looked away, shut it out of my mind and didn't mention it to Ian for fear of putting him off. Later he told me that he also had seen it, but hadn't told me for the same reason.

We reached the ledge just before dark, glanced down and saw two figures climbing up towards us. We were not glad to see them. On the Eiger it is much better to be on your own with the companion you have chosen and in whom you have complete trust. Everything is very simple—if you get into trouble, you get yourself out of it. I should never expect anyone to come to my help on the Eigerwand—in most cases a rescue operation is impractical, and anyway, what right have I to expect others to risk their lives when I have chosen to go into a place, knowing full well its dangers. If there is another party on the face with you, whether they are competent mountaineers or insufficiently experienced, you are tied to them. If they get into any kind of trouble, you would have to go to their help; if you were in trouble, they would feel the same obligation, even though in doing so they might sacrifice their own lives. Whether we liked it or not, there was now another party. The next thing was to find out who they were.

As soon as they came within hailing range, Ian called out.

"Hello. Who are you?"

The man in front replied in German, but then to our surprise his companion called out in broad Scots.

"And who the hell do you think you are?"

"Chris Bonington and Ian Clough," I replied. "Are you Tom Carruthers, by any chance?"

I knew that Tom Carruthers, a well-known Glaswegian climber who, the previous year, had been with Brian Nally on

Ian Clough at the bivouac below the Difficult Crack.

Chris at the bivouac below the Difficult Crack (*photo Ian Clough*).

the North Face of the Matterhorn, was planning to go on the Eiger.

"Aye," he replied.

"Who's your mate?" asked Ian.

"I only met him today. I was hoping to go on the face with Bill Sproul but he sprained his ankle and had to go home. This bloke's partner backed down at the last moment so we decided to team up."

"Do you know anything about him?"

"He's pretty good, I think. He's been to the Caucasus."

"What's his name?"

"Anton Moderegger—he's Austrian."

We were astounded by the whole business. Not only were they complete strangers, but they could hardly speak a word of each other's language. Nevertheless, I suggested—

"If we are climbing at the same speed, we might as well join forces, but if one party is faster than the other, I think the fast one should press on."

"That's fair enough by me," agreed Tom, and the two settled down on a ledge just around the corner.

Conditions seemed perfect for the Eiger. As soon as the sun dropped below the low foothills to the West, it grew cold—there was no doubt about it—it was freezing hard: there would be no stones coming down early the following morning. Ian and I settled down for the night with a feeling of complete confidence—in each other and in the weather. All the early fears I had experienced were now gone, replaced by a pleasurable anticipation of what lay in wait for us in the next day or so.

"We might as well have a feast tonight," I suggested. "We're carrying miles too much food—I could hardly lift my sack this afternoon."

We cooked a thick stew over our small gas cooker, opening all the tinned food we had brought with us. I have found on long climbs in the Alps that I can go for several days with very little solid food, provided that there is plenty to drink at night —well-sugared tea and soup. During the day there is no time to eat; you are keyed up to such a pitch of nervous tension, your concentration is so complete, that you feel no desire for food.

The pool of light from Ian's head torch and from the steady purr of the cooker seemed homely and peaceful. Our ledge was positively luxurious—we could spread our equipment over it, could even lie down, and were protected from the threat of falling stones by an overhang jutting overhead.

"I reckon this is the best bivouac I've ever had," observed Ian.

"It's a lot better than the Swallow's Nest—I doubt if we'll be as comfortable tomorrow night," I replied.

"How far do you think we'll get?"

"It's hard to say; I suppose we could just make the top. It's been done in a day. Anyway, let's get some kip."

We both had down jackets and pieds d'éléphant. We were dry and sufficiently warm. I quickly dropped off into a dreamless sleep, happily unaware of the thousand-foot drop a couple of inches behind me.

We slept too well! It was past dawn when we woke up; we could hear the other pair moving just round the corner.

"Come on, Ian," I urged. "We want to be sure of getting away first."

We were at the foot of the climb, it would be safe and easy to turn back; at this stage, therefore, I felt no compulsion to join forces with the other party. If we had overtaken them half-way up the Face and they had been in trouble, it would have been a different matter.

After a hurried breakfast, we packed our sacks and I started up the Difficult Crack—it was the first time I had led it, this had always been Don's pitch. I had a momentary pang of guilt as I looked up at it, wondered what would be Don's feelings if we succeeded, but then put the thought aside for I knew he would have done the same in similar circumstances.

The crack was both dry and clear of ice—a pleasant augury of what was to come. We crossed the Hinterstoisser Traverse, moving quickly and easily.

"I've never seen it in such good condition," I assured Ian. "If we don't get up this time, we never shall."

"Don't count your luck too soon," he muttered.

Beyond the Hinterstoisser, conditions remained good. We were able to scramble on rocks up the side of the First Ice-field, where the ice had shrunk from the face, and then at the top of the Ice Hose, across bare rocks to the foot of the Second Ice-field. The atmosphere was different from what it had been when I was with Don just a few weeks before. There was not a cloud in the sky, but, more important, the face was still and silent—no rattle of falling stones.

Chris, wearing duvet and pied d'éléphant, settled down for the night in the bivouac below the Difficult Crack (*photo Ian Clough*).

SUMMIT ICE-FIELD

The North Wall
of the Eiger (*photo
John Cleare of
Gamma*).

EXIT-CRACKS

SPIDER

TRAVERSE OF THE GODS

RAMP

DEATH BIVOUAC

FLAT IRON

SECOND ICE-FIELD

ICE HOSE

SWALLOW'S NEST

HINTERSTOISSER TRAVERSE

"Last time we cut right across the ice-field," I told Ian. "This time we'll go straight up. There should be a good gap at the top which we can use as a handrail."

It was much quicker going straight up. We cut the odd step, but for the most part went up on the front points of our crampons, sharing the lead all the way. At the top I was pleased to find a good gap between ice and rock and we traversed across quickly with hardly a pause. It was only nine o'clock in the morning. But things were going too easily: we had to cross the entire length of the Second Ice-field, a distance of some hundred yards, and it was here that I made a stupid mistake in the route-finding. The vast scale of the face caught me out. We were sharing the lead and now it was Ian's turn to go in front, up a little gully which seemed to reach the Flat Iron. Without thinking, I accepted his judgement, in spite of the fact that I had been beyond this point when we rescued Brian Nally; then I led up a thin crack in a corner. Something was wrong here—it was as hard as a Gritstone problem, and there were no pegs in place. I was soon a hundred feet up and extended near my limit—a fall would have been fatal. There were some loose blocks in the back of the crack—be careful with those—I cocked a foot out behind me, swung out of balance and could feel the weight of my rucksack dragging me down. There were another fifteen feet of difficult climbing, and I had nearly run the rope out before I reached a ledge.

"I'm bloody sure this isn't on the route," I shouted down. "You'd better come up all the same."

Once Ian had joined me, we traversed across a series of ledges and soon saw that we were too high; there was nothing for it but to abseil down to the ice-field. We had wasted at least an hour on our little excursion; the only consolation was that others had made the same mistake—we could see a rusty peg in a crack just above.

Back on the ice-field we were soon at the start of the climb to the Flat Iron. A fantastically twisted piton marked the point where Brian Nally had held Brewster's fall. It was my turn to lead. I took off my crampons and pulled up a steep wall. This was the route all right, it was much easier than where we had just been. After a few feet the steepness relented and I reached a region of easy-angled slabs. It all looked deceptively safe, but this was the most dangerous spot on the entire Eigerwand— the Flat Iron. After midday this place would be a death trap subjected to a constant bombardment of falling stones; everywhere I looked the rock was scarred by their impact. As I brought Ian up towards me my eye was drawn by the trailing loop of the climbing rope, to a small patch of white on the grey ice-field a hundred and fifty feet below—the ledge where Brewster had spent his last night. There was something lying on it that I couldn't make out, a rucksack, or perhaps an anorak. All the way up the Eiger there are these grim tokens of other people's misfortune—a tattered piece of material, a broken axe, a piece of old rope; and this all combines to give the face an atmosphere of brooding menace, even when it is in perfect condition and no stones are coming down.

At the top of the Flat Iron we looked back to see how the other pair was getting on; at first we couldn't see them and then, straining our eyes, could just discern two tiny dots at the end of the Second Ice-field; they were moving so slowly that it was difficult to distinguish them from rocks embedded in the ice.

"I wonder why they're going so slow?" asked Ian.

"God knows, but if they don't hurry up they're going to reach the Flat Iron when the stones start coming down. Look, they're trying to cut across the ice-field. They'll take too long."

We shouted to them to cut straight up to the top, but they were too far away to hear.

"Come on," I urged. "It's no good waiting for them. There's bugger all we can do; we'll be sitting ducks ourselves if we stay here much longer—it's right in the line of fire."

"You know, I reckon their morale's cracked," Ian suggested. "This face is so bloody terrifying that I reckon you need someone with you whom you really know and trust. It must be desperate if you can't even speak each other's language. You might just as well do it solo."

We watched them for another minute: two tiny ants on a sweep of grey ice. Even at that distance we could sense their uncertainty; it was infectious for we suddenly realised the danger of our own position, and turned without speaking to the Third Ice-field.

"We'll have to cut steps here," Ian called back. "It's bloody steep."

He hammered away rhythmically, the pick of his axe scattering particles of ice that hissed out of sight down the slope. It was a relief to reach the shelter of the Ramp, a narrow rock-gully stretching up into the Face.

On the ice-fields we had felt naked and exposed; it was pleasant to feel rock around us once more: our world confined to rock walls on either side, rock soaring above our heads. I bridged up a chimney—no more delicate teetering on the points of my crampons, but back against one wall, feet against the other, thrusting with all my might against the hard un-yielding rock. It had been cold on the ice-fields, but soon we were warm as we struggled pitch after pitch up the Ramp. The chimney opened out into a bay at the back of which was a deep-cut corner that closed down near its top to a narrow gash. This was the famous waterfall pitch. I remembered reading of the struggle that Hermann Buhl had to climb it when he fought his way against the weight of water thundering about his head. Today it was still—there seemed to be not a drop of water on the entire face. It was Ian's turn to lead, and he started up confidently, but suddenly his progress slowed.

"It's plastered with verglas!" he shouted down. "Watch the rope."

He now had to chip away the invisible film of ice from every hold; even so it was impossible to clear it completely, for it clung to the rock with the tenacity of treacle. Slowly, patiently, he cleared the holds, eased his way up the chimney. This was by far the hardest part of the Ramp. The next pitch was easier, but a bulge of opaque overhanging ice barred the way.

"You're getting all the good pitches," I told Ian, with a trace of envy; with dry clothes, and being certain of the weather, we could relish technical difficulty for its own sake as something that made the climbing all the more interesting. He now had to cut foot and hand holds in the ice, hanging back out of balance. Fortunately he was able to use the wall of the gully behind him to get some support. When he pulled out of sight over the bulge I could still hear the thud of his axe but the rope was running through my hands more swiftly.

"Come on up, Chris."

I negotiated the bulge and found myself on the narrow ice-field that we knew marked the top of the Ramp. Somewhere up there was the start of the Traverse of the Gods—the way back into the centre of the Face. We had to find the right line: if we went too high here, we could land ourselves in serious difficulties. To make matters harder, we were now in cloud, an eerie silent world of plunging rock and dirty, rubble-strewn ice.

There was a shout from above; we glanced up and saw a figure outlined against the cloud on the arête high to our right. We hadn't known that there was anyone climbing above us, and immediately wondered what they could be doing, how we had come to catch them up. Could they be in trouble? If so, what on earth could we do about it; this was the most inaccessible part of the entire Face.

As I climbed up a steep wall towards the figure, I couldn't help remembering our experience with Nally only three weeks before; I poked my head over the ledge, and found two climbers seated there, grinning a welcome. They just weren't the kind of people you would expect to meet half-way up the North Wall of the Eiger. One of them, as far as I could gather from his stream of broken English, had only been climbing for a year, though he had trained hard for the North Face by cycling to work every day throughout the winter. His companion seemed more experienced; but their progress that day had been pathetic: they had climbed only three hundred feet, having spent the previous night in the Ramp. At four o'clock they were going to settle down for the night.

"We are tired," they told me.

I couldn't help feeling responsible for them; I didn't like the thought of leaving them behind, any more than I liked the prospect of taking them with us. But I offered:

"Would you like to join us—we can all go up together. I think we should push on tonight as far as possible."

"No. It is quite all right. We shall stay here and go on to-morrow."

We left them with a feeling of relief mixed with guilt, and started across the Traverse of the Gods, a line of rubble-strewn ledges, clinging to the sheer wall. We could hear the cow horn at the Kleine Scheidegg blow a lugubrious tune and, nearer, the rattle of the rack railway; the sounds emphasised the isolation of our position more than the wildest mountain could have done. We seemed so close to safety, and yet, if anything went wrong, nothing could help us. At the end of the Traverse, I started into the White Spider, a terrifying place of converging walls and steep ice. As I edged round the corner, there was a high-pitched whistle. I ducked instinctively and a stone bounded past my head: the afternoon bombardment had begun. I retreated hurriedly.

"There's no point going any further today," I told Ian.

Chris on the Hinterstoisser Traverse (*photo Ian Clough*).

Looking back on to the Second Ice-field from the top of the Flat Iron.
The two dots are Carruthers and Moderegger (*photo Ian Clough*).

"We'd be asking for trouble. It should be safe here for the night, and we can press on in the morning when the stones have stopped.

"This is as good a place to bivouac as any," he agreed. "We'll have plenty of time to get sorted out."

It was little more than five o'clock. We could probably have reached the summit that night, but the risk of being hit by a stone was too great for it to be worth while—the only justification for fast ascents is greater safety; in trying to climb the Eiger in a day the danger factor is definitely increased, for its upper parts must inevitably be climbed after the stone-fall has begun.

We had no sense of urgency: the weather seemed settled. The rock was bathed in a warm yellow light from the slowly sinking sun, a sea of low cloud engulfed the valleys and lapped around the tops of the foothills. At the other end of the Traverse we could just see a tiny red blob—our two Swiss friends. Contentedly we prepared our resting place, cleared stones from the narrow ledge and searched for patches of snow to make a brew. We had dry clothes to sleep in, enough food and plenty of gas for our stove—what more could a climber want. As night fell we watched the myriad of lights in the valley below, feeling detached from the rest of the world. The bivouac wasn't quite as comfortable as our first—we couldn't lie down on the ledge—but we dozed off for long periods, occasionally waking and brewing tea or coffee. The night didn't drag as it does on a cold, wet bivouac, and all too soon the horizon to the east began to pale with the coming of dawn.

I started, once again, into the Spider. There was no stone-fall, but the very silence suggested a lurking menace. I have never been in such an oppressive place on a mountain. On three sides, dark walls converged on the triangular strip of ice; looking down, the rest of the Face was cut away and only the Alpine pastures 4,000 feet below were visible. Around me stones embedded in the ice were a reminder of the bombardment we should suffer if we didn't get out of the Spider in time. I suddenly realised that I was cutting large steps, moving slowly, oppressed by the threat of the place. I forced myself to move up on the points of my crampons, kicked hard into the ice, teetered up on an eighth of an inch of steel—a hundred and fifty feet of rope ran out, and I seemed to have barely started on the ice slope. Ian came up to me, said nothing; I think he had the same feeling of oppression, almost claustrophobic, in these close confines.

Looking up from the bottom it had seemed only a couple of hundred feet, but we ran out five lengths of rope before reaching the top. Suddenly, once out of the Spider, we had a wonderful feeling of release—the top of the Exit Cracks, a network of gullies seaming the final rock-wall between us and safety, looked quite close. We read the description, "Climb easy slabs for two hundred feet, then a steep black nose. (Grade V)". Ian ran out the first rope length, a full hundred and fifty feet; I led through and started looking for the black nose; a pitch of grade V—it must be hard, for there are only two or three others of that standard on the mountains. I quickly scrambled up another hundred feet, shouted down to Ian:

"I wonder if we're on the wrong line—this is dead easy—it can't possibly be V. Can you see any steep black noses down there?"

"There's a horrible looking groove just above me," he replied doubtfully. "It's certainly steep enough, looks bloody desperate. I suppose you could say that it was on a nose—the rock's black."

I came back down—we both gazed up at the groove—it would give some hard climbing, there was no doubt about that. It was about sixty feet high, near vertical, bunged up with ice. If you are not quite sure of the way it is all too easy to convince yourself that a certain line is the right one; you then fit almost any rock feature to the route description, turning arêtes into gullies to substantiate your reasoning. Ian and I very quickly convinced ourselves that this was the route.

The next thing was to decide whether to tackle it in crampons or ordinary boots, for there were pieces of rock projecting from the ice. Since I have always been a rock climber rather than an ice expert I decided to trust to my boots and what rock there was.

It was one of the hardest pitches I have ever done—much harder than it looked from below, but after the first few moves there was no turning back. I couldn't possibly have climbed down and there were no cracks for my pegs—the rock was either compact, or so shattered that the peg would have been pulled straight out. I balanced up from one rocky projection to another, soon realised that it was even steeper than I had thought, found myself thrust backwards out of balance. I knew

On the Third Ice-field (*photo Ian Clough*).

Cutting steps into the White Spider from the end of the Traverse of the Gods (*photo Ian Clough*).

that if I slipped I should almost certainly be killed and take
Ian with me; yet this was climbing at its best—I was right at
the edge of my own limits and at the peak of my form. I had
no feeling of fear. I caressed a shattered flake, calculated
whether it would take my weight, decided it could, pulled
gently, and was bridged across the groove sixty feet above Ian,
the rope dropping straight down to him without a runner. The
rock was covered by a glass-like film of ice, there was nothing
solid to hold on to—all one could do was to use the balance of
limbs counterpoised on two rugosities. I didn't notice the time
but when I reached the top Ian told me I had been an hour. He
followed up quickly, calling for a tight rope.

"You got your hard pitch," he gasped. "It was more like
VI to me. Are you sure that was on the route—there should
have been some pegs in it."

"They might have been covered by the ice. Anyway, we'll
soon see—there's another crack over there."

Ian climbed over towards it—everything was plastered in
ice, making progress desperately slow.

"We're definitely off route," he called back. "I'm now on the
wrong side of the Spider—it must go up where you turned
back."

Meanwhile the two Swiss had caught us up. It was quite
obvious that they would never have succeeded in leading the
pitch I had just climbed so I gave them a top rope and hauled
them up the groove. Now all four of us had to abseil back down.
We discovered, at this point, that our two Swiss friends had no
idea of how to abseil. It seemed unbelievable that they could
have ventured on the Eiger with such a scanty knowledge of
any rock techniques, though in all fairness to them they were
thoroughly competent on ice. Ian gave them a hurried lesson
in the elementary principles of abseiling and soon we were all
back at the foot of the groove.

After this pitch the Exit Cracks seemed child's play. Once
again we were very lucky with conditions: they were free of
ice. I could imagine just how hard they might be in bad
weather, for the route ran up a series of smooth, polished
gullies of compact rock. When free of ice, it was just a scramble,
and after a time we even took off the rope, but when heavily
iced it would be a different story: all the holds were sloping
and there were no cracks for pitons; the easy gullies would
then turn into glassy chutes.

We were still unroped when we reached the summit ice-field. I suddenly noticed the clean sweep of ice dropping away below my feet, straight down to the woods and valleys 6,000 feet below, and felt naked and exposed without the security of a rope.

"I reckon we could do with a rope," suggested Ian.

I agreed whole-heartedly; we cut out a proper ledge, roped up and finished the climb in orthodox manner, using peg belays, moving one at a time. Only a few years before, two Germans had fallen to their deaths at this very point, just a stone's throw from the top.

Ten minutes, and a hundred feet later, we were on the Mitellegi Ridge, following the well-marked trail of footsteps left by other climbers. It was all over; we had climbed the North Wall of the Eiger. My strongest feeling was one of gratitude for our good fortune, that the face had been in such perfect condition, and above all that we had been able to enjoy the actual process of climbing, while on it. It was not just a question of retrospective satisfaction at having survived a stern struggle, a feeling of relief at the end of several days' acute discomfort and danger. This must be the feeling of the majority of the people who climb the Eiger, for all too often the Ramp and every other chimney or gully on the face is a torrent. Once you are soaked to the skin there can be no question of enjoyable climbing and the nights are then sheer purgatory; there is a real satisfaction in this kind of strife over hard conditions, but to me, this cannot compare with the sheer physical pleasure of climbing over difficult terrain, of picking out a complex route when I am sufficiently warm and dry to appreciate it. We were always aware of the potential menace of the face—I have never been on a climb with such a grim atmosphere, partly gained of course from our knowledge of its history and my own experience on it, but also from its very structure, the sheer compact walls, plunging slopes of grey, rock-scarred ice, and the dark shadows contrasting with sunlit woods and pastures below. We were aware, too, that an unexpected change in the weather could turn the face into an inferno, that suddenly we could find ourselves fighting for our lives, that then we should have to use our last reserves of strength—all the skill and experience we had ever gained in the mountains.

But all that was over. We sat on the summit, munched some

dried fruit, basked in the sun, enjoyed the exquisite pleasure of having space all round us, of seeing mountains on every side, and no longer confined to the one view from the prison we had just escaped. Another few minutes and we left the summit— it was a joy to be able to scramble unroped down the easy slopes of the West Ridge. We heard a shout from below, and saw the two Swiss work their way up the final ridge; they would soon be on the top.

We reached Kleine Scheidegg in a couple of hours, and then all the elation was knocked out of us. Herr von Almen, the proprietor of the hotel, asked us into his study.

"Could you tell me the names of the two climbers who were behind you?"

"Yes—they were a Scot, Tom Carruthers and an Austrian. I think his name is Moderegger. Why do you ask?"

"I'm afraid I have bad news for you. They are dead."

"But—how?"

"We do not know. The face was covered in cloud all afternoon. I watched them on the Second Ice-field in the morning. They were very slow. Then, when the cloud lifted in the evening, I couldn't see them."

"Couldn't they be out of sight in the Ramp?"

"No, I'm afraid not. I searched the lower part of the face with my telescope and was able to pick out their bodies. The guides are going up this moment to bring them back."

Even in those seemingly perfect conditions, the Eiger had made its claim.

EPILOGUE

THE ship was slowly pulling out from the wharf; tugs hooted, people were waving, a woman near me was crying. I held Wendy closer to me, just to convince myself that she really was there beside me, that we were both on board this ship bound for South America. The previous month had passed in a breakneck whirl of lectures, telling the story of my ascent of the Eiger, building the foundations for a new freedom and earning enough money for both of us to go to Patagonia.

We were on the threshold of a new life; there was to be no more compromise between leading a conventional career and my love of climbing. I could not quite see what the future would bring, at times I even had moments of doubt, but beyond that I felt a deeper happiness than I had ever known. I was at last basing my life on the things that I loved.